Financing California Real Estate

T0361860

California was at the epicenter of the collapse of the real estate market in 2008, which had a devastating effect on the world economy. Taking this diverse and powerful state as a case study, this book presents a financial history of the property business from the time Spanish Missions were established to the Great Recession.

Financing California Real Estate provides the history of expansions and contractions in the real estate market, and describes factors in the state and nation which may have triggered changes in the direction of growth in real estate lending. It explores how financial institutions which provided funding for building and buying homes changed over time, from the establishment of Spanish Missions in 1769, to the Gold Rush, to rail transportation, all the way through to the real estate bubble that peaked in 2005. Using detailed information on financial institutions to explain the changing nature of the real estate market, this book ultimately suggests an alternative theory for what led to the Great Recession.

This book will be of interest to researchers working in the area of real estate cycles in the economy, historians interested in the economy of California, and financial historians.

Lynne P. Doti is the David and Sandra Stone Professor of Economics at Chapman University, USA.

Banking, Money and International Finance

Financing California Real Estate

Spanish Missions to subprime mortgages

Lynne P. Doti

Routledge
Taylor & Francis Group

LONDON AND NEW YORK

First published 2017 by Routledge

2 Park Square, Milton Park, Abingdon, Oxfordshire OX14 4RN
52Vanderbilt Avenue, New York, NY 10017

Routledge is an imprint of the Taylor & Francis Group, an informa business

Firstissuedinpaperback2020

British Library Cataloguing in Publication Data
A catalogue record for this book is available from the British Library

Library of Congress Cataloging in Publication Data
Names: Doti, Lynne Pierson, author.
Title: Financing California real estate: Spanish missions to subprime mortgages/Lynne P. Doti.
Description: Abingdon, Oxon; New York, NY: Routledge, 2016.
Identifiers: LCCN 2016002699|ISBN 9781848936010 (hardback)| ISBN 9781781448687 (ebook)
Subjects: LCSH: Real property–California–Finance–History.| Housing–California–Finance–History.|Mortgage loans–California–History.| Real estate investment–California–History.
Classification: LCC HD266.C2 D67 2016|DDC 332.7/209794–dc23
LC record available at http://lccn.loc.gov/2016002699

ISBN: 978-1-8489-3601-0 (hbk)
ISBN: 978-0-367-59646-0 (pbk)

Typeset in Times New Roman
by Deanta Global Publishing Services, Chennai, India

Dedicated to:

Dr. John Butler
Dr. Rita Mehta
Dr. Mark Kobyashi

Contents

Graphs

Graphs

Introduction and overview

Importance of real estate cycles

In 2016, the United States still struggled to fully recover from the Great Recession, one of the deepest economic downturns since the Great Depression. Food stamp usage was at an all-time high, some ninety-three million Americans had stopped looking for jobs entirely, and the number of full-time jobs was still low compared with the labor force. That eight years after the 2008 financial crisis, which included the collapse of several of the nation's largest investment banks and the government bailout of others, the economy has recovered so slowly is a story in itself. But perhaps an even more intriguing story is why the greatest economic debacle of the young twenty-first century occurred in the first place. Increasingly, research points to real estate and the housing market as the origin of the disaster.[1]

Housing prices rose at an increased pace through the mid-1990s and sky-rocketed in the early 2000s, changing the incentives for why people acquired property.[2] After 2005, the rate of increase in prices slowed, then declined, then, in several places, completely crashed. The federal government's takeover of bankrupt real estate lenders Fannie Mae and Freddie Mac in 2008 was one of the early aspects of the financial chaos that followed. Yet, at the time, few experts appreciated the connection between the housing crash and credit crisis.[3]

The connection between the housing price decline and the recession is explained by a loss in asset value. The collapse in the boom or "bubble" of rapidly rising real estate prices slowed consumer spending because buyers no longer had a cushion of home equity to borrow against. In addition to the loss in value of real assets, which would affect spending, the financial markets were thrown into turmoil. The rise in real estate prices had produced a variety of innovative investment instruments that channeled funds into real estate markets. Fannie Mae and Freddie Mac, at the time independent entities (but with implied government backing of their assets), sold bonds and other investment instruments and used the funds to purchase mortgages and mortgage-based products. They were anything but non-political: their purchases were designed to perpetuate the American ideal of home ownership, but also to advance a social agenda by making loans available to lower-income groups. Through Fannie Mae and Freddie Mac, enough funds were fed into the market to finance an astounding half of all the mortgages in the country by 2008. The fact that the first major event of the financial crisis was the September 7 2008 government takeover of these two entities to prevent their failure is telling. The effect of their failure was judged to be so dangerous that President George W. Bush, who called himself a free market advocate, insisted "the only way to preserve the free market in the long run was to intervene in the short run" with a "breathtaking intervention .... [that] flew against all my instincts."[4] The Treasury, the Federal Reserve System and other parts of government then instituted a flurry of unprecedented programs. If these programs helped, they did not prevent the capital markets from collapsing.

The sequence of events leading up to the 2008 financial meltdown led to an increased interest in past linkages between real estate cycles and economic cycles. It appears that many recessions were preceded by real estate cycles where prices rose dramatically, then fell. In the publication *The 4% Solution: Unleashing the Economic Growth America Needs*, Edward Leamer found a similar pattern in eight out of ten previous post-World War II US recessions.[5] Each recession was preceded by a real estate bubble that broke before the recession had begun. Steve Gjerstad and Vernon Smith in 2012 showed that a housing downturn in 1926 preceded the Great Depression.[6]

After the Depression, economists preferred to watch the stock market as an indicator of future spending. If the market fell, people and businesses felt poorer and spent less. However, they may have been watching the wrong thing. In the latest economic cycle in the United States, the value of residential property may have replaced the wealth role previously played by shareholder value. Then economists, most notably Steve Gjerstad and Vernon Smith, noted that a housing bubble in the 1920s preceded the Depression. Many economists now have directed their research toward testing whether financial crises and recessions may have developed after real estate cycles.[7]

The connection between real estate values and the economy is not easy to establish using United States historical financial data. Price indexes for real estate were not developed until very recently. Robert Shiller and Karl Case began an index in 1987, which they projected back to 1890.[8] The Case-Shiller Index shows the highest housing prices ever in the United States in 2006 and the very sharp drop from 2006 to 2008.[9] They projected the index into the past to give some perspective, but, as important as it is, the usefulness of the index is somewhat limited as it is based on resale of the same properties from year to year in certain target neighborhoods.

There are challenges linking real estate prices to financial crises also. Nationally chartered banks disclosed their lending and this information is available through the Federal Deposit Insurance Corporation (FDIC), but, subsequent to the 1863 National Banking Act, the federally chartered banks were forbidden to lend on real estate.[10] Until the enactment of the Federal Reserve Act in 1913, no real estate loans appeared in the books for national banks, and, even after 1913, the national banks supplied only modest funds to the mortgage market. Links between the real estate market, financial markets, and the economy can only be established with information from all the sources of funding for real estate, including state-chartered banks, savings banks, building and loan societies (B&Ls), savings and loan associations (S&Ls), and insurance companies.

California is a particularly useful test market for theories about financial markets due to its large size, varied economy and available data. While nationally chartered banks were forbidden to lend on real estate, the many California state-chartered commercial and savings banks lent heavily. At times, building associations, insurance companies and mortgage banks added substantial amounts to real estate funding. In addition, in the nineteenth century San Francisco, California, was the entry and distribution center for capital in the western part of the United States. The financial system of the state developed almost entirely in historical times and, while mostly it has been a free market environment for capital, it has initiated unique regulations also. As housing prices are difficult to measure for the past, real estate lending is used here to indicate fluctuations in the price level and the volume of activity.

Data sources

This study, unlike other analyses of US financial markets, includes the records of various California state regulatory authorities. It also uses information from regional and national newspapers, and federal data sources, as well as previously published material. Data on funding sources, lending and investment has been collected from state regulators' reports on commercial banks, savings banks, savings and loan institutions, and B&Ls.

Most studies of the financial system use data on banks chartered by the national government. However, in the United States, each state also charters financial institutions, thus giving the United States a "dual banking system." In fact, it is in reality a triple or quadruple system because depository institutions can also choose to be commercial banks, B&Ls, savings banks, or S&Ls. Until the FDIC began insuring all depository institutions, a researcher had to collect data on state-chartered banks from each state.[11]

The FDIC was formed in 1934, but few state-chartered banks joined. It was the 1990 Financial Institutions Recovery and Reform Enforcement Act (FIRREA) that brought most financial institutions—national banks or not—into the FDIC insurance plan, and it was only then when the FDIC data on "insured institutions" became meaningful. This lack of data on earlier state-chartered institutions creates a bias, because there are systematic differences in the sizes and investments of the insured banks as against non-insured banks. Moreover, the regulatory structure governing the state-chartered banks differed from the federally chartered institutions. While these disparities have been reduced over the years, they still exist. Even today, institutions choose their regulators by changing between national and state charters.

In California, various state financial departments printed annual reports on state-chartered financial institutions and on out-of-state institutions operating in the state. The California State Banking Department was started in 1878, and reported the balance sheets for commercial banks, savings banks, and trust associations. Twelve years later, B&Ls had a state department reporting on their activities. When S&Ls gradually replaced the B&Ls, starting in the 1950s, yet another separate Commission reported on the status of state S&Ls. The FDIC publishes data on insured financial institutions by state, starting in 1966. Despite all these reports, boards, Commissions, and sources, it is not always possible to distinguish lending on California real estate from other types of loans. For example, sometimes a loan listed as a personal loan was used to buy a house. However, using state regulator-reported data and other information pertaining only to California allows a more detailed view of the boom and bust cycles of the state's real estate markets.[12] Real estate lending is used as an indicator of whether the market is in an expansionary or contractionary phase, and makes bubbles obvious.

In the 2006–10 recession, property value in the entire United States dropped by around 20 percent.[13] California came closer to the "crash" definition: property value in the Golden State declined by about 30 percent. Yet California had climbed higher than almost any other state prior to that downturn, which nationally saw US housing prices increase 150 percent between 1998 and 2006.[14] The latest real estate cycle was an example of how financial markets—and the laws restricting them—play a major role in business cycles. Identifying California's expansions and contractions in the real estate market reveals they often coincide with changes in the financial markets and the economy.

Summary of California real estate cycles

California of course had real estate cycles and bubbles throughout its history. The first documented rise in values occurred with the arrival of the Spanish Catholic Missions in the eighteenth century, which created an increase in requests for land grants of nearby property. Several of the Missions thrived as trading centers for passing ships, which attracted neighbors. This expansion ended with Mexico's dismantling of the Missions between 1830 and 1840. The nearby ranches ("Ranchos") often gained land and livestock when the Missions closed, but suffered from the transition and from frequent droughts. The Gold Rush of 1848 created a well-documented bubble in the period 1848 to 1854, when prices of land and buildings rose to heights unimaginable in the rest of the country. In 1855, there was a financial crisis in the city of San Francisco, which was followed by a crash in real estate prices.

Vast amounts of silver were discovered in an area called Virginia City, east of the Sierra Nevada Mountains, in 1859. While this city eventually became part of the state of Nevada, the economy was fully integrated into San Francisco during the height of the silver mining era. The silver mined there brought another boom to California. While Virginia City developed the attractions dear to miners—saloons to theatres and shacks to mansions—with the mining wealth, San Francisco became one of the major cities of the world. The wealthy formed banks in the city to finance the expansion of the deep mines, which required capital for engineering, transportation, and pumping out persistent floods. An active stock market provided additional capital.

San Francisco then became a financial capital for the western United States and even financed trade and railroads in Asia. The availability of money created a "Big Bonanza" period from 1874 to 1878, while the rest of the country languished.[15] By 1879, Virginia City production was tapering off. Mining stocks stopped paying dividends and interest waned. Virginia City declined and took San Francisco with it. The banks, stock markets, and other financial institutions began to fail.

As the stimulus of the silver era tapered off, another boom period was already under construction. In 1859, an engineer, Theodore Judah, was petitioning Congress for one of the most ambitious projects ever attempted in the United States, the transcontinental railroad. Surveying the Donner Pass, he saw a relatively easy way across the Sierra Nevada Mountains to bring Virginia City silver to San Francisco Bay for shipping. Four Sacramento merchants, Charles Crocker, Mark Hopkins, Collis Huntington and Leland Stanford, offered financing for further exploration of the idea. Congress wanted more than a way to transport silver over the mountains: they wanted a direct connection to the eastern parts of the United States to tie the country together. In 1862, President Lincoln signed a bill that promised 400 acres per mile and $48,000 of government bonds to the Central Pacific Railroad for each mile built from Sacramento west to meet the Union Pacific Railroad being built from the Missouri River toward the west. The building commenced in 1863 and again California land rose in value in anticipation of access to the markets in the rest of the United States.

The transcontinental railroad was completed in 1869. The first effect was a giddy round of tourism. After only a week of travel, easterners could see the fabled golden land, and, along the way, perhaps glimpse the fabled buffalo or Native Americans. Even as the transcontinental railway was under construction, other local lines were being built for more commercial purposes. By the 1880s, the easy access provided by the railroads to the rest of the nation produced another land boom. The railroads reached Southern California in 1885, where cattle ranches had been closed by drought.[16] Speculators bought land once deemed nearly worthless, subdivided it, and sold or leased it for small farms. Aided by cheap railroad tickets, promoters lured thousands of prospective farmers to these "developments." The developer or the speculators were backed by San Francisco banks, but I.W. Hellman, president of the Farmers and Merchants Bank in Los Angeles, was himself a developer of much of west Los Angeles.[17]

At the end of the century, California was an efficient statewide capital market. In 1880, San Francisco banks had 23 percent of all their property loans on land outside the city.[18] Lending was not all from San Francisco, still the financial center of the state (and the entire western United States).[19] Banks loaned frequently on distant real estate, and more local banks developed in the 1880s, providing local sources for real estate developers' funding.[20] Los Angeles showed an increase in the number of banks between 1884, when there were only three state-chartered banks, to nineteen in 1889, and twenty-four in 1894.[21]

In 1891, the California Bank Superintendent bragged that the financial storms that raged in the rest of the world created hardly a ripple in California.[22] However, by 1893, the problems were evident. A panic started with the closure of the

Riverside Banking Company on June 14. In a few days banks had suspended payments of deposits in San Francisco, San Bernardino, Los Angeles, San Diego, and in other towns.[23] The panic ended the boom of the 1880s in Southern California, but growth in small family farms would return at a slower pace. Well-planned towns continued to serve the surrounding farms until after World War II. The trend of subdividing large ranches continued even longer. The continued growth of the real estate market was well supported by the banking system.[24]

The national oil boom of the early 1900s had less of an effect on the California real estate market. Oil was discovered in enough places that almost any area could yield a bonanza. Upton Sinclair's novel, *Oil!*, featured a character who achieved great wealth buying up land that was best suited for raising goats, but was over an oil field. The largest oil deposits would not be discovered in California until the 1920s. By then much of the land had been divided into small properties, and the oil interests purchased only the mineral rights under the land, but an oil pump rocking in the backyard is still a possibility in Huntington Beach.

Los Angeles was the center of the 1920s oil, real estate, and movie booms that drove California's economy. The oil and the movie boom did not seem to generate large demand for real estate. However, the oil discoveries and the growing motion picture industry certainly boosted awareness of the area and increased population. One author reported that 100,000 people came to Los Angeles every year.[25] During the 1920s, 3,233 subdivisions embracing 49,608 acres of 246,612 building lots would add to its size, as well as the two million extra people in the state.[26] People settled in the cities and small towns and on ample suburban lots where they could do some farming. Most of this growth occurred between 1920 and 1924. This boom paused in 1926, recovered slightly, and ended with the Depression.

Building activity in 1927 had been quieter than in the last five years. In spite of that, employment, manufacturing output, wholesale trade, retail sales, and auto distribution numbers were all up. Only agriculture had continuing problems with loan repayment. [27] In fact, 1928 was a temporary reprieve. Assets of deposit institutions were up slightly after a decline in 1927. B&Ls continued to grow until 1930, and then declined at a modest pace, but the assets for state and national commercial banks, savings banks, and trust associations virtually crashed.

Loans in California and the nation both continued to drop through the Depression. The population increased in California, since there were immigrants from the Midwest, but housing was unavailable, although transient camps were built with some help from local and federal government sources. Some land and simple shelters even sold. The government instituted several programs to help homeowners, including the Federal National Mortgage Association (FNMA), later called Fannie Mae. FNMA sold federal government-backed bonds and used the funds to buy real estate loans from banks. This became a model for other housing organizations established later, like the Government National Mortgage Association (GNMA)—"Ginnie Mae," for veterans—and the Federal Home Loan Mortgage Corporation (Freddie Mac).

When World War II started, private housing construction was banned by the federal government. However, since many defense workers were recruited from outside California, there were loans during the war for temporary housing for essential labor. Because California benefited disproportionately from the war expenditures, this did allow some housing construction during the war. As a result of the extra workers, bank deposits increased dramatically, allowing construction financing. The housing market did pick up again in California in 1944, anticipating victory.

An early sign of the long post-war housing boom came from the B&Ls. Less regulated than other financial institutions, they were able to quickly respond to the pent-up demand for personal residences. In 1944 they first showed a substantial increase in real estate loans. By 1945, the Building and Loan Commissioner noted that there was "marked inflation in the selling prices of real estate, particularly homes, both old and new."[28]

After World War II, the housing market exploded nationwide. In addition to the family formation known as the "baby boom," very low interest rates, the Federal Housing Administration (FHA) programs implemented in the 1930s, and the "G. I. Bill" with its low-interest, low down-payment loans soon made home ownership more accessible than it had ever been before. In-migration to California, especially the suburbs of southern California, dramatically added to the demand for housing. The growth in California relative to the rest of the nation was so rapid that moving funds from outside the area into real estate development, construction and mortgages became a challenge to the financial industry.

Post-war developers no longer provided land ready for farming, even for a "gentleman farmer." People wanted homes within driving distance of the factories or office buildings where they worked. The solution to providing this type of home was the same as it had been in the 1920s: buy a farm and subdivide it into buildable lots. Already, in 1946, the state's real estate Commissioner noted that several thousand acres of California's best farmland was being lost to housing. Prices were rising rapidly, and the only complaints about realtors were that the realtor had allowed the client to move too slowly and the property had been lost to someone else. In April 1946, the Commissioner noted that "the subdivision market is rapidly approaching a speculative stage." People bought these lots with only the promise of streets and utilities to come, and tracts sometimes sold in a matter of days.[29]

The 1950s real estate boom would completely change the structure of the financial system.[30] Commercial banks, B&Ls, savings banks, and insurance companies all played a role in this massive inflow of funds. In California, during this period, national life insurance companies also played an important role in channeling funds to developers, and the S&L industry became the most frequent provider of home mortgages. The S&L industry had been unimportant, compared with the other financial institutions in California, until its rapid growth in the 1950s and 1960s to finance the housing boom. Newly established institutions were the main source of the growth, with B&L conversions and existing S&Ls and the savings banks adding to the funding. For all S&Ls, in this time period, the business consisted almost entirely of generating funds through savings and time deposits, and lending for real estate development, construction or acquisition.

From 1960 to 1965, the entire economy's growth was slow, but California had some particular problems. The housing market turned down sharply in the early 1960s. Defense was a major industry. Aircraft manufacture, aerospace, and defense contracts were important remainders of the war and were kept growing by the Cold War. California received about 40 percent of all aerospace contracts from 1962 to 1978 and, mostly, these contracts were concentrated in the Los Angeles area.[31] The slow-down in California started as early as 1957 as the first projects closed. Other companies opened in other states and many of California's technical employees moved to follow the jobs. This trend continued through the early 1960s.

The next boom came in the 1970s with inflation and some special circumstances particular to the state. Four major changes occurred to affect the real estate market. First, California was a leader in environmentalism and passed laws that had the effect of restricting building. Second, the state legislature required public access to be available to nearly every part of the 840 miles of coastline along the Pacific Ocean. Third, the public passed an initiative to limit property taxes. Fourth, the California Supreme Court ruled that customers, not banks, owned the mortgages they had been granted. All of these changes created a chaotic real estate market. In addition, commercial banks nationwide increasingly complained of uneven regulations that seemed to favor the S&Ls, mutual funds, life insurance companies, and investment trusts. Because of this greater legal freedom, especially in California, these non-bank financial institutions were developing new products to compete directly with the commercial banks.

The 1970s started with a decline in the real estate market. New home construction fell dramatically between 1969 and 1971. Sales of existing homes also slowed in the beginning, in 1969.[32] Recovery came by 1973. A *Los Angeles Times* article reported the price of all homes was rising. In Orange County, it was "skyrocketing." This area, one of the nation's "hottest" housing markets, experienced an increase in average sales prices for single-family, three-bedroomed, detached dwellings between 1,400 and 1,500 square feet from $28,000 in the first half of 1971 to $35,800 in the first half of 1973.[33] In 1978, while many experts predicted nationwide housing prices were in danger of imminent collapse, the prices in California, particularly Southern California, continued to climb.

There was a brief downturn in the real estate market between 1978 and 1982. After 1982, they rose until 1986.[34] The steadily rising interest rates were a frequently cited factor in the downturn, but legislation and environmental factors also played a role. In 1982, Congress tried to help the S&Ls to better compete with commercial banks, in the 1982 Garn-St Germain Depository Institutions Act. The law provided for continued liberalization of asset powers for S&Ls.[35] That same year, California allowed the S&Ls and the banks to become direct partners in real estate development.[36] Unfortunately, these moves into new areas of business did not turn out well for many of the financial institutions. Even in 1980, twenty-two California S&Ls failed.[37] The problem quickly became epidemic. By 1994, in the California S&L industry, forty-three federally chartered institutions, with assets of $39 billion, were "resolved" by the federal government.[38] Another seventy state-chartered savings institutions, with total assets of $95 billion, made California the biggest problem the FDIC had to deal with among all the states.[39]

The United States was in recession from 1990 to 1992. While California had recovered quickly from the 1981–2 recession, it lagged in recovery from this recession. Real estate prices levelled off then declined. Unemployment rates exceeded the national average. Forced to cut costs, California businesses began to leave the state, looking for lower costs and, not incidentally, less regulation. Things were particularly bad in Southern California, where the decline in the real estate values led to declines in one of the major industries, construction. Other problems included the strong environmental movement, which was the new embodiment of "no growth" policies, the state's complex and costly workman's compensation insurance plan, and a decline in military spending.

The stimulus for the next real estate boom started after Congress enacted affordable housing goals in 1992. The legislation required Fannie Mae and Freddie Mac (the latter created in 1970 for residential mortgages that did not meet the Fannie Mae requirements) to purchase an increasing quota of loans that were made to borrowers at or below the median income level in their region. The quota was increased over the years and it became increasingly difficult for Fannie and Freddie to find sufficient loans to fill the quota. So they decreased their underwriting standards.[40] The demand for these "subprime" loans created a market that many saw as a business opportunity. Investment funds were started to create these innovative mortgages. The fund would originate subprime mortgages and sell shares in the entire pool of mortgages to investors. Some of these funds grew at a startling rate. Values for shares in these funds were derived from values of other securities, and thus were called "derivatives." Even though investment in a type of derivative brought about the largest municipal bankruptcy in history, of Orange County, California, derivative securities became popular in the mortgage market.

In the early 2000s, Ameriquest and Countrywide were two of the biggest and best-known mortgage originators in the United States. Both started in the Los Angeles area. Another company, New Century Financial Corporation, in Orange County, was featured on *60 Minutes* for its phenomenally rapid growth. According to Alan Greenspan, these and other companies were "pressed" (by demand) to originate mortgages and sell them to securitizers.[41] The securitizers would package these loans into "silos" and sell shares in the silos, or even pieces of several silos combined, to investors. These innovative securities fueled the real estate market, which expanded rapidly from 2000 to 2005, levelled off, and then began to drop.

While the economy had been experiencing other problems since 2005, the signs of trouble were not widely noticed. Unemployment was around 5 percent in 2005, and was still around that level in 2008.[42] One of the signs of trouble was the over-building of housing. In 2000, US builders started 1.6 million new homes, but in 2005, they started 2.1 million.[43] Yet by 2005, the housing market was slowing. By 2008, housing prices were clearly falling. In 2008, this turned into an international financial meltdown. Aside from the prevalence of the securitizers in California, which were closed, failed or were acquired, after 2008 the real estate problems were national in scope. Recession gripped the nation. Growth rates of gross domestic product (GDP) did not become positive until 2010, and remained historically low even in 2016.

The financial system and the real estate market in California is not just a microcosm of the United States as a whole. This study is intended to provide as much information as possible about the financial history of California and the factors that affected the real estate market, with the particular goal of finding the factors that triggered the beginnings and ends of real estate expansions. In so doing, perhaps it will provide clues to the roles of regulations, financial structure, and other factors affecting real estate markets and the economy.

The administration and my colleagues at Chapman University have provided unwavering support over many years for my research. Many of my students helped with various critical aspects of this work, including Joe Ramirez, Mohammed Alnuami, Meagan O'Reilly, Sabrina Gladstone, Julie Zerbo and Olga Zoria. My husband, Jim Doti, and our family have been understanding in many ways. Thank you all.

Lynne P. Doti
The George L. Argyros School of Business and Economics
Chapman University
Orange, California
2016

Notes

1 See for example Steven Gjerstad and Vernon L. Smith, *Rethinking Housing Bubbles* (Cambridge, England: Cambridge University Press, 2014); Peter J. Wallison, "Get Ready for the Next Housing Bubble," *The Wall Street Journal* (December 5 2013), A19; Barry Eichengreen, *Hall of Mirrors: The Great Depression, the Great Recession and the Uses—and Misuses—of History* (Oxford, England: Oxford University Press, 2015); Charles Calomiris, and Stephen Haber, *Fragile by Design: The Political Origins of Banking Crises and Scarce Credit* (Princeton, New Jersey: Princeton University Press, 2014).

2 There is also a rising interest in the cause of booms and busts in the housing market itself. See for example: Craig Burnside, Martin Eichenbaum and Sergio Rebelo, "Understanding Booms and Busts in Housing Markets," National Bureau of Economic Research Working Paper no. 16734. (Cambridge, Massachusetts: National Bureau of Economic Research, 2011). Available online at www.nber.org/papers/w16734.

3 Alan Greenspan, *The Map and the Territory: Risk, Human Nature, and the Future of Forecasting* (New York: The Penguin Press, 2013), 64.

4 George W. Bush, *Decision Points* (New York: Crown, 2010), 458–9.

5 Edward Leamer, "Housing is the Business Cycle," *The 4% Solution: Unleashing the Economic Growth America Needs*, edited by Brendan Miniter (Danvers, Massachusetts: Crown Publishing Group, 2012), finds a similar pattern in eight of ten previous post-World War II US recessions.

6 Steven Gjerstad and Vernon L. Smith, "At Home in the Great Recession," in *The 4% Solution: Unleashing the Economic Growth America Needs*, edited by Brendan Miniter (Danvers, Massachusetts: Crown Publishing Group, 2012), 50–79.

7 Examples of early articles include: Penido de Freitas and Maria Cristina, "Asset Inflation and Deflation Triggered by the US Housing Financial System," *Revista de Economia Politica/Brazilian Journal of Political Economy* 28, no. 3 (July 1 2008): 414–33; Wayne R. Archer and Brent C. Smith, "Residential Mortgage Default: The Roles of House Price Volatility, Euphoria and the Borrower's Put Option," *Journal of Real Estate Finance and Economics* 46, no. 2 (February 2013), 355–78; Margarita Rubio, "Fixed and Variable-Rate Mortgages, Business Cycles and Monetary Policy," *Journal of Money, Credit and Banking* 43, no. 4 (June 2011), 657–83. Rubio studies the differing impact of monetary policy in situations where real estate loans are fixed-rate versus variable-rate, finding little difference in impact; Brent C. Smith, "Mortgage Reform and the Countercyclical Role of the Federal Housing Administration's Mortgage Mutual Insurance Fund," *Federal Reserve Bank of Richmond Economic Quarterly* 97, no. 1 (2011), 95–110. Xi Chen, "Real-Time Warning Signs of Emerging and Collapsing Chinese House Price Bubbles," *National Institute Economic Review* 223, no. 1 (February 1 2013). R39; Viktor Dorofeenko, "Real Estate Price Bubbles: the Impact of Shocks on the Risk House Prices Volatility and the Volatility of Investment in Residential Real Estate," *Perspektiven der Wirtschaftspolitik* 12, no. 2 (January 1 2011), 151–69.

8 Robert Shiller. Online data. Available online at www.econ.yale.edu/~shiller/data.htm.

9 Robert Shiller, *Irrational Exuberance* (Princeton, New Jersey: Princeton University Press, 2005), 13.

10 Federal Deposit Insurance Company, "The Historical Statistics on Banking." Available online at www5.fdic.gov/HSOB.

11 They still do not insure credit unions, but set the rates and furnish information about them. Non-depository mortgage banks and insurance companies also play an important role in real estate lending.

12 Superintendent of Banks of the State of California, *Annual Report* (Sacramento: State Printing Office, 1920), 10.

13 Bruce McKinnon, "1968–2008 Median Price on Home Sales," US National Association of Realtors (June 25 2008). Covers only existing home sales.

14 Thomas E. Woods Jr., *Meltdown: A Free-Market Look at Why the Stock Market Collapsed, the Economy Tanked, and Government Bailouts Will Make Things Worse* (Washington, DC: Regnery Publishing, 2009), 63.

15 Richard E. Lingenfelter, *Bonanzas & Borrascas: Gold Lust and Silver Sharks, 1848–1884* (Norman, Oklahoma: The Arthur H. Clark Company, 2012), 212.

16 J. A. Graves, *My Seventy Years in California: 1857–1927* (Los Angeles, California: The Times-Mirror Press, 1927), 99.

17 Robert Cleland and Frank Putnam, *Isaias Hellman and the Farmers and Merchants Bank* (San Marino, California: Huntington Library, 1965), 46.

18 Lynne Pierson Doti, *Banking in an Unregulated Environment: California 1878-1905* (New York: Garland Publishing, 1995), 88.

19 Kerry O'Dell, *Capital Mobilization and Regional Financial Markets: The Pacific Coast States, 1850-1920* (New York: Garland Publishing, 1992). *Passim.*

20 Doti, *Banking in an Unregulated Environment*, 72.

21 Ibid., 123.

22 Board of Bank Commissioners, *Annual Report* (Sacramento, California: Office of the Board of Bank Commissioners, July 1 1891), 5.

23 Board of Bank Commissioners, *Annual Report* (Sacramento, California: Office of the Board of Bank Commissioners: July 1 1893), 3.
24 Doti, *Banking in an Unregulated Environment*, 87.
25 W. W. Robinson, "The Real Estate Boom of the Twenties," *Quarterly Journal of the Los Angeles Historical Society* 24 no. 1 (March 1 1942), 25.
26 Marquis James and Bessie R. James, *Biography of a Bank: the Story of Bank of America NT & SA* (New York: Harper & Row, 1954), 236.
27 Superintendent of Banks of the State of California, *Annual Report*, (Sacramento: State Printing Office, 1928), 5.
28 Building and Loan Commissioner of the State of California, *Annual Report* (Sacramento, California: California State Printing Office, 1945), 4.
29 California Department of Investment, Division of Real Estate, *Report for Governor's Council* (Sacramento, California: State of California, 1946), 2.
30 Lynne Pierson Doti and Larry Schweikart, "Financing the Postwar Housing Boom in Phoenix and Los Angeles, 1945–1960," *Pacific Historical Review* 58, no. 2 (May 1989), 173–94.
31 Allen J. Scott, "Interregional Subcontracting Patterns in the Aerospace Industry: The Southern California Nexus," *Economic Geography* 69, no. 2 (April 1993), 142–6. Available online at www.jstor.org/stable/143533.
32 John Lawrence, "Homes, Loans Scarce; Worst May Be Ahead," *Los Angeles Times* (1923–current file, July 11 1969); ProQuest Historical Newspapers *Los Angeles Times* (1881–1987), A1. Available online at www.proquest.com/products-services/pq-hist-news.html.
33 Dick Turpin, "Waiting Costly in Purchasing Home," *Los Angeles Times* (1923–current file, October 21 1973); ProQuest Historical Newspapers *Los Angeles Times* (1881–1987), H2.
34 California Department of Real Estate, *Deregulation of Financial Institutions: How has it Affected the Real Estate Industry in California?* (Los Angeles, California: California Department of Real Estate, 1988), II-7. Prepared by the Institute for California Real Estate Research.
35 Ibid., II-15.
36 Ibid., II-18.
37 The Federal Deposit Insurance Corporation, *The FDIC and RTC Experience: Managing the Crisis* (Washington, D.C: August 1998), 860–1.
38 Ibid., 834.
39 Ibid., 832. The Texas financial system virtually collapsed, with 226 failures. Texas banks were all independent as branching was not allowed, limiting their size. Also Texas problems were specialized, as they related closely to lower oil prices.
40 Peter J. Wallison, "Get Ready for the Next Housing Bubble," *The Wall Street Journal* (December 5 2013), A19.
41 Alan Greenspan, *The Map and the Territory*, 64.
42 Alan S. Blinder, *After the Music Stopped: The Financial Crisis, the Response, and the Work Ahead* (New York: The Penguin Press, 2013), 16.
43 Ibid.

1   Serra's Missions to Sutter's Fort
To 1848

Financing real estate in California undoubtedly started long before any record of it. Even for highly civilized societies in prehistoric and, even early historic periods, most history focuses on war, rulers, and social trends, not everyday business life. While more attention is being paid by today's historians and anthropologists to this part of history, few of them have the training to recognize money, banks or purely financial transactions in early history. Only recently, for example, has the temple of Delphi been identified as a sort of central bank for the region, the treasures brought to the Oracle providing backing for their representative money.[1]

Native California economy

California was first inhabited more than 15,000 years ago, but even the most significant history in the pre-European times seems to be irrecoverable.[2] Even the peak population of native Californians is unknown, although 300,000 is a popular estimate. At least thirty major tribes have been identified, with a great diversity in language, habits, and lifestyle between the tribes throughout the state.[3] Considerable evidence exists showing early forms of money, and extensive trade, two conditions that are precursors to a financial system. Small, isolated societies may exist without money, utilizing barter, but as trade expands a form of money is ultimately required. This money is designed or, more usually, selected to obviate the need for complicated exchanges, and to increase the ease of transporting, hiding, and protecting value. Thus, most early monies consist of a commodity—gold, silver, salt—that is durable, divisible, and portable. Several items may coexist as money, but one type of money usually is used as the standard of comparison. In the case of California, the Native Americans used shells.

One early type of money was dentalium shells, small tubular molluscs that look like little unicorn horns. While this species lives throughout California, they live partly buried in the sand in deep water. They were most accessible where rivers fed onto broad ocean shelves, which is more common in the northern part of the Pacific coast.[4] The early inhabitants of the Pacific Northwest thus initiated the use of dentalia as a standard of monetary exchange and a sign of wealth. There are over 300 species of dentalia, but *Antalis pretiosum* was the species most used by Native Californians as money. These shells are most associated with the tribes of Northern California. However, even for Northern Californians, most of their dentalium shells came in trade from even further north.[5]

The largest shells could grow to 2.5 inches or longer, and were most prized. In one report, a small boat cost one strand of dentalium shells about the length of a man's arm.[6] The Native Americans strung the shells on fiber thread in alternating directions, so the cone-shaped shells would not nest into each other and confuse the size or number. The shells on one strand tended to be of a common size, furnishing a denomination of sorts. The string would be long enough to easily space the shells into groups, allowing easier counting or, perhaps, creating smaller values.[7] The Yurok tribe, in northern California, stored the strands in elk horn "purses" and had five named denominations determined by the size of the shell, plus adjectives to distinguish if the strand was deficient in some way. The wealthier men in the Pacific Northwest decorated their ceremonial clothing with both large and small dentalium shells.[8] A Northern California tribe with permanent settlements along the banks of rivers that were near the ocean, the Yurok used dentalia, but rarely possessed the largest shells.[9] They also used other objects to make payments including deerskins, obsidian blades, and flint.[10]

The dentalia strings spread as far as the Dakotas through trade, but were rare in southern California.[11] There, the common money was carved from a thick clamshell. This shell in its natural form is too common to make good money. To create money from a clamshell, a carver created a disc, pierced the disc in the center like a doughnut, and then strung the discs on fiber strands. The discs were roughly shaped, bored, strung, and then rounded and polished on a sandstone slab to about one-third of an inch in diameter. These strands of shells were the most common money among the Native Southern Californians even into the 1800s. The Chumash, who not only inhabited much of the southern California coast, but also many of the Santa Barbara Islands, were the main supplier of this labor-intensive money. In central California, the Pomo played a similar role. The coastal Miwok and the Pomo tribes gathered clam shells of *Saxidomus aratus* or *gracilis*. These were sometimes traded to inland tribes for the manufacturing step. From Morro Bay to San Diego, the pieces were made from the *Tivela* or *Pachydesma crassatelloides* shells.[12] For most southern California tribes, the length of the strand determined its value, and the unit of measurement was a wrap around the palm.[13] In eighteenth- and early-nineteenth-century trade with foreigners, eight yards of these beads were considered equivalent to one Spanish dollar.[14]

Many Europeans were oblivious to the intricacies of native California money. "There is very little occasion for money in a country where there is nothing to be purchased. Beads are the only money of the Native Americans," J. F. de G. de Laperouse noted in his diary of a trip to California in the late eighteenth century.[15] However, for items to be "purchased" property rights had to exist. That concept was for goods that were scarce, not for items, such as land in the seventeenth century, that were in such abundance that they could be had without cost.[16] In the earliest days of California, scarce items, such as boats, and also wives, most definitely involved monetary transactions, but most land was without value.[17]

The Spanish Missions

California was a largely neglected and ignored dependency of Spain for around a hundred years before the founding of the Missions there. Spain moved into "Alta California" in 1769 to protect the silver mines of northwestern New Spain from a feared Russian or English advance. They eventually created twenty-one Missions, four military bases ("presidios"), and three civilian settlements.

The planned economic relationship of the Missions with Spain was mercantilist: Alta California would produce raw materials for Spanish Mexico, and buy their manufactured goods. Foreign trade was forbidden.[18] Local Native Americans were recruited to provide the labor force. It is not known if the labor force was attracted "with flattery and presents" to receive instruction in the Catholic faith and the skills of farming, as two naval officers claimed after visiting California in 1792.[19] There are many who think the Native Americans were not a contented labor force, and some who present evidence of a state of serfdom or even slavery. The model provided that the Mission would set up a community of Native Americans, convert them to Catholicism, and teach them to grow food for themselves and the soldiers. This food would be periodically supplemented by visits from Spanish ships with extra supplies until the settlement grew enough to be self-sufficient and allow the export of goods. There were also plans for independent towns, and for the presidios.[20] The original plan specified that once an established economy existed, the Missions would revert to ordinary churches serving the community.

Father Junipero Serra founded the first of the Missions in San Diego in 1769. He walked there from "Baja California" with Gaspar de Portola and his expeditionary force. Portola left Father Serra, two other priests, eight soldiers, fourteen civilian volunteers (who were too ill to continue), eight Native Americans from Baja California and a few other individuals in San Diego, while he continued north. This group founded a combination presidio and Mission on July 16 1769.[21] After setting up a camp, Serra's group was visited by local members of the Diegueno tribe. The Dieguenos politely laid aside their weapons and helped themselves to the possessions of the priests and soldiers. As this practice continued, skirmishes with the soldiers became common and relations deteriorated. On August 15 1769, the Dieguenos launched a full-scale attack on the camp. Most of the Spaniards survived. Afterward, they built a stockade, and the foundations of a small chapel inside.[22] This, unfortunately, was located in an area that the local natives considered their own. Naturally, after these incidents, Serra had trouble recruiting candidates for baptism, and then he had trouble providing food for those who applied. Only fifty-five people were baptized between 1769 and 1772. Serra felt the soldiers were interfering with the process by harassing the Dieguenos, using work animals for military purposes, and taking more than their share of deliveries from the Spanish ships bringing supplies. In 1774, the Mission moved five miles east of the presidio. Unfortunately, again the spot they selected was an area already occupied and inhabited by the Dieguenos. Their leaders recruited members of the Kumeyaay tribe who lived in villages nearby, and encouraged them to petition in large numbers to be baptized. Since the Mission could not feed all these recruits, Father Luis Jayme, now heading the Mission while Serra travelled north to establish new Missions, left them living in their villages rather than in the Mission community. In fact, these recruits may have been part of a plot to regain the Dieguenos' land. On November 5 1775, in the night, bands consisting of around 600 members of several local tribes attacked the Mission and the presidio. They killed Father Luis Jayme along with one-third of the soldiers, a carpenter, and a blacksmith. Most of the other soldiers were wounded. The attackers burned all of the buildings at the Mission and killed several cattle. After Spanish ships arrived, and brought military reinforcements and more supplies, the Mission was re-established. It eventually became one of the largest in the system.[23]

The Missions were constantly challenged by the unreliable arrival of Spanish supply ships.[24] By 1820, vessels from many other countries stopped regularly (though illegally) along the coast for the purpose of trade. They brought goods from Mexico and picked up tallow (rendered cattle or deer fat) and hides to take back home.[25] The tallow was used to make soap and candles, and also was used as a lubricant. Hides made horse tack, upholstery, clothing accessories, and the belts used to transfer water wheel power to machinery of the early industrial revolution. The Spanish also encouraged the production of hemp, for rope production, and sea-otter fur, which they traded to China for mercury, necessary for silver refining in Mexico.[26]

By the 1780s most of the Missions could be deemed successful at producing food for their recruits.[27] By then, Father Fermin Lasuen headed the California mission project. He emphasized quick baptism and a focus on teaching practical skills for converts. There were fewer shipments to supply the Missions, so it was more important to be self-sufficient. The Mission residents learned to farm, and make adobe bricks. A few even learned carpentry, blacksmithing, stonecutting, masonry, weaving, tailoring, milling, and decorative painting. Many became cowhands ("vaqueros"), as the Missions soon learned that, most of the year, cattle and horses could simply be left unattended to graze the arid but expansive lands. Once a year the animals were rounded up to cull the herd for the hides and tallow, and to brand the newborn.

Most of the Missions did become the fairly self-sufficient operations envisioned. Several not only produced enough wheat, corn, barley, beans, and livestock for themselves, but also provisioned the local military, and supplied passing whaling and trading ships. Some had tens of thousands of cattle in their herds. The trading ships supplied the Missions with manufactured goods, often in large quantity for resale to other settlers, according to William Heath Davis, a trader whose father also ran a trading ship in the Pacific.[28] When supplying the presidios, Missions received a credit, which was redeemed, through agents, on goods from Mexico City.[29] Clearly many of the Missions became successful business enterprises and attracted other settlers. Spain granted vast amounts of land to any Spanish citizen who would farm or raise cattle, although, in fact, the Spanish grants were usually only of "grazing rights," not actual ownership, which always resided with the King of Spain. The grants allowed buildings on the property only for the use of the owner ("ranchero") and the vaqueros needed as seasonal workers to round up the stock on the ranch ("rancho"). Ironically, the cowhands were almost always the Native Americans of local tribes. Some of these Spanish land grants turned out to be of so little value that grantees abandoned the land. Even in the early 1770s, when Spain founded a Mission, requests for land grants near the Mission increased, showing Missions increased surrounding land values.

By the 1820s, populations at some Missions numbered more than one thousand persons. Native Americans provided all the physical labor and received payment in kind: food, housing, religious instruction and clothing. While the exact nature of the laborers' contract with the missionaries remains unclear, they were not always allowed to come and go as they pleased, and their labor was at times contracted out by the friars to the soldiers, or to nearby Ranchos. And certainly not all Native Americans in California were attached to Missions. The friars sometimes hired members of these independent groups to work on Mission harvests, building projects, or other occasional jobs.[30] Individual Native Americans attached to Missions also used their holidays for outside work to earn coins or European goods at nearby Ranchos.[31]

No banks existed, but the Missions, located a day's journey apart, likely made loans to each other, and perhaps to local rancheros. William Heath Davis' mother told him that when she visited California aboard her husband's ship from 1814–16, the missionaries paid for goods in Spanish doubloons, other silver, or with gold coin, and otter skins.[32] The Missions probably served as banks, holding and lending coin for the rancheros and some of the workers. Bankers of the day accepted coin in deposit, but as long as payment could be made on demand, not all of it had to be on the premises. This would allow the missionaries to also make loans. It is also possible that the goods purchased from one ship could be sold later, for coin, to other ships. Certainly there were some bank-like activities occurring. Davis (the son) also worked as a trader in the Pacific by the mid-nineteenth century. He wrote of one transaction where he sold some goods to Father Mercado of Santa Clara Mission in 1844 and was provided with a letter to Father Muro of Mission San Jose requesting Muro complete payment for the goods with 200 cattle hides.[33]

Mexico became independent of Spain in 1821 and evicted the missionaries, taking land from the church in 1823 and gradually secularizing the Missions. Between 1836 and 1842 the Governor of Alta California, Juan Bautista Alvarado, leased or sold the former Mission lands to private owners.[34] In one exception, land surrounding Mission San Juan Capistrano was given to the Native American inhabitants of the Mission, but a civil administrator sold most of the land to settlers.[35] The Missions were not completely dismantled until 1845.[36] The fading of the Missions shifted the economy to the rancheros.

The rancheros and coastal trade

Various Spanish, Mexicans, Russians (at Fort Ross), and Americans settled in Alta California during the mission period, but there were so few people in the San Francisco Bay area in 1838 that Captain Davis claimed to know all the

564 non-Native residents personally.[37] The people in the state other than Native Americans certainly did not number more than a few thousand until after 1846.[38] San Jose, Monterey, Los Angeles, and San Diego each had multiple Ranchos at that time. After 1823, Mexican citizens (but only Catholics or those married to Mexican Catholic citizens) had the right to be granted up to 50,000 acres if they would settle on the land. Most of the twenty or so Spaniards working their existing grants then kept their grants by becoming Mexican citizens.[39]

In spite of the Mexican government continuing Spanish prohibitions on foreign trade, ships were coming regularly to buy tallow, pelts, and hides. Private individuals wanted to share in the production of these goods. When Mexico became independent and started to secularize the Missions, the missionaries voiced opposition, as taking the land from the Missions left most of them without enough land to be self-supporting. Mexican land grants accelerated after 1840 and by 1846 numbered around 750.[40] Britain, Russia, and most alarmingly, the United States had made their interest in California clear, and the government wanted more settlements in California to keep it from foreign influence.

While Mexican land grants were often subdivisions of the old Spanish grants, they still encompassed thousands of acres. The Mexican land grants, unlike the Spanish, gave full ownership rights, instead of only the right to use the land for specific purposes. Land not granted was assumed to belong to the Mexican government. Especially in the south, the large ranches were semi-arid and required vast amounts of land to support the roving herds of cattle and horses. The Ranchos became self-sufficient empires, with a variety of crops and livestock, but were marked by the abundance of cattle. A ranch could have tens of thousands of head, and often nearly as many horses. Even as the density of certain areas increased, the cattle roamed free for most of the year. A yearly roundup brought the widely dispersed cattle and the vaqueros who tended them to the Rancho. There, the new generation of cattle was branded and some of the older generation slaughtered. The roundup created a social occasion and a market.[41] Little money traded hands. Cowhands traded the wages due for special food, clothing, and hats. Most cash still due would usually be kept on account by the ranch owner, who also was the source of loans. After the roundup (called, along with the celebration, a "fandango") the ranch resident workers cut some of the beef into strips and dried it for preservation. They rendered tallow to use for cooking, and for making soap and candles. Hides were scraped and dried in the sun. The leather was extensively worked and softened, then made into clothing items, horse tackle, parts of furniture, rugs, and anything else that could be made of leather. The owners then journeyed to a seaside town where trade with passing ships provided what the less rural world enjoyed. They brought their stock of dried hides and leather bags of tallow to barter with the local trader, who gathered and stored these goods for the arrival of the ships.

Richard Henry Dana, a Boston schoolboy who travelled to California as a sailor, kept a journal that was published as *Two Years Before the Mast*, and is still perceived as a remarkable slice of history. In his journal, Dana described what happened when his ship visited the capital town of Monterey in 1835. The sailors took a small boat to the beach to retrieve the hides and tallow they had come for. He said there were large piles of bullock hides on the high part of the beach. They were doubled lengthwise and "nearly as stiff as boards."[42] He observed sailors from another boat don soft wool hats and lift the hides onto their heads. The leather bags of tallow were so heavy that two sailors joined to put one on their shoulders. The loaded boats were then rowed through the surf back to the ship.[43]

Dana's ship, the *Pilgrim*, operated a general store while they were in port at Monterey. For a week to ten days the crew ferried customers to and from the shore. On the boat, customers could use the coin or credit earned from hide and tallow sales to buy virtually anything. Dana names spirits, teas, coffee, sugars, spices, raisins, molasses, hardware, crockery-ware, tin-ware, cutlery, clothing of all kinds, boots and shoes, calicoes and cotton fabric (from Lowell, Massachusetts), crepes, silks, shawls, scarfs, necklaces, jewelery, hair ornaments and combs, furniture, Chinese fireworks, and cart wheels.[44]

Many sources report the use of tallow and hides as money in the early 1800s. Robert Glass Cleland referred to dried cow hides as "California Bank Notes," but Dana first used this term. "The truth is, they have no credit system, no banks, and no way of investing money but in hides—which the sailors call 'California Bank notes'."[45] On the other hand, Dana remarked, "I certainly never saw as much silver at one time in my life, as during the week that we were at Monterey." As Monterey was a major trading center, it is likely that silver coins (probably Spanish) were used as money, to separate the value of the hides from the purchase of items from the merchants and the ships, and to ease trade. In other words, the rancher might have deposited the hides with the trader before the arrival of a ship, and received silver. This silver would then allow the rancher flexibility in his purchases. In this situation, it was unnecessary to take the silver back to the ranch and the trader might have held it, and acted as a banker. Hence, most of the silver would stay in Monterey with a trader/banker until a ship arrived. There are reports of ranchers with strongboxes of silver in their possession, however. The hides were actually too bulky to serve as money.

A house sale

In 1841, the first recorded house sale occurred in California. Land grants were common, and perhaps there were a few sales of the Ranchos. But this story seems unique. Mission San Francisco de Asis was founded in 1776, ten miles south of the presidio that Spain had founded on the southern side of the entrance to the expanse of the bay. Unlike other Missions, it did not attract settlers to the vicinity. Closer to the presidio was a sheltered cove called Yerba Buena that attracted some early settlers. William Richardson, an English seaman, reached the bay area aboard a whaler early in the 1830s. His jumping ship may have been motivated by love, as he married the daughter of the Comandante of the presidio. In June 1835, he lived in Yerba Buena in "a shanty of rough boards" and occupied himself by studying the tides, currents, and channels around the bay. San Francisco dates his residence as the beginning of the city.[46] An American merchant, Jacob Primer

Leese, soon settled near him and treated the area residents, numbering a few less than twenty, to an Independence Day party on July 4. Leese was the first merchant in Yerba Buena. "I have concluded to stop in this place for good," he wrote in a letter dated August 3 1836, "in consequence of the great prospect ahead, which is plainly foreseen. I have made a contract with a couple of Men to Build a house for 4 hundred and 40 dollars paid in Goods. I think it is a good Traid."[47] Leese married a sister of Mariano Vallejo, Comandante of San Francisco, and soon moved to Sonoma, north of Yerba Buena and the Mexican capital of Alta California. When he moved, Leese sold his property to the Hudson Bay Company.[48]

The Hudson Bay Company had operated as a trading company since 1670. They had a department headquartered in Vancouver with trading facilities at Astoria, Oregon and other points along the Columbia River, but nothing further south. In 1840, the head of the Vancouver department, John McLoughlin, decided to set up a post in Yerba Buena. He purchased the house owned by Jacob Leese, with the land, about two-thirds of the modern city block bounded by Montgomery, Sacramento, Clay, and Sansome streets. William Rae, the son-in-law of McLoughlin, arrived and opened a trading post there. The house was described as a large wooden building with two stories. The price was $4,600, half in coin and half in goods. The house purchase was finalized on September 9 1841. The remaining third of the block that contained the Hudson Bay trading post (and the home of Rae, his wife and two or three children) was a public house with a billiard room and bar. The owner of the "pub," Jean Jaque Vioget, known as John, from Switzerland, lived upstairs with his family.[49]

William Rae sent small boats to the Ranchos around the bay, collected hide and tallow, and delivered items in trade that had arrived from the Hudson Bay Company by way of Monterey. The establishment never did well, at least partly due to a drought in 1841 that killed wheat and cattle. The Hudson Bay Company management complained of the excessive price of the building, contending that for a few hundred dollars a few men could have constructed a better space. The company was, in general, cutting costs by reducing the number of trading posts and probably did not realize the price of lumber in Yerba Buena. They closed the post after William Rae committed suicide in 1845, having developed a decided drinking problem and possibly a too-public romantic entanglement. The house was sold to Mellus and Howard, a mercantile establishment, for $5,000. They opened a store there, which would flourish in the Gold Rush and make them both very wealthy men. In the winter of 1849–50 the building was converted into a hotel after other structures replaced it for retailing.[50]

Sutter's Fort

Another early settlement would play a more significant role in the California real estate market. John Sutter left Switzerland, his wife, five children, and large debts behind when he came to the United States in 1834 with some of the fine, costume-like clothing he loved. He would become one of the most influential of the rancheros in California and would play a major role in developing the Sacramento area. When he arrived in New York, he met John Laufkotter. When Laufkotter opened a grocery store in St Charles, Missouri, Sutter joined him there. By the next spring, Sutter's engaging personality, flashy dress, and glamorous, but fictional, military history were offset by his substantial debts. He left town with some French trappers headed to Santa Fe. He returned in the fall with a barrel of wine and seven mules, perhaps obtained from trading some of his wardrobe. Back in St Charles, he lived by borrowing from his friends, including the widow who boarded his mules.[51]

The apparent success of Sutter's trip to Santa Fe allowed him to collect $14,000 from seventeen Missouri investors to buy goods for trade in another trip to the town. Forming a wagon train, he and the investors travelled to Council Grove, in a sort of moving drinking party, to join other wagons for the perilous journey. By then, Sutter was out of funds and lacked several essentials for the trip. Most of his disgruntled party returned to St Charles. Sutter arrived safely in Santa Fe and stayed there, trading with apparent success. He also had a side business of illegally purchasing horses from Apaches, which they in turn had stolen from settlers. He returned to Missouri in the fall of 1836, with 100 horses and an employee named Gutierrez, who stayed with him until Sutter's death.[52]

Sutter's next venture was to build an upscale hotel in Missouri. Sutter's debts were rising quickly, and a court date loomed when Laufkotter visited. Laufkotter had been in California during the winter of 1837, perhaps coincidentally the year when 1,500 stolen horses spent the summer there before being sold in New Mexico. Somehow Sutter raised the funds to go to California and left town the day before his court date. He brought two horses, some cloth, and a gold watch chain. Gutierrez and a Mr Wetler accompanied him as he started the 2,000-mile journey. The group, too small to survive the journey alone, joined a larger group as soon as possible, and followed the route west known as the Oregon Trail. Sutter's small group, now enhanced by two more German-speaking men and Native American slave boy who spoke English, crossed the Cascades and rested in Willamette Valley until October. Then, convinced that it would be a faster, if less direct, route to California, Sutter took his slave and Wetler to Hawaii by ship.[53]

Sutter was stranded, quite productively, in Hawaii for months. He met several people there, including young William Heath Davis, who was now the stepson of the American consul. He also met prominent Hawaiians, perhaps even King Kamehameha III, and through them arranged for eight Hawaiian men to come to California with him. Two brought their wives.[54]

Impatient with waiting for a ship to California, Sutter and his group joined a trading expedition to Sitka, Alaska, to purchase seal and otter pelts. After the Alaska stop, the ship headed south to California, arriving in San Francisco in 1839 with "starving" passengers and crew. As San Francisco was not a legal entry port, the Mexican commander of the presidio gave the ship forty-eight hours to provision and leave. A few days later it arrived at Monterey, the official port of entry. They were in time for a Fourth of July party thrown by American merchant Thomas O. Larkin, then one of the most successful traders in California. The party-goers also included David Spence, a prominent Scottish ranchero married to a Mexican woman, and the Governor of Northern California, Juan Bautista Alvarado.[55]

The next day, Sutter met with Alvarado and described his wish to settle in California. They agreed that he could choose land on the Sacramento River, in the San Joaquin Valley, a fertile area that occupies the center of the state (also called the Central Valley). While current law required Mexican citizenship as well as possession of land for ten years to receive title, Alvarado was anxious to stabilize the sparsely populated inland region. There, Miwoks, Yokuts, Mexicans, and "adventurers of all nations" traded and stored stolen horses. Alvarado gave Sutter a title to indicate he had government authority, but warned him to avoid Comandante General Mariano Vallejo and the northern bay area he policed. Sutter promptly disregarded Alvarado's plea and proceeded north to pay his respects to the Comandante, then went on to Fort Ross, which he saw as a model of the trading post he wanted to establish.[56]

When he returned to San Francisco, Sutter acquired two schooners and a large rowboat. He added weapons and tools. His Hawaiian companions and nine other men sailed with him up the Sacramento River. One of them was teenager William Heath Davis. Over the next eight hot August days, the party made its way inland, stopping occasionally for Sutter to determine if the area would be suitable for settlement. At night, sleep on the boats was disturbed by an "immense multitude of mosquitoes."[57] About 200 miles south of the present site of Sacramento, hundreds of Native Americans appeared on the riverbank. Sutter bravely stepped off the boat alone and attempted a Spanish greeting, which proved successful. Two other men came forward and conversed in Spanish, volunteering to guide Sutter upriver. On the American River, about a mile upstream from the point where it joined the Sacramento River, Sutter chose a spot to settle.[58] As most of the party was departing back to the coast on the two schooners, Sutter dramatically fired his cannons. Davis recorded witnessing a sight that illustrated the wildness of the place:

> As the heavy report of the gun and the echoes died away, the camp of the little party was surrounded by hundreds of Indians, who were excited and astonished at the unusual sound. A large number of deer, elk, and other animals on the plains were startled, running to and fro, stopping to listen, their heads raised, full of curiosity and wonder, seemingly attracted and fascinated to the spot, while from the interior of the adjacent wood the howls of wolves and coyotes filled the air, and immense flocks of water fowl flew wildly about over the camp.[59]

Yet he named his settlement New Helvetia (New Switzerland) and proceeded to build a shelter, firing his cannon occasionally, which maintained the respect of the Native Americans, but may also explain his pleas for meat from San Francisco when there was so much wildlife nearby.

Sutter was not the only non-Native American in the Sacramento area. John Marsh lived about forty miles away on a land grant he had obtained in 1837. They probably knew each other, perhaps even back in Missouri, where both had questionable reputations. Don Ignacio Martinez also had a ranch nearby. By this time the local Native Americans were familiar with Europeans and Americans. They had experienced, or heard about, missionaries, trappers, and traders. The local Miwoks and Nisenan were mostly hunter-gatherers, but horse theft and trading was a lucrative sideline for many.[60]

Sutter was soon successful at making some of the Miwoks his friends and employees. One of their villages relocated to be closer to Sutter, who soon had adobe walls around his first buildings. He had already rebuffed several armed attacks from small groups of tribal members. Their goal had been to steal more of the goods Sutter had gifted them. In 1840, he lost cattle and horses to raiders. With eight men and his cannon, Sutter attacked the suspected thieves' village and killed around thirty people. Soon after, he executed ten Native Americans guilty of raiding a tribal village near New Helvetia. The suspects had arrived "to trade," but went to a nearby village, killed the old and young, and kidnapped the others to sell them to rancheros. Sutter mentions that this "was common in those days." However, Sutter pursued the perpetrators and punished the leaders. This cemented the loyalty of the local tribes.[61]

Soon, Sutter had a sort of company town. He paid his workers with a special tin disc, punctured with a star-shaped hole. These discs could be redeemed at his store. His operation grew rapidly. He soon had a protective force of around 150 men, most with some sort of uniform, in keeping with his own fondness for fancy dress. It is hard to imagine how Sutter financed his fast-growing "fort" without one activity. He himself described it this way: some Native Americans "brought some sore-backed horses to me that they had stolen from some settlers." Sutter bought the horses, "pastured them until they were well," and then returned them to the owners, "who paid me back what I had paid."[62] Vallejo and Alvarado felt that this description of Sutter's activities was not quite accurate, that in fact he was encouraging horse thieves (as long as they did not steal horses near him) and profited from the operation. Their tolerance came from the fact that Sutter was maintaining control and increasing the population of rancheros in the previously wild area. Sutter's operations continued to grow, but his recurring failure to pay his debts quickly escalated and soured relationships with Martinez, Alvarado, and Vallejo. When he agreed to pay debts in coin, he often paid with cow hides or beaver pelts. Hides were worth $1.50 to $2.50 during the 1840s, but Sutter also tended to stretch his repayment times beyond tolerable limits.[63] His reputation worsened, both for being a poor credit risk and also for his well-known inclination toward heavy drinking. In spite of these problems, by 1840 he had a herd of 1,500 cattle, tended by Native Americans, and he became a Mexican citizen to secure his land ownership. A Frenchman who visited that year noted that there were around 200 people attached to "Sutter's Fort."[64]

Sutter then had an opportunity to expand in a new direction. Fort Ross, the Russians' ocean-side trading post, was offered for sale. Vallejo wanted to purchase it, but the Mexican government balked, noting that it was an illegal settlement on their land anyway. Sutter agreed to pay $30,000 worth of wheat for everything at Fort Ross. The land was included, although there really was no evidence of ownership. Sutter's employee, John Bidwell, promptly began moving cattle, sheep, tanning and other tools, windmills, and millstones from Fort Ross to New Helvetia. Soon, Miwok and Nisenan employees wore Russian uniforms when they were on guard duty.[65]

More Americans were moving into California. In 1841 a group consisting of thirty-two men, one woman, and a child came overland from Missouri.[66] Sutter took them in and gave them jobs. By 1844, New Helvetia was a destination for overland immigrants coming from the eastern United States to California. Kit Carson and John Fremont headed there when their party nearly perished travelling in the Sierras. Fremont would make the trip, and California, famous in the report he wrote back in Washington, D.C. The report also fuelled President James K. Polk's interest in acquiring California for the United States.

In California, the inhabitants were beginning to take sides in the inevitable struggle. A few favored an independent California. Sutter took the side of Mexico. On January 1 1845, Sutter launched a military display of, according to his memory, about 400 men. Miwoks and members of other tribes made up the ranks, while an assortment of Europeans and Americans led the group. Three African-Americans were the backbone of a small band. After a rousing display, the army marched toward San Jose in support of the Mexican-appointed governor Manuel Micheltorena. As the army moved, they swept horses from rancheros along the way.[67]

By March 1845, Sutter was back at Fort Sutter. Unfortunately, the time had come to settle the bill for Fort Ross. He focused on planting wheat and managed to deliver a portion of what he owed. Sutter issued a mortgage on New Helvetia for the balance and decided to sell. Before that was possible, Fremont returned and asked for Sutter's help in the ill-fated Bear Flag Revolt, in which a small group of Americans tried to take California from Mexico.[68] Sutter provided some pack animals and provisions, in spite of his status as a Mexican citizen, but then warned Vallejo of Fremont's intentions. Fremont retaliated by taking over Sutter's Fort and imprisoning Vallejo there.[69] These events were interrupted by the Mexican War.

The Mexican War

Polk was determined to fulfill the manifest destiny and worked to solidify a northern border for Oregon. He also wanted California for the United States, and promoted the numerous skirmishes between the Mexican government and settlers there from the United States. When part of the Mexican army battled with the US army on April 26 1846, on the American side of the Rio Grande River, Polk brought the news to his cabinet. They unanimously voted to request Congress to declare war. Congress complied on May 12.[70]

A naval force commanded by Commodore John D. Sloat, which had been off the coast of Mexico in the spring, took possession of Monterey, California in July 1846. Commodore Robert F. Stockton took San Francisco, and then sailed down to Monterey. In the meantime, Stephen Kearny brought his "Army of the West" across the desert. All in all, the fighting in California was minimal, and in fact more about personal issues and score-settling than about the governance of the state. Little government control of this vast, sparsely populated region was possible, anyway. Probably the biggest effect of the Mexican War was not the acquisition of California by the United States, which by then was nearly inevitable, but that the soldiers who came to California to serve in the Mexican War made Americans aware of the vast, empty land, and rich, fertile valleys of California. Many would leave the army and return in a scenario to be repeated in every US war afterwards.

The American victory did bring one influential official to the government. Walter Colton was appointed and served three years as the "Alcade" (Mayor) in Monterey starting July 16 1846, just nine days after the US flag was permanently raised over the town. His many observations have provided a great deal of detail on the California of the time. For example, he reported in the 1840s, the usual rate of interest for money loaned in Monterey on good security was 24 percent.[71] He also reported that merely raising the US flag raised property values 40 percent.[72] By October 1846, emigrants from the United States who were originally heading for Oregon were pouring into the rich San Joaquin Valley. Colton quoted a letter from one of those immigrants saying that "no less than 2,000 are now in the interior."[73] In addition, Colton reported that a convoy of 2,000 Mormons was on its way to settle in the state.

In fact, after Joseph Smith, the leader of the "Latter Day Saints," was murdered in Carthage, Illinois in 1844, the new leader, Brigham Young, sent various groups out to find a place for the religious group to live undisturbed. He took the largest group overland toward the west, and would stop in 1847 at what became Salt Lake City, Utah. A group of about 200, led by Samuel Brannan, headed to Yerba Buena, hoping the relaxed governing that Mexican California experienced would make it an attractive home. When they arrived, they were disappointed to find a US warship in the harbor and the US flag flying. The area had around 150 people in 1845. When the 200 Mormons arrived in 1846, there was no surplus housing. Some attempted to make the abandoned Mission Delores livable. Many lived in tents.[74]

The Mexican War ended quickly, by concession of California to the United States by the Treaty of Guadalupe Hidalgo, February 2 1848. This was a generous settlement asking only that the citizens acknowledge the US government. In spite of the promise that no existing legal land ownership would be disturbed, problems immediately developed over property rights. Many of the rancheros could not provide evidence of the Mexican land grant to the new government to prove their ownership. Even those who had proof soon had difficulty with encroachment due to the "meets and bounds" system of granting land, used by the Mexican government. This system used geographic features to establish property parameters rather than the precise surveys insisted upon by the founding fathers in the eastern United States. Many of the Mexican grants had overlapping boundaries, and the size of the average claim was over 15,000 acres.[75] The California Land Act of 1851 set up a land claims commission and a court system. Individuals had to present their documents and testimony of witnesses. By the 1852 deadline,

813 claims had been filed. The Commission would make a decision, which could be appealed, by the claimant or the federal government, to the California district court, and from there up to the Supreme Court. Once the matter was settled, the property was surveyed and the owners received a patent or title to the land. The remaining land belonged to the US government.

There are many stories of land titles lost in the legal process through missing documents or lack of money to finance the claim process, but research indicates that most of the claims were, ultimately, proved. Squatters who settled illegally on properties were not so easily dealt with. The United States had a long history of favoring those who used and improved land over "idle" or absentee landlords. It was hard for eastern farmers to understand the vast size of the land needed for a western cattle ranch. There were not adequate personal or government resources to deal with people settling on land that was owned by others, and many of the property owners lost their property to squatters.[76]

When the fighting ended in January 1847, many of the Native Americans who had joined the fight, on both sides, returned to horse thieving. In April, Stephen Kearny, now Governor, appointed Sutter as Indian Agent to bring the Sacramento area under control. This position brought a salary and Sutter gradually regained his empire. He embarked on two projects. One was a water-powered gristmill. The other was a sawmill on the American River. This project would dramatically change California real estate, and the state.

Notes

1 Laurence R. Iannaccone, Colleen E. Haight and Jared Rubin, "Lessons from Delphi: Religious Markets and Spiritual Capitals," *Journal of Economic Behavior & Organization* 77 (2011), 326–38.
2 A. L. Kroeber, *Handbook of the Native Americans of California* (New York: Dover Publications, 1976). Originally published by the GPO as Bulletin 78 of the Bureau of American Ethnology of the Smithsonian Institution (1925), 43.
3 Albert Hurtado, *Native American Survival on the California Frontier* (New Haven, Connecticut: Yale University Press, 1988), 1.
4 Kroeber, *Handbook of the Native Americans of California*, 22.
5 Trinidad Trading Company, "Dentalium Shells Were Money to American Native Americans," Available online at https://trinidadtrading.com/dentalium. info@trinidad trading.com. Hupa, Tolowa, Yurok, Wiyot, Karuk, and Wintu used dentalium shells.
6 Trinidad Trading Company, "Dentalium Shells Were Money to American Native Americans."
7 Kroeber, *Handbook of the Native Americans of California,* 23.
8 Trinidad Trading Company, "Dentalium Shells Were Money to American Native Americans."
9 Kroeber, *Handbook of the Native Americans of California*, 25.
10 Trinidad Trading Company, "Dentalium Shells Were Money to American Native Americans," 22.
11 Ibid., 25.
12 Kroeber, *Handbook of the Native Americans of California*, 177.
13 Ibid., 565.

14 Susanna Bryant Dakin, *A Scotch Piasano in Old Los Angeles: Hugh Reid's Life in California, 1832–1852, Derived from his Correspondence* (Berkeley, California: University of California Press, 1939), 43.

15 J. F. de G. de Laperouse, *A Voyage Round the World in the Years 1785, 1786, 1787, and 1788*, vol. 3 (London: 1798), vol. II "Life in a California Mission: Monterey in 1786," 231.

16 Terry L. Anderson and Peter J. Hill, *The* Not So *Wild, Wild West* (Stanford, California: Stanford Economics and Finance, 2004), 43.

17 Kroeber has various descriptions of these transactions among different native groups. In *A Patriot's History of the United States: From Columbus's Great Discovery to the War on Terror* (New York: Sentinel, 2004), 404, Larry Schweikart and Michael Allen point out that the lack of well-established property rights to land allowed the Native Americans to be more easily exploited.

18 Steven W. Hackel, "Land, Labor and Production: the Colonial Economy of Spanish and Mexican California," *Contested Eden: California before the Gold Rush*, edited by Ramon A. Gutierrez and Richard Orsi (Berkeley, California: University of California Press, 1998), 113–17.

19 Donald Cutter, *California in 1792: A Spanish Naval Visit* (Norman, Oklahoma: University of Oklahoma Press, 1990), 129.

20 James A. Sandos, *Converting California: Indians and Franciscans in the Missions* (New Haven, Connecticut: Yale University Press, 2004), 70.

21 Rose Marie Beebe and Robert M. Senkewicz, *Junipero Serra: California, Indians, and the Transformation of a Missionary* (Norman, Oklahoma: University of Oklahoma Press, 2015), 206–9.

22 Sandos, *Converting California*, 49.

23 Serra blamed the uprising on neophytes who were members of the Mission and "gentiles from forty Rancherias." However, the number of Rancheros seems too high, and he was not present. Beebe and Senkewicz, *Junipero Serra*, 324; Sandos, *Converting California*, 56.

24 Hackel, "Land, Labor and Production," 114.

25 Ibid., 129.

26 Ibid., 119.

27 Sandos, *Converting California*, 93.

28 William Heath Davis, *Sixty Years in California: A History of Events and Life in California: Personal, Political and Military, Under the Mexican Regime; During the Quasi-Military Government of the Territory by the United States, and After the Admission of the State Into the Union, Being a Compilation by a Witness of the Events Described* (no publisher: General Books, 2009). OCR scan of original book (published 1889), 176. Davis's father died young, but his mother had travelled on several trading voyages with him.

29 Hackel, "Land, Labor and Production," 117.

30 Ibid., 126.

31 Ibid., 122.

32 Davis, *Sixty Years in California*, 176.

33 Ibid., 349.

34 Leonard Pitt, *The Decline of the Californios: A Social History of the Spanish-Speaking Californians, 1846–1890* (Berkeley, California: University of California Press, 1966), 9.

35 Sandos, *Converting California*, 109.

36 Pitt, *The Decline of the Californios*, 8.

37 Davis, *Sixty Years in California*, 333.
38 Population of Native Americans : soldiers and settlers according to Hackel, "Land, Labor and Production," was 1770 59,700 : 150; 1780 57,000 : 480; 1790 43,600 : 1,060; 1800 35,850 : 1800; 1810 25,900 : 2,300; 1820 21,750 : 3400; 122.
39 Helen Bauer, *California Rancho Days* (Sacramento, California: California State Department of Education, 1957), 9.
40 Karen Clay and Werner Troesken, "Ranchos and the Politics of Land Grants," *Land of Sunshine: An Environmental History of Metropolitan Los Angeles*, edited by William Deverell and Greg Hise (Pittsburgh, Pennsylvania: University of Pittsburgh Press, 2005), 57–66.
41 Davis, *Sixty Years in California*, 19.
42 Richard Dana, *Two Years Before the Mast* (New York: A. L. Burt Co., 1840). For example, page 66.
43 Ibid., 67.
44 Ibid., 86.
45 Ibid., 89.
46 Gunther Barth, *Instant Cities: Urbanization and the Rise of San Francisco and Denver* (Oxford, England: Oxford University Press, 1975), 95.
47 "Old Letters Tell of First S. F. Building: Documents, Hoary With Age, Reveal Founding of Original St Francis Hotel 75 Years Ago," *San Francisco Examiner* (June 12 1921). Available online at www.sfmuseum.org/hist11/oldletters.html. Quote is from a letter "recently discovered."
48 Barth, 95.
49 Davis, 71.
50 Ibid., 70, 74.
51 Albert L. Hurtado, *John Sutter: A Life on the American Frontier* (Norman, Oklahoma: University of Oklahoma Press, 2006), 13.
52 Ibid., 25–7.
53 Ibid., 29, 35, 40–2.
54 Ibid., 45.
55 Ibid., 52, 54.
56 Ibid., 59.
57 Ibid., 63
58 Ibid.
59 Ibid.
60 Ibid., 68–9.
61 Ibid., 73, 75.
62 Ibid., 76.
63 Ibid., 83.
64 Ibid., 88, 94.
65 Ibid., 97–100.
66 Ibid., 89.
67 Ibid., 141–3.
68 Karen Clay and Werner Troesken, "Ranchos and the Politics of Land Grants," *Land of Sunshine: An Environmental History of Metropolitan Los Angeles*, edited by William Deverell and Greg Hise (Pittsburgh, Pennsylvania: University of Pittsburgh Press, 2005), 64.
69 Hurtado, *John Sutter*, 147.

70 Allan Nevins, editor, *Polk: the Diary of a President 1845–1849* (London: Longmans, Green and Co., 1952), 83.

71 Walter Colton, *Three Years in California* (Stanford, California: Stanford University Press, 1949), 68.

72 Ibid., 52.

73 Ibid., 72.

74 Roger Lotchin, *San Francisco, 1846–1856: From Hamlet to City* (1973. Reprint. Lincoln, Nebraska: University of Nebraska Press, 1979), 7–8.

75 Karen Clay and Werner Troesken found 80 percent of the claims in Los Angeles were patented. "Ranchos and the Politics of Land Grants," 64.

76 Ibid., 65.

2   Gold Rush to land rush
1848–1855

The discovery of gold and the subsequent population increase caused a land boom like few others in history. Because of the difficulty of travel to California, prices became astronomically high for the simplest items—a barrel of flour could cost $50, which in the East would be two months' wages. Land prices similarly soared. In just a few years, land went from having no value at all to prices that astonished the rest of the country. According to Robert Glass Cleland,

> during the four years of the Gold Rush, rents and real estate values in San Francisco and other cities skyrocketed to dizzy levels. Leases on hotels and gambling houses ran as high as a hundred thousand dollars a year … Lots in Sacramento went from two hundred dollars to thirty thousand a year later.[1]

The Gold Rush attracted people from all over the world to California. Most of these people came by sea, through San Francisco and Sacramento, where population was scattered and few buildings existed. The United States had just won the Mexican War, two years before, and acquired Alta California from Mexico. The US government honored the Mexican land grants, but new immigrants quickly squatted on land that was not obviously occupied. Miners quickly developed their own rules of property ownership and staked out lots for mining. A hastily-drawn map, certified at a government office, constituted an official, legal deed. For a while, the Gold Rush was a land rush. It was a short boom, however. As soon as the most accessible surface gold was picked off, the mania calmed and several minor bank runs preceded foreclosures and slower growth.

Sutter and the Gold Rush

It was January 24 1848 when James Marshall discovered gold at John Sutter's sawmill on the American River, and four days later when he arrived in Sacramento to show Sutter. Sutter agreed the metal was, in fact, gold and travelled to the mill construction site. Marshall and his men had been collecting gold and could identify several places with rich deposits. They also scattered some for Sutter to find, hoping that this would result in him passing around the bottle of liquor he always carried with him. Marshall and Sutter arranged a lease with Yalisumni Nisenans, a tribe which lived a short distance downriver from the mill, hoping to strengthen Sutter's legal claim to the land.[2]

The discovery of gold should have made Sutter wealthy. He owned large areas of land in the path of the hordes that came to search for gold. In Sacramento, he had the best-known trading post in the state. By mid-February, word of the gold discovery had spread throughout California via crews of the coastal trading ships, and people from all around were arriving to mine. Sutter recognized the danger to his property and tried to secure legal possession to Coloma from then-Governor Richard Mason. While he seemed willing to grant Sutter rights, unfortunately the Treaty of Guadalupe Hidalgo had been signed only days before their meeting. Although the treaty upheld land grants under Mexican law, there was insufficient clarity regarding Sutter's claim. Then some of the Mormons from the sawmill went downriver and made a rich gold strike, in what came to be known as Mormon Island, or Diggings, causing others to enter the area and start mining. Sutter no longer had the power to protect his land.[3]

Meanwhile, workers completed the saw mill, but the loss of workers to the mines meant the gristmill in progress could not be completed before the harvest, forcing Sutter to pay for milling his wheat. Sutter now began to use the gold discoveries to request delays in paying his debts. When that was insufficient, he began renting his land, then his fort, for cash.[4] He really had no choice, and the land around the fort soon filled with squatters in "low ranges of buildings ... occupied as hospitals, stores, drinking and gaming shops, and dwellings."[5]

Still hoping to profit from sales of his land, Sutter created a subdivision of lots on a bluff three miles southeast of the fort, and called it Sutterville. Lansford Hastings and John Bidwell laid out the new town in return for shares of the profit on the lots. George Zins built the first brick house there in 1846, but most people thought the land was too far from other settlements to be attractive.[6] Now the subdivision land also began to fill with squatters as they stopped on their way to the gold region.

Sam Brannan, who brought the Mormons to San Francisco in 1846, had urged Brigham Young to relocate the Salt Lake City settlement to California. When Young disagreed, Brannan decided he would stay. By 1848 he was a prosperous and prominent merchant, and publisher of the *California Star*. He was not impressed by the stories the mill workers told him about the gold discovery, nor was his editor, who visited Coloma. However, after Brannan went to Mormon Island he was more enthusiastic. Always visionary, he returned to Sacramento and made plans to rebuild a dock and add a warehouse and store to the riverfront on the Sacramento River. Then he galloped on to San Francisco and urged more of the Mormons to go to the mines. Many did. Brannon frantically bought goods to fill his new Sacramento warehouse while word of the gold spread and the trickle of miners became a stream. Everyone in California came to try mining.[7]

Colonel Richard Mason was one of the visitors. As the newly appointed military commander, he toured the state with Lieutenant W. Tecumseh Sherman in July, remarking on the fact that San Francisco was nearly deserted. Travelling to Sacramento and the mines, he also noted that along the way, "mills were lying idle, fields of wheat were open to cattle and horses, houses vacant, and farms going to waste."[8] At Sutter's Fort, visitors rented rooms for $100 a month, and recently opened stores and hotels dotted the neighborhood. Mason and Sutter continued up the American River to the "diggings." There they noted around 200 men working in the hot sun. Some of the men had tin pans, others had baskets, and some used a "cradle." This device was operated by four men: one dug the streambed dirt, the second carried it to the cradle and deposited it, the third man rocked the wooden device, while a fourth added water from the stream. The gold, heavier than the dirt from the stream, tended to sink to the bottom of the cradle and was caught in baffles nailed there, as the water flowed through the device. The finer flakes were separated when the sand was emptied from the cradle and left to dry. Again, the heavier gold settled below the finer sand, which could be blown off. With this technique, the four men retrieved between one and three ounces of gold per person in an average day. Mason estimated there were 4,000 miners working, half of whom were Native Americans.[9]

Late in the summer, Sutter tried mining himself, or, more precisely, took around 100 Native Americans and fifty Hawaiians to work the American River between the sawmill and Mormon Island. He didn't stay long, however. Word came that his twenty-two-year-old son, August, had travelled from Switzerland to see him, and was waiting at the fort.[10]

August Sutter had been sent as a sort of advance party for Sutter's family, still waiting, still impoverished, in Switzerland. He must have heard of the gold discovery when he reached New York, as by then word was spreading to the east coast. When he reached San Francisco, he immediately learned a different story, of his father's business problems and debts. In spite of his youth, he accepted his father's ploy to avoid creditors: a grant to him of all his father's land. Unfortunately, the financial problems still mounted as the senior Sutter continued to acquire partners and commit to unfulfillable promises. His Coloma workers, unpaid, took the gold they mined, while Sutter looked for glory.[11]

After one intoxicated and unusually scandalous evening, Sutter embarked for Coloma. There he became a partner in a store. Sam Brannon opened a competing store in Coloma, leaving a clerk in charge and making sure the prices reflected the shortages. According to the clerk, prices were high: "Crackers and flour, one dollar a pound; six quart tin pans, sixteen dollars apiece; pickels [sic], sixteen dollars a quart … whiskey sixteen dollars a bottle and everything in proportion."[12] Col. Mason, himself, opened a third store, to allow his (rapidly deserting) officers and men an opportunity to supplement their military income. They were also allowed to mine. There was no one who wanted work at anything other than mining. Faced with such challenges, Sutter soon sold both his store and the sawmill.[13]

While Sutter was in Coloma, stranded by heavy snow, Sam Brannan presented August with a new idea. He proposed a new town in the area between Sutter's Fort and the Sacramento River. August hired Captain William Warner to survey the new town in December, and Warner laid out the town on the American plan, with First, or Front, Street parallel to the Sacramento River, and regularly spaced numbered streets to Thirty-Two just beyond the Fort. At right angles he put streets A to Y. Each block contained eight lots divided by an interior alley. He designated twelve blocks for public use. Also in accordance with US Federal practice, Warner made no accommodations for variations in geography, like ponds or swamps, keeping each lot perfectly square. August then hired an agent, Peter Hardeman Burnett, to sell the lots for $250 to $500 each, and he rented out, and then sold off, the last of the Fort, piece by piece. Lt Tecumseh Sherman reported that the rooms there were rented for $100 a month, when his own salary from the military was only $70.[14] August moved out of town to "Hock Farm," a pleasant country home Sutter already owned. Burnett sold the lots near the Sacramento River and the money was sufficient to pay Sutter's debts, even the eight-year-old debt to Russia.[15] When Sutter returned from Coloma, squatters populated his remaining land in Sacramento. His herds and wheat fields succumbed to the credit burdens, and he ran out of options. August managed to bring the rest of the family to California, and Sutter settled into a relatively quiet life, surrounded by his family, at Hock Farm. The man who had established his empire in the path of the California Gold Rush had not personally benefitted from one of the great discoveries in American history, although for years he petitioned Congress for compensation. Eventually he received token payment in recognition for the role he played in the state's history.[16]

Squatters were a common problem in California during the Gold Rush. In American tradition, squatters were generally favored over landowners, based on the long-established principle of "pre-emption," in which landowners were required to work their lands. The principle came from opposition to "land barons" whose property never produced goods that benefited the community. With this American tradition, the large Mexican land grants became vulnerable. In fact, huge acreage was often necessary to maintain the massive herds of cattle and horses on native vegetation. However, to prospective tenants the land appeared unused. This led squatters to occupy land where someone else had the title. Around San Francisco, Sacramento and Stockton, this became a problem almost immediately. In August 1850, a group of around forty squatters marched toward a Sacramento lot that had been reclaimed by the rightful owner, and later threatened to attack a prison ship that housed the offending squatters. The Mayor and a number of citizens attempted to stop the mob. The Mayor was shot. The riots continued, with several deaths, until troops arrived two days later.[17]

In San Francisco, most of the land near the bay had been granted or sold under the Mexican government. But, during the Gold Rush, it was the general practice to simply occupy any unused land, regardless of ownership. When Theodore Shillaber received a lease on Rincon Point from the Federal government, he had to bring out twenty soldiers from the Presidio to clear a group of Australian immigrants who had created a tent and shanty town on the property. When fires destroyed the fragile "downtown" of the city, shop owners rushed to maintain their property against squatters before the site had even cooled.[18]

Initial mine finance

As stories of unimaginable riches spread, many wanted to come to California. However, the gold discoveries were not only far from any cities, they were far from any settled area. There were three choices for people from the eastern United States who wanted to get to the west coast. One, overland wagon trains from the St Louis area, entailed covering vast, empty land—empty that is, except for several tribes of notoriously unfriendly Native Americans. Two, the east coast US inhabitants could sail from New York around the tip of South America and up the west coast. Three, they could sail to Central America, cross overland at Panama or Nicaragua, then catch a passing ship to finish the journey to San Francisco. Numerous international "'49ers" seeking gold usually took a sea route from Canton, Chile, or even Europe through New York. All of these trips took from four months to more than a year, depending on circumstances, and all involved an interesting variety of bad outcomes.

To make these trips possible, entrepreneurs put together companies to travel together and share in any small amount of expertise available on how to reach the gold fields. Many of these companies were cooperatives, with plans to share mining profits. Each member of a cooperative company bought into it for around $300 (a year's average wage). In return, the investor was provided transportation, supplies, mining equipment, and goods for trade. One source estimates there were at least a thousand of these ventures formed just on the US eastern coast in 1849 and 1850, which raised at least $20 million. Disappointment with the arrangements caused many, if not most, of these companies to break up even before reaching California, and few, if any, succeeded in the transition to mining activities. The most valuable aspect of the companies was facilitating the travel, but fortunes were made by some entrepreneurs. George Gordon, formerly known as George Cummings, a London speculator who came to Philadelphia to escape his debts, organized Gordon's California Association. He collected $160 from 127 shareholders to sail around the horn, and $225 from 113 more to sail from New York to Nicaragua then cross Nicaragua and sail from there to San Francisco. The first group made it to San Francisco, but the second group, like many others, found themselves stranded in Nicaragua. Some of this group walked a grueling 2,500 miles to San Diego, California. There they eventually found ships headed north. Gordon travelled with this group, buying lumber in Nicaragua and later making a fortune selling it in San Francisco.[19]

More funds were earned by companies with owners who stayed behind. The Curtis California Mining Company sold 2,000 shares at $5 each and contracted with ten men to travel to California, work for two years, and send the company one-sixteenth of their earnings. In London, eight of these companies formed in January 1849 and raised $12.5 million. In Paris this investment was even more popular, probably due to the fact that France already allowed limited liability companies. Over eighty companies formed in two years and raised $70 million.[20] Expeditions of this type were made from many countries, including China and Chile.

Miners' property rights

Since California became part of the United States in 1848, but not a state until two years later, the Gold Rush occurred in the absence of clear laws as to the property involved. The United States did not even start surveying there until 1851.[21] According to the Treaty of Guadalupe Hidalgo, any land without a Mexican claim or other "encumbrance" belonged to the US federal government. The early gold-mining lands did not belong to any one previously, as they were so far from settled areas. Since the majority of miners were Americans, the assumption was that anyone could settle and use the land. Col. Mason briefly considered ways the government could tax the miners, but realized he had insufficient resources. In fact, miners actually worked out their own system of land ownership. In *A Theory of Property Rights with application to the California Gold Rush*, John Umbeck showed how an excellent scheme developed in the absence of any pre-existing legal system.[22] Even in 1848, when there seemed to be gold everywhere, certain areas (like Coloma) became congested enough that there was conflict between neighboring miners. The solution miners developed was to call a meeting and make up rules about which miner could work a certain area. Once decided, all the participants would enforce each miner's "claim" against outsiders. The group would also make decisions in the event of disagreements among the members.

While these agreements were often only verbal, diaries and a few surviving copies of written agreements reveal that the "miners' meetings" almost always contained certain provisions. First, claims always specified a physical dimension and belonged to individuals, although in fact more than one person usually worked a claim. The workers could be employees or have neighboring claims and work cooperatively. Second, miners had to continually prove they were still actively working their claims, either by actual physical activity, or by reposting their notices of ownership frequently. This satisfied the principle that there should not be absentee land-owners and, very practically, insured that if enforcement was necessary, the participants in the agreement would be close at hand. Exceptions to the rules about active ownership included illness and provision for months when the weather did not allow mining. Third, these miners' groups also invariably made decisions by majority rule.[23] James Williams, a fugitive slave, recalled "we miners constituted a law for ourselves" and that his vote was once crucial in an occasion to try another miner for the crime of stealing $50. He voted for the prevailing side, which did not hang the man, but forced him to return the money and leave the camp.[24]

Umbeck described a written agreement, one from the miners at "Jackass Gulch," from 1849, which he judged to be typical:[25]

1 Each person can hold "one claim by virtue of occupation" that would be one hundred feet square.
2 A claim or claims if held by purchase must be under a bill of sale, and certified by two disinterested persons as to genuineness of signature and of the consideration.
3 A jury of five persons would resolve any dispute. [More often, all the miners voted.]
4 Notices of claims must be posted upon the ground chosen, and must be renewed every ten days "until water to work the said claims can be had."

5 As soon as there is a sufficiency of water for working a claim, "five days of absence from said claim, except in case of sickness, accident or reasonable excuse" shall forfeit the property.
6 These rules shall extend over Jackass and Soldier gulches and their tributaries.

Even though this system of property rights started in 1848, when miners still used pans to mine, claims made under these agreements were so consistently recognized that miners felt perfect security in their ownership. They demonstrated this over the years by making heavy physical investments in their property, and by sales and stock issues.

The land bubble in San Francisco and Sacramento

San Francisco was almost always the entry point to California. By the early spring of 1848 the town, still called Yerba Buena, had about 800 inhabitants. Bayard Taylor was a new arrival then and described "hundreds of tents and homes that were scattered all over the heights, and along the shore for more than a mile." The streets were dirt, and lined with "canvas sheds, open in front." Stored out in the open were "great quantities" of goods.[26]

In Sacramento in July 1849 the situation was similar. Several thousand people were residents, most doing some sort of business in canvas tents or cloth shanties. William Prince set up shop to supply the prospectors on their way to the mines. He paid five dollars a day for half of a canvas store. He then acquired a lot and a wooden store and planned to rent that out for $600 a month.[27]

The '49ers rapidly swelled the ranks of both cities. Since crews often deserted when a ship arrived in San Francisco, the bay was almost solid with hundreds of vessels. Those closest to shore became more like buildings, used for housing and storage of goods. Wooden walkways wove among them in the shallows. But, by 1854, San Francisco had churches, hospitals, a public market, newspapers, at least one school, and several blocks of lighted streets with kerosene lighting and wooden walkways. Many brick and stone structures punctuated the canvas neighborhoods. 500 saloons provided the usual leisure activities for the predominantly young male population.

Financing for the mines

Organized mining companies and shares of stock developed early. From the beginning, East Coast and European investors were the main targets for securities-bearing messengers holding specimen rocks streaked with gold.[28] The Rocky Bar Mining Company is an early example. In the summer of 1849, forty men joined together to mine a promising bar on the American River. They found 107 pounds of gold, but felt that more investment would allow them access to "the source or matrix of all the gold in the country."[29] James Delavan, a physician, went to New York, rented an office, and displayed an array of gold in various forms, including a ten-pound quartz rock streaked with gold veins. He raised only

$20,000. On his next trip, he increased the number of shares, and exaggerated the prospects. He brought back $100,000 from New York, then went to London in 1852 and sold more stock for $125,000.[30]

Horace Greeley and John Fremont each sold stock in their own gold mining companies; Fremont attracted buyers with gold samples purchased for the occasion.[31] By 1851 there was so much mining stock trading that New York tried to open an exchange specifically for mining shares. It was not successful, even though the accumulated value of mining stock sold in the year 1853 alone was about $6 million between New York, London, Manchester, and Paris.[32]

San Francisco had its own market for stocks. There were over 600 men in San Francisco and Sacramento with individual wealth of more than $5,000, but unlimited liability for debts and familiarity with the risk made them cautious of lending to mine projects. Occasionally a merchant would offer a miner a "grubstake": supplies for a season of prospecting in return for a share in any gold found.[33] This obviously was too uncertain and insecure an investment to become a major source of funds. Real estate, especially in property located in San Francisco, seemed to be the favored investment. However, steamboat, wharf, telegraph, water, warehouse, and many other large companies developed in the 1850s, to serve the growing population, and these companies often were financed by issuing shares. Brokers set up business along Montgomery Street and bought gold dust and foreign exchange as well as company shares. Trading was informal among the brokers.[34]

Mining techniques progressed in just a few years. The first miners used pans to sift through sand near the rocky bottoms of creeks to find gold flakes, dust, and even nuggets that had settled there. Cradles were slightly more sophisticated. It was even more efficient to build dams to increase the water pressure and make the streambed dirt below the dam easier to access. Washing dirt from surrounding river banks and bluffs with water hoses came next. This hydraulic mining became more and more sophisticated as hand pumps were supplemented with mechanical. Quartz mining, or tunneling after gold veins (which, although starting with a man with a pickaxe, required shoring for the tunnel and a "car," often on rails, to take the material out), came later, and was the most expensive.[35]

When banks appeared in California, banking was well established in the rest of the world. The process by which banks came into existence in different parts of the United States was common: usually a person who was established as responsible, often a merchant, would accept deposits from local business owners or individuals who wanted safe storage for their gold. They evolved into bankers by making loans, which would be in the form of paper notes issued by the individual bank. Borrowers circulated these notes as they were spent. If any holder of a note appeared at the bank which had issued the note, they could trade it for gold, usually at the prevailing rate of $15 per ounce. But the accepted value in San Francisco was $16 per ounce of assayed gold (assayed to establish the purity).[36] However, notes were more convenient to carry and store than gold, so holders did not usually rush to redeem them and the notes functioned as money. It was vital for bankers to be always able to redeem these notes promptly to prevent panic, so these bankers probably loaned only around 50 percent of the deposits. Bank notes were unpopular in California and merchants often refused to accept them. However, the existence of these note-issuing banks expanded the money supply beyond the value of the circulating gold, which allowed growth of the economy and contributed to the high prices.[37]

Companies that shipped gold also soon found themselves in the exchange business, with Adams & Co., one of the first important express companies in California, becoming one of the major exchange dealers prior to 1855. Likewise, in Stockton, south of Sacramento, C. M. Weber, who started the town's first express company, had built a vault and obtained a safe in 1851 for the purpose of accepting packets for storage.[38] Wells Fargo, long associated with its stagecoach and express business, entered banking in California in 1852 when it issued certificates of exchange in July of that year.[39] The banking services at Wells Fargo had grown so important that an advertisement in the *San Francisco Business Directory* in 1852 only mentioned the express business in tiny letters, while below, in a huge headline, proclaimed "Bankers and Exchange Dealers." Wells Fargo's banking operations grew so fast that by 1855 the company had expanded its services to Sacramento, Stockton and Portland, and, when Wells Fargo opened its office in Los Angeles, its capital quickly reached $1 million.[40]

A common breeding ground for early financial institutions was the general store. The merchant had to handle money and had a chance to establish the trust of customers. Most merchants allowed reliable customers to "run a tab"—an early form of credit extension—and many already had safes to protect their own daily cash balances. Even Luzena Wilson, who started her career making biscuits as her husband dug for gold in Nevada City, then quickly evolved into a boarding house owner, described herself as a "banker," too. She kept bags of gold dust in her kitchen, in milk pans, and in the oven, and she made loans at 10 percent interest.[41] One merchant, Darius Ogden ("D.O.") Mills, left a budding career as a bank clerk in New York to follow his older brothers to California. Abandoning the rigorous life of a miner shortly after he arrived, Mills purchased a stock of goods which he transported to Sacramento and quickly sold. The profit from this operation was so much greater than he could make in the gold fields that D.O. returned to New York, found a financial partner, and brought more goods to take back to Sacramento. After a year as a storekeeper, Mills made another trip to New York to present his business partner with $40,000 in profits from a $5,000 initial investment![42] When Mills travelled back to Sacramento in the winter of 1849–50, he left orders for a number of goods to be shipped after him, including a large safe, which became the key feature in the new "Bank of D.O. Mills." He would become one of the most important bankers and the richest man in the state.

Rent rose quickly in gold rush San Francisco. Thomas Wells, a newspaper publisher, moved to California from New England to establish a branch of Willis & Company, a Boston banking house. In August 1849, Thomas Wells opened his Specie and Exchange Office that consisted of only a fourteen- by twenty-two-feet room with a wooden plank counter, used as a teller's window and a bed. The *Bankers Magazine* reported the rent for this room was $800 *per month*.[43]

Wells was out of business in a few months, but bankers came early to the Gold Rush and mostly did well. Bankers built some of the earliest and most substantial buildings in San Francisco. Once a businessman had gained a reputation and acquired a safe, the final step in becoming a successful banker was to construct a building. The bank building was the physical "symbol of safety" upon which a banker's business rested. An aspiring banker made it a matter of urgency to construct a facility that not only provided physical protection of assets but also suggested that it was an establishment of permanence and strength.[44] The building itself often contained the most ornate furnishings and finest wood and brass, matched by few other buildings, save for a saloon, in a typical western town.[45]

John Parrott constructed one of the most interesting financial buildings in early San Francisco. He had been an early immigrant, from Mazatlan, Mexico, and owned many lots in the town. In Mazatlan he had been a banker. In 1852, he decided to create a truly unique structure for a bank. From China he ordered a building facade of stone. Many Chinese were in San Francisco by then, and the assembly instructions in Chinese presented no challenge. Unfortunately, the construction workers quickly informed Parrott that the building had poor "Feng Shui," and they would not work on it. But they did finish the building, and, with some proper rituals enacted, it survived without incident as a financial institution until the 1900s.[46]

After seeing the rich lode at Coloma, Lt Tecumseh Sherman left California for New Orleans. There, he was offered a job as manager with St Louis-based Lucas Turner & Co., when that company opened a branch in San Francisco in 1853. Henry Turner himself opened the branch early in 1853 by renting a space across the street from the Parrott Building for $600 a month and hiring two employees. Sherman arrived to assess the prospects in late April after a two-month trip marked by a pair of shipwrecks on the same day: "not a good beginning for a new peaceful career," he wrote.[47] Finding the prospects good, Sherman returned home, resigned his Army commission, collected his family, and journeyed back to California. By the end of the year, he started planning for a permanent building for the bank. He paid $31,000 for a lot at Montgomery and Jackson in February 1854.[48] Sherman, who would later gain fame on his "March to the Sea" with the Army of the West in the Civil War, then constructed a three-story building at a cost of 27 percent of the of the bank's total capital. The building survives today, although it lost the top story to the 1906 earthquake. While it was obviously a solid structure, Sherman built it for investment purposes. It housed the bank, but had other office space that could be rented out.[49]

End of the land boom

Ultimately, the rush of the '49ers to California created only a short surge in land values. According to bank historian Ira Cross,

> in the early months of 1850 it began to appear, however, that the future of business in practically all lines had been greatly overestimated. Real estate

values had been inflated to a ruinous degree by the unbounded confidence of the people.[50]

The most probable cause of the slowdown in the economy was an extremely dry 1849–50 winter, which impeded gold mining. Businesses supplying the mines clearly suffered. This recession brought foreclosures. In Sacramento, Cross estimates that probably less than a quarter of the amount originally loaned was repaid.[51] The next winter was also dry.

Snow and rain came in the 1852–3 winter, and the spring thaw attracted many miners up to the high hills again. But the decline continued in gold production by individual miners, and increasingly the successful operations needed expensive equipment and expertise to reach the profitable veins of gold. Many quit and returned to their original home, with lifetime tales of adventure but little yellow ore.

In 1854 and 1855, financial markets in San Francisco experienced several panics. When the St Louis-based Page, Bacon & Co. failed, it triggered a disastrous run on all banks in San Francisco. The main office of Page & Bacon had invested heavily in a Midwestern railroad, but still had sufficient capital to keep the bank open by shipping California gold back to St Louis by steamer. But word reached San Francisco that the St Louis branch of Page & Bacon had folded, and the subsequent run shut down the company, as well as other banks, including Adams & Co. and Miner's Exchange Bank. Most offices of Wells Fargo closed.

Another panic occurred when prominent San Francisco citizen Henry Meiggs, who had supplied much of the city's lumber, and built Meiggs Wharf, unexpectedly left town owing $800,000 secured with forged city warrants.[52] Meiggs' abrupt exit could be traced to the constant harassment he received from Sherman regarding his debts. Dwight Clarke's collection of letters from Sherman shows that the future general mercilessly hounded Meiggs for payments in the period prior to the latter's hasty departure.[53] Meiggs' voyage triggered several bank failures. The Savings Bank of California failed in 1855. The Pacific Loan and Security Bank, which opened in 1854, paid one to 1.5 percent a month interest on deposits (not an unusually high rate), and closed in 1856.[54]

In the bank panic of 1855 "hundreds of businesses went under." Between 1855 and 1860 there were "a plethora of bankruptcies—a condition reflected in the other chief centers in the State."[55] Yet gold mining continued to stimulate the California economy through the late 1800s with smaller, localized discoveries all over the state. By 1860, gold mining had produced an accumulated value of output of $44 million, more than ten times the next-largest industry, flour. However, the Gold Rush as a phenomena was over by 1860, when the US census of manufacturing listed "Flouring and Grist Mill Products" as the largest industry in the state, with an aggregate annual value of $9 million. Milled quartz (rock crushed for gold content) was the fourth-largest industry, with $3.4 million of output.[56] Ultimately, the land rush spread from San Francisco and Sacramento to the surrounding farmland.

The fact that the 1870 census showed the largest industries were flouring and grist-mill products ($12 million), slaughtering ($7.9 million), molasses and refined sugar ($4.7 million), foundry and machine shop products ($4.7 million), and boots and shoes ($4.5 million), did show that the state was no longer dependent on mining.[57] By then there were over half a million people residing there, and the need for residential land overtook the demand for land laden with gold.

Notes

1 Robert Glass Cleland, *From Wilderness to Empire: A History of California 1542–1900* (New York: Alfred A. Knopf, 1944), 269.
2 Albert L. Hurtado, *John Sutter: A Life on the American Frontier* (Norman, Oklahoma: University of Oklahoma Press, 2006), 217–18.
3 Ibid., 218.
4 Ibid., 224–30.
5 Rockwell D. Hunt, *California and Californians: The American Period* vol. 2 (Chicago, Illinois: The Lewis Publishing Company, 1930), 63.
6 Hurtado, 175.
7 Ibid., 225–8.
8 Richard Mason, "Official Report on the Gold Mines," (San Francisco, California: The Virtual Museum of the City of San Francisco, August 17 1848). Available online at www.sfmuseum.org/hist6/masonrpt.html.
9 Ibid.
10 Hurtado, 234.
11 Ibid., 239.
12 Ibid., 240.
13 Ibid.
14 Dwight L. Clarke, *William Tecumseh Sherman: Gold Rush Banker* (San Francisco, California: California Historical Society, 1969), 14–15.
15 Hurtado, 249.
16 The house at Hock Farm was destroyed by arson in 1865. Sutter relocated to Washington, D.C., then later retired to Pennsylvania. He died in 1880, in Washington, D.C., still working to get his claims verified. Hurtado, *John Sutter*, 321.
17 Hunt, 288.
18 Ibid., 290.
19 Richard E. Lingenfelter, *Bonanzas & Borrascas: Gold Lust and Silver Sharks, 1848–1884* (Norman, Oklahoma: University of Oklahoma Press, 2012), 45–6.
20 Ibid., 49.
21 Hunt, 293.
22 John Umbeck, *A Theory of Property Rights with application to the California Gold Rush* (Ames, Iowa: The Iowa State University Press, 1981).
23 Ibid., 94.
24 James Williams, *Fugitive Slave in the Gold Rush: Life and Adventures of James Williams* (Lincoln, Nebraska: University of Nebraska Press, 2002), 23.
25 Umbeck, 94.
26 Hunt, 206.
27 Hurato, 250.
28 Lingenfelter, 57.
29 Ibid., 55.
30 Ibid., 56.

31 Ibid.

32 Ibid., 61.

33 Ibid., 54–5.

34 Leroy Armstrong and J. O. Denny, *Financial California: An Historical Review of the Beginnings and Progress of Banking in the State* (1916. Reprint. New York: Arno Press, 1980), 157.

35 Umbeck, 103.

36 Ben[jamin] Cooper Wright, *Banking in California: 1848-1910* (1910. Reprint. New York: Arno Press, 1980), 7.

37 Lynne Pierson Doti and Larry Schweikart, *California Bankers 1848-1993* (Needham Heights, Massachusetts: Ginn Press, 1994), 15.

38 Ira Cross, *Financing an Empire: History of Banking in California* vol. I (Chicago, Illinois: S. J. Clarke, 1927), 90.

39 A merchant could deposit gold in a financial institution in San Francisco. The certificate of exchange, when presented to another institution in a different location, allowed gold to be paid. Pamphlet. Wells Fargo History Department, *Historical Highlights* (Wells Fargo Bank: 1982), 5.

40 W. Turrentine Jackson, "Wells Fargo: Symbol of the Wild West?" *Western Historical Quarterly* 3 (April 1972), 179–96. Also see his many articles on Wells Fargo, including "A New Look at Wells Fargo, Stagecoaches, and the Pony Express," *California Historical Society Quarterly* 45 (1966), 291–324; "Stages, Mails and Express in Southern California: The Role of Wells, Fargo & Co. in the Pre-Railroad Era," ibid. 56 (1974), 233–72; "Wells Fargo Staging Over the Sierras," ibid. 44 (1970), 99–133; and "Wells Fargo's Pony Expresses," *Journal of the West* 11 (1972), 412–17.

41 JoAnn Chartier and Chris Enss, *With Great Hope: Women of the California Gold Rush* (Guilford, Connecticut: Twodot, 2000), 59.

42 Lynne Pierson Doti, "D.O. Mills," *Encyclopedia of American Business: Banking and Finance to 1913*, edited by Larry Schweikart (New York: Facts On File, 1990), 316–20.

43 Cross, 91.

44 More unorthodox methods of protecting money and valuables are discussed in Doti and Schweikart, *Banking in the American West*, 19–37, and Larry Schweikart, *A History of Banking in Arizona* (Tucson, Arizona: University of Arizona Press, 1982), chapters 1 and 2.

45 Doti and Schweikart, *Banking in the American West*, 39.

46 Doti and Schweikart, *California Bankers*, 24–5.

47 Clarke, 17.

48 Ibid., 22.

49 Ibid., 18.

50 Cross, 91.

51 Ibid., 92.

52 Ibid., 177.

53 Clarke, 155–7.

54 Cross, 177.

55 H. W. Brands, *The Age of Gold: The California Gold Rush and the New American Dream* (New York: Doubleday, 2002), 350.

56 Kerry O'Dell, *Capital Mobilization and Regional Financial Markets: The Pacific Coast States, 1850–1920* (New York: Garland Publishing Company, 1992), 52. Compiled from the Census of Manufacturing data.

57 Ibid.

3 The silver boom and the golden spike
1860–1880

California's slowing economy in the mid-1850s was interrupted by the discovery of a massive silver lode east of the Sierra Nevada Mountains, a discovery almost as significant to California's growth as the Gold Rush had been a decade earlier. As that growth tapered, the transnational telegraph was completed in 1861, and the transcontinental railroad connected in 1869, both of which expanded California's role in the world market for agricultural products. While the silver boom brought enough money into the economy that San Francisco experienced yet another new wave of building and emerged as the financial capital of the West, the connection of the telegraph and the railroad also stimulated real estate prices. Agriculture continued to expand, particularly in the San Joaquin Valley, in coastal communities and inland in the south.

San Francisco develops into a financial center

San Francisco was surveyed to its current plan in 1847 by order of the American "Alcade" (mayor). The US grid system used seemed poorly suited to the hilly city, and Market Street, which runs diagonally on the relatively level land, now seems a strange accommodation as it creates traffic havoc in the city's busiest areas. When the Gold Rush started, a few swampy areas had been filled in, but the majority of the city remained "largely in a state of nature."[1] Heavy rain in the winter of 1849–50 created streets deep with muck, but in the summer of 1850 businesses contributed to a government effort to add planks and sewers to the streets. The northern coast of the United States supplied plentiful lumber, and it was used to create deck-like roads and sidewalks. Unfortunately, frequent fires consumed the flimsy town, and the wooden streets often fell victim to them. The bay at the foot of Market Street was promptly filled with "water lots" sold in the expectation that the cove next to the downtown would be filled in. It did become part of the city, starting with incorporating the ships abandoned early in the Gold Rush. The infill continued until Market Street reached its current terminus in 1851. By then, no indentation of the cove remained.[2] By 1856, some very large commercial buildings existed in the city. St Mary's Church, still standing in 2016, was almost complete. George Gordon had finished the first sugar refinery on the west coast and built the South Park neighborhood.

George Gordon first became known to Californians as the leader of the first expedition to the west coast to cross Nicaragua. The expedition became stranded in the land crossing and most passengers had to make their own way up to gold country. When Gordon finally found a ship to take his by then diminished group from Nicaragua, the lumber he also included in the transport made him a fortune when he arrived in October 1849. He then attempted to establish a regular shipping line to run from San Francisco to New York by purchasing ships that had been abandoned in the bay. Buying and selling more lumber, Gordon built wharves, imported prefabricated buildings, and purchased buildings elsewhere that could be broken down easily for reassembly. Included among the buildings he advertised for sale was, one "got out of Liverpool," a church with Gothic windows, and a thirty-two-room hotel. It is likely that the oldest residence in San Francisco today, the "Abner Phelps house," was imported by Gordon, probably from Louisiana.[3] He was also building houses by 1851, and extended his wharf-building activities to other coastal towns. Constructing "iron houses and buildings" in his foundry and on site, he sold plank roads, docks, wheat threshers, building foundations, water and gas pipes, mills of all types (lumber, grist, quartz, and so-on), and steam engines.[4]

In 1852, Gordon bought twelve acres on the south side of Rincon Hill and put together plans for an elegant neighborhood bounded by Second, Third, Bryant, and Brannan streets. He bought six lots, and then broke them down into sixty-eight town house lots. The neighborhood was centered by a boat-shaped garden 550 by 75 feet. A newspaper advertisement appearing in January 1855 stated that the lots would be auctioned, and terms would be offered of one-third cash down with the balance in six and twelve months, at 2 percent interest per month. Seventeen houses had been built at a cost of about $150,000.[5]

Unfortunately, Gordon offered the houses for sale just as the economy slowed in 1861, forcing him to offer loans on 90 percent of the value.[6] South Park became a fashionable neighborhood, in spite of remaining unsold lots, and continued to be a preferred neighborhood until Nob Hill became its main competition in the 1870s. George Gordon had moved into other industries by that time. His chief project was a beet sugar refinery, a massive building financed by a stock issue. Local owners had half the stock and the rest of the funding came from the east coast. At this time, the ironworks, too, had been incorporated. By 1865, Gordon was one of the wealthiest men in San Francisco. To celebrate his new status, he decided to build a country house.[7]

Gordon chose a location just south of San Francisquito Creek, which divides Santa Clara and San Mateo counties. He built a "very respectable house," then planted grapes and sugar beets.[8] He and his neighbors, including banker William Ralston and railroad builder Leland Stanford, would develop widely varied agricultural and industrial activities in the 1860s, using the earnings from silver mining.

The Silver Bonanza

Two miners looking for gold discovered silver in 1859. This "Comstock Lode" would turn into the biggest silver discovery in history and fuel the next boom in California. Another rush began, known as the "Silver Bonanza." The area where rich veins existed was in the desert just on the other side of the Sierra Nevada Mountains from the San Joaquin Valley; however, for political reasons this area became part of the new state of Nevada. Since little else existed in what would become Nevada, in the 1800s the bonanza economy was entirely Californian, and profits made in mining for the next twenty years fueled the building of a new San Francisco. California notables such as William Ralston, Charles Crocker, Leland Stanford, George Hearst, John Mackay, and William Flood all made their fortunes in silver mining. Silver mining offered fabulous opportunities for wealth, but involved considerable risk. Silver was unlike gold. It was not on the surface, but had to be pursued where the vein of metal led, and veins often dove deep into the mountains, becoming accessible only by digging mines. While silver miners might easily discover a vein of the blackened metal near the surface, the pursuit of silver veins required deep mines with reinforced tunnels, ore cars and rails, and pumps and blowers to keep the water and noxious gasses at bay, as well as elaborate mills and separators to process the ore. The timber had to be brought to the desert from the Sierra Nevada Mountains rising precipitously west of the town. Equipment for the mines was shipped from San Francisco docks to Sacramento, then hauled to the mountains, and then over the mountains to Virginia City. This all required extensive capital. Hydraulic gold mining had originally initiated the use of mining shares, and mine stock examples exist for the 1850s.[9] But with the higher costs of the silver mines, a lively market for silver mine stocks soon developed, as people realized that capital invested in a mine might not pay off for years or could make one rich in a day, depending on what the miners found. Flooding, gas leaks, and collapsing timbers all provided variations in production, all risks better shared.[10]

By 1862, there were at least fourteen stockbrokers in San Francisco. While they mostly handled trades in mining shares, they were also brokers for the bonds issued by utility companies, steamboats, wharves, insurance companies, and the scrip occasionally issued by the city in lieu of payments. The same brokers handled currency exchange.[11] Buying low and selling high proved traditionally lucrative, but the broker's fee for matching buyers and sellers provided a steadier income. In 1862, forty members formed the San Francisco Stock and Exchange Board. In 1863, two more boards formed, the San Francisco Board of Brokers and the Pacific Board of Brokers, also with forty members each.[12] The San Francisco Stock and Exchange Board doubled its size within a year and sold seats for $250 to $1,000 each. Prices for the seats rose in spite of being fixed at $2,000 each in 1867. Two seats traded in 1873 at around $10,000.[13]

The stock market in San Francisco quickly became as sophisticated as any in the world. In 1868 there was a contest for the control of a $1 million-a-year mine, the "Hale & Norcross." The stock went to $2,925 a share, then, in a week, to $7,100. Short sales became a problem, as it seemed the stock had become unavailable at any price. It was briefly delisted to allow time for the market to find equilibrium.[14] By 1875, Virginia City silver mining stocks were traded heavily. The prices ranged from around $20 to $800. Hundreds of thousands of dollars of stock were traded before the official daily opening of the market at 11.00 a.m., and the opening was moved to 9:30 a.m. Then the market closed at 11.00 a.m. to record the transactions. Another short session occurred in the afternoon.[15] A broker reported the orders for mining stock came in from "the kitchen to the pulpit; from every shade in life, and every nationality represented in San Francisco."[16] The Chinese population was singled out as particularly active traders. About $350 million in trades were conducted that year.[17] The stock profits often ended up in the facades of the rather fabulous buildings erected in San Francisco in this era.

The brokers lived well then, as brokers often do in boom times, some making more than $1,000 a month.[18] By the mid-1870s the stock exchange seats went for up to $40,000. In 1874, the "California Mine" and the "Consolidated Virginia" struck very rich veins of silver, precipitating a short but spectacular bubble. Major owners of stock in the mine, including E. J. "Lucky" Baldwin, suddenly became extremely rich. "Lucky," it should be noted, earned his nickname because a large tract of land he received, in lieu of his deposit, from the failed Temple and Workman Bank of Los Angeles rocketed in value when the railroad chose his property for the first route south from the bay area to Southern California.[19]

Silver Kings' banks

The Virginia silver mines provided cash for some very large banks, which changed the face of San Francisco and supplied funds from there to the economy of the rest of the state. The impetus for starting a new bank was the ability of the bank to invest in the stock of other companies. Until 1930, banks freely invested in stocks. Starting a bank multiplied the funds available for the purpose by investing the deposits. The Bank of California, built on the silver rush, was started by the "Atlas of the Pacific": William Ralston. Ralston had been influential since he started for California in 1849. He quickly discovered that serving the other gold seekers could be more profitable. On his way to California, he stopped in Panama and ran a Cornelius Vanderbilt-backed business helping book passage to San Francisco. Once he arrived at the town himself, he set up a steamship business, imported merchandise, started a dry goods store, and joined a banking firm. In 1864, he rounded up some of the most prominent California citizens, including pioneer banker D. O. Mills, and started a new bank. Ralston wanted his new bank to stand out as the most important in the state, and accordingly he named it The Bank of California (with "The" always capitalized in the title). Mills became the new president, bringing his famous wealth and reputation to the position, while Ralston took on the daily management job of cashier, deciding the investments and loans that the bank would make. When The Bank of California opened on July 1 1864 its charter specifically listed its business as banking, the first bank allowed under an 1862 revision of the state's Constitution. The Bank of California was the first incorporated bank in California, which would grow with the increasingly successful Comstock silver mines.[20]

With its earnings from silver, The Bank of California financed woolen mills, a sugar refinery, an insurance company, a railroad equipment manufacturing company, a winery, lumber mills, gas and water companies, and the Sacramento Valley Railroad, as well as investing in other existing projects, such as the Vulcan Foundry. Ultimately, so many businesses owed at least some part of their existence to The Bank of California that Ralston biographer George Lyman called Ralston the "Atlas of the Pacific," for upon his shoulders "rested the financial structure of the Pacific Coast."[21]

Ralston suited his title, building the most elaborate financial headquarters west of the Mississippi, with tall arched windows and nineteen-feet-high ceilings capped by ornamental vases. The bank's interior sported polished dark wood counters, and, while it lacked the traditional tellers' "cages," The Bank of California advertised its four massive vaults, each formed of a three-inch-thick wall of stone. Enclosed in glass were inner offices where Ralston and the cashier worked. Contrary to the layout of most banking houses in other parts of the country, there was no "ladies banking room." The bolder sort of women who lived in California deposited their funds with the same dark-suited tellers who served the men. To attract Chinese customers, Ralston employed Chinese tellers, whom he exempted from his dress codes by allowing them to wear their customary dark silk robes and braided long hair.[22]

Beyond the bank, however, Ralston's influence ran deep. He built the huge, unrivalled Palace Hotel, and, to reduce the costs of construction, he created furniture and hardware businesses. He even loaned money to the Japanese government to buy railroad engines from California. In 1874, he created a new silver coin, called the "trade dollar," to encourage Asian suppliers to hold money earned in trade, increasing the demand for silver. By August 1875, however, Ralston's overextended empire caught up with him. That year, a nationwide financial panic that had started in 1873 finally reached California, sparking runs that closed the Bank of California. Ralston, the day after the bank closed, perhaps crushed by the impending bankruptcy of his personal estate, went for one of his occasional swims in the San Francisco Bay. He was observed in a brief struggle, but died before he could be brought ashore. "Atlas" had put down the globe for good, but the bank managed to reopen in October of the same year under the leadership of William Sharon, backed by the return of D. O. Mills.[23]

Nevada Bank, which began business in 1875, was one of the largest banks built on wealth from the silver mines. It was named for the location of the silver mines, but the bank was in San Francisco. James Flood, W. S. O'Brien, James Fair and J. W. Mackay started it with capital of $5 million. Within a year the capital was paid up to $10 million. There were only five stock holders: the four "Silver Kings" mentioned above plus Louis McLane, first president of the bank.[24]

James Flood had worked with William S. O'Brien in the mines, and the two renewed their friendship in San Francisco. In 1857, determined to try a recession-proof venture, they opened a saloon. Their establishment became an institution by the 1860s. O'Brien was happy with the social life this business produced, but Flood had other ambitions. He began to speculate in silver stocks, soon proving himself a keen investor. By 1868, he hauled his partner out of the bar and into upstairs offices on the "Wall Street of the West," Montgomery Street.[25] A few months later, the pair joined with John Mackay and Charles Fair, who had par-layed their mining skills into mine shares and were substantial owners of Virginia City silver mines. Mackay and Fair recognized potential in the Hale & Norcross mine, and approached Flood and O'Brien with a plan to gain control. Mackay had cash to buy a three-eighth interest with the profits he had saved from his "Kentuck" mine, but the other partners borrowed to pay for their shares.[26] Flood began to quietly buy the stock on their behalf.[27]

With Mackay and Fair's mining skills the Hale & Norcross began to pay nicely, and the four looked to repeat their success at another mine.[28] They also bought a silver-stamping mill (which crushed ore to extract the silver), and a water com-pany. Although they owned several mines, the one that kept the stamps busy and made the fortune of the Silver Kings was the "Consolidated Virginia." The mine had been worked over by numerous owners but had yielded only low-grade ore, containing little silver per ton of rock, when the talented miner Fair began to tun-nel under the property from a neighboring mine. In May 1872, he pursued silver through more than a thousand feet of rock, 1,200 feet below the surface. The heat was so oppressive that the pick crews had to be relieved every fifteen minutes. In mid-summer Fair finally spotted a thin line of silver. Within weeks, this opened up into the richest silver and gold discovery of all time.[29] The Comstock Lode, two miles long and a couple of hundred feet wide, in just a few years produced $400 million-worth of gold and silver, and "made enormous fortunes for half a dozen men, besides creating a score of mere millionaires and putting hundreds in possession of nest-eggs that ranged from a hundred thousand dollars upwards."[30] Less than four years later, the Silver Kings were enjoying an income of half a million dollars a month.[31]

Crime of '73

Inevitably, the boom would end. One setback was the federal government's decrease in the money supply and the availability of loans on real estate. Then, in a move particularly damaging to California, they decreased silver purchases. Also, the changes in state law stifled the budding stock market, and the produc-tion from the silver mines slowed. To supplement their finances during the Civil War, the US treasury tried issuing paper money for the first time. The Civil War did not directly reach California. However, to fund the war, the Union govern-ment centralized and nationalized control over the American financial system through the National Banking Act. This act established the federally chartered National Banks, which, in turn for buying Union bonds, issued a note that had to be redeemed by any other nationally chartered bank in coin at face value. When the federal bank charters proved unpopular, notes issued by private, state-chartered banks were taxed nearly out of existence. To supplement the availa-ble money, the US Treasury issued "greenbacks," which promised to pay like notes. Greenbacks were disliked by creditors everywhere, but especially in California. Most California transactions required gold in payment, leaving the US customs collectors as almost the only people in the state willing to accept greenbacks. One San Franciscan remembered, "we saw very little currency on this Coast except to pay government taxes … All of our transactions were made in gold."[32] Accordingly, in 1870, Congress amended the National Bank Act to provide for the creation of National Gold Banks, with new notes payable in gold coin. But Congress required that the banks hold a 25 percent reserve in specie—substantially higher than most antebellum private banks would have held—and limited the total amount of outstanding gold notes to $45 million. National banks could not lend on real estate and showed no real estate loans on their books. They did, however, hold repossessed property, so personal loans may have included real estate as collateral. However, just as California was discovering the profits that could be made in farming, a new banking system limited the loans needed to buy land.

The next blow to the market was the federal government's demonetarization of silver in 1873, known as the "Crime of '73." Since 1787, the nation had recognized silver as an official currency as well as gold, in what was known as a "bimetallic standard." Until 1873 the federal government minted both gold and silver coins, with metal purchased on the market without limit. After the Virginia mines and several other silver discoveries in the western United States, silver prices fell. The federal government stopped buying silver to mint silver coins until the 1890s, when silver coining began again, with pressure from western interests.

State increases financial regulation

The state also moved to slow lending. California began examining the state-chartered banks in 1878, and published the balance sheets. Of the first five banks examined, examiners closed the first; the second managed to pass; and the next three closed before the inspectors' arrival.[33] The first reports of the bank examiners were incomplete, but seem to reveal twenty-eight incorporated savings banks, fifty-two commercial banks and four branches of foreign banks in the state. When the examiners started looking at the books of the individual state-chartered banks, they found five insolvent. A number of other banks were discovered to have impaired capital. It seemed an unusual number of banks had failed in 1877 and 1878, causing speculation that they had anticipated poor reviews.[34]

California's assembly re-wrote the state's constitution in 1879, and, wary of all financial businesses, included detailed laws limiting the activities of stockbrokers. Stocks could be sold with a 50 percent margin, refundable.[35] This further slowed the waning mining stock frenzy, as the brokers were not willing to take the extra risk of margin sales in this circumstance, and left the mine owners without the funds needed to mine ever deeper. Combined with that problem were the increased costs due to flooding in the Virginia City mines. A pick applied to rock could result in a powerful spray of scalding water which quickly expanded to a torrent as miners fled in terror. Powerful, and expensive, pumps were needed to keep underground pockets of water at bay. After years of trying to get cooperation from the mine owners, Adolph Sutro built a tunnel to drain the water, completing it in 1879. He partly funded it with a "safety" tax on the miners. By the late

1880s, the price of silver fell to a point that the deep, costly mining in Virginia City was no longer profitable. Most silver mines were abandoned. Consolidated Virginia Company stock fell to $2 a share in 1885. As Virginia City quieted, silver was discovered in Tonopah, in Southern Nevada, which provided another burst of activity in the San Francisco Stock and Currency Exchange. However, this turned out to be a relatively modest discovery and it did not change the fact that the silver boom was over. Fortunately, while the silver boom slowed, a period of railroad-building would ready the state for the next boom.

Transcontinental railroad

When the Union Pacific and Central Pacific railroads linked up at Promontory Point, Utah, on May 10 1869, the event produced a transformational change in the American economy. While Robert Fogel was the first to investigate its actual dollar impact, and argued that railroads' completion pre-empted canals, wagon roads, and other forms of transportation, there is no doubt that, for California, it was one of the most important events in its history.[36] The vast emptiness between the Mississippi and the state, and the hundreds of dismal accounts of travel over that barren and sparsely populated area, argued in favor of shortening a danger-ous trip of several months to only a week on a relatively comfortable mode of transportation.[37]

The transcontinental railroad was made possible by federal government sub-sidies in the form of land and bonds. Since the mid-1700s, the government had granted public land to subsidize transportation. There is economic justification in this. Private owners of roads, canals or trains can only make the travelers pay, but the benefit of improved transportation is even more to the land-owners. Transportation facilitates the movement of customers, supplies and finished goods, which makes the land more valuable for business or residential use. Governments' power to tax the property owners and supplement the transportation costs ensure that more transportation is provided.[38]

The idea of a transcontinental railroad was prompted by the Gold Rush mass exodus through St Louis to California. Congress started to seriously discuss the idea, and in 1855 the Secretary of War presented a report to Congress, which based the need mostly on the safety of Americans travelling the route.[39] Congress approved aiding the effort in 1862 and amended the bill in 1864, now spurred by the recognition of the need to move troops in wartime. The Union Pacific Railroad Company was to commence building from St Louis west, and the Central Pacific Railroad Company would build east from Oakland. They would each proceed to Nevada, or wherever they met.[40]

Congress granted each company a right of way 400 feet wide and twenty odd-numbered sections of land beyond that to sell. This is roughly 12,800 acres per mile of track built. Congress granted The Central Pacific, assembled in 1861 by business leaders Collis Huntington, Charles Crocker, Leland Stanford, and Mark Hopkins, an additional twenty sections per mile to compensate for the more rug-ged terrain it had to cross.[41] In fact, much of the land was not very valuable, as it was mountainous, riverbed, swampy, or otherwise unsuitable for farming. If the land granted was previous occupied, the railroad could swap that land for other land.[42] The railroad land grants were in the usual rigid checkerboard pattern, so the railroad owned plots corresponding to red, while the government retained ownership to the black plots. Both were anxious to sell, the government for the revenue, and the railroads both for income and to put farmers and ranchers in place that would become customers.[43] As Collis Huntington put it:

> What we get by the sale of the lands is not the object; but it is that we may have a title to convey to others, so that they can put on the necessary improvements and cultivate the same so as to give the railroad something to transport.[44]

There had been considerable land speculation anticipating the completion of the Transcontinental Railroad. When it was finished in 1869, the possibilities of exports were not immediately obvious. There was far too much empty distance between California and the more densely populated regions of the United States. Plus, there was the difficulty of getting the crop production from rural areas to the railroad terminus. While some short rail lines were built before 1869, including one from Sacramento to Folsom, which opened in 1856, regular routes for bulk exports did not exist when the transcontinental line connected.

Congress then subsidized a rail line to connect the Central Pacific route via a roughly north-south line through Sacramento to Oregon. In 1887, this line reached Ashland, Oregon.[45] As the railroad went through Sacramento, the wheat growers in the San Joaquin Valley also had railroad access to the river to San Francisco Bay and to the transcontinental railroad. The railroad grants in the Valley were occupied by the ranchers and farmers, with the expectation that the railroad would "prove" its grants by finishing the required mileage, and then that it would sell the land to the farmers at a low price. The resulting tension between the wheat farmers and the railroad when the land grant was signed over to the railroad culminated in the armed clash known as the "Mussel Slough" incident, which was fictionalized in Frank Norris' *The Octopus*.[46] The incident was real, but in the book the tension was exaggerated. While the railroad company spent ten years finishing the line, settlers had been making improvements to their land. In the Norris book, when the railroad offered the land for sale, they asked for the ten to forty dollars that the improved land would be at market value, instead of the two dollars that federal land usually sold for. The railroad, in reality, promptly offered discounts to existing settlers. The Mussel Slough incident occurred, but most of the issues proceeded to the courts, with widely varied outcomes.[47] Congress and the state gave numerous grants for railroad building, totaling eleven million acres, or about 11.4 percent of the state's area. The Southern Pacific railroad received around seven million acres in total.[48] After 1900, the Southern Pacific changed their policy to develop their properties themselves, rather than selling. Railroads, especially the Southern Pacific, still owned significant amounts of land in California for the next century. But in the 1870s, they saw the need for more customers, and built more branch lines to accommodate the growing agricultural industry.

Early development in agriculture

As population continued to increase after the Gold Rush, farming in the central valley known as the San Joaquin was becoming necessary to the economy. The earliest farming came with the Missions, of course, but even before the Gold Rush the fertile land and abundant water between San Francisco and Sacramento attracted farmers. Wheat was the easiest crop to grow, and was in demand from the passing trading ships and whalers. Even William Ralston bought an island where he grew wheat, and John Sutter promised shipments of wheat to the Russians at Fort Ross. Champion Hutchinson came to Sacramento in 1850 when his warehousing operation in Kenosha, Wisconsin, failed. His Kenosha business had warehoused wheat for spring shipment, but when he bought a ranch south of Sacramento in 1851 he planted 800 acres of fast-growing barley before adding wheat.[49] While most development in the 1860s and the 1870s occurred in and near San Francisco and Sacramento, immigrants were arriving to start new ventures and new towns in other parts of the state. Most of these towns focused on agriculture.

Wine-making was one of the earliest of these ventures. Many visitors spoke of the friars' vineyards and wineries. Missionary Juan Crespi described grapes growing near the Santa Ana River in 1769. At first he said it appeared they had been planted, but he also mentions that they grew wild in many places.[50] In 1856, Agoston Haraszthy, a Hungarian immigrant who had already served as mayor of San Diego and director of the San Francisco mint, started a winery called Buena Vista, in Sonoma. By 1858, he had 57,000 vines on 100 acres. Haraszthy focused on developing a grape from combinations of native vines, and imported New York and fine European grapes. His wine aged in caves carved by Chinese laborers from solid rock, and visitors could buy plants from his nursery. He is credited with starting the commercial wine business in the state, and probably developed California Zinfandel wine.[51]

Other agricultural communities developed first in the period 1860 to 1880. The valley that came to be known as San Bernardino had been known to the Spanish missionaries, and a chapel in the area served priests from the San Gabriel Mission. Pedro Fages had visited the area when tracking a missing soldier. Several tribes of Native Americans lived in the area, then and long afterward. Some Spanish land grants dotted the valley, but they had vanished by the 1830s, leaving only the name San Bernardino. When the Mexican government took the land, it granted land to the three sons and a nephew (Diego Sepulveda) of Antonio Maria Lugo, who already owned a legendary amount of land in the state. The four men attempted cattle and horse ranching, but suffered from frequent raids by Native Americans. Even Utes from the Great Basin area would travel through the area, sweeping horses before them. Finally, the Lugo brothers asked Lorenzo Trujillo, a trader from Santa Fe, to bring families to settle the area. Families came from New Mexico, but did not stay more than a year. Then a band from the Cahuilla tribe agreed to relocate from the nearby mountains to the ranch. This still apparently did not make the ranch attractive to the Lugo family, because, in 1851, the ranch was sold to the Church of Latter Day Saints (Mormons). The Mormon Battalion had passed through San Bernardino on their way back to Salt Lake City from San Diego, where they had served in the Mexican War. They were impressed enough to ask a price they could name to Brigham Young. The valley would serve as an outpost to Salt Lake City, where the resources were too limited to accommodate all the converts. The gold discovery intervened, but eventually around 450 Mormons came to live in the valley.[52] They industriously began cutting down trees, building homes, and planting grains and vegetables for local use. They built a road to the nearby mountains to facilitate harvesting and hauling timber to Los Angeles for sale. In 1857, Young called the Mormons in San Bernardino back to Salt Lake City. Not all went, but the number of empty houses attracted new settlers, and the town continued its development.[53]

Anaheim, south of Los Angeles and now part of Orange County, also developed early. A group of around fifty German immigrants in San Francisco decided to seek a more rural environment. In 1857, they cooperatively bought 1,100 acres of a Mexican land grant southeast of Los Angeles. The colonists divided the land into small plots, and planted grapes. It was necessary to irrigate the land, so the settlers dug wells and a ditch from the Santa Ana River. It is likely the river, named by Portola on his 1769 expedition, was the source of the town's name.[54] In spite of an apparent lack of experience with wine-making, the colony thrived. The wine made there was exported via a harbor and wharf they built on the ocean, at Alameda Bay, about twenty miles away.

Disease killed the wine grapes in 1885, but, even by the 1870s, Anaheim had schools, churches, fraternal organizations, and at least one bank. Anaheim also had neighboring towns. Santa Ana was the chief rival, and the town leaders fought each other for a rail terminus. Anaheim won, and the first train from Los Angeles arrived at their station in 1875. Two years later an extension brought it to Santa Ana. In the mid-70s there were several years virtually without rain. This slowed the growth of both towns, but also caused the sale of most of the remaining Ranchos in the area. When the rain returned, several other small farm towns developed in Orange County.[55]

In the 1860s and 1870s, growth continued, but at a much slower pace than during the bubble of the Gold Rush. The 1860s and '70s did not experience anything approaching a bubble. The growth during this period was not steady, mostly due to the two major droughts, but there was development of the foundations that were necessary to catch up with the frenzied settlement of the early 1850s. The state gained the massive infusion of funds from the silver mines, the transportation infrastructure of a railroad system, and the foundations of a more diversified economy. Most importantly, growth occurred in the area that would create the next real estate bubble: agriculture.

Notes

1   Roger W. Lotchin, *San Francisco 1846–1856: From Hamlet to City* (Lincoln, Nebraska: University of Nebraska Press, 1974), 165.
2   Ibid. Map, xxii.
3   Albert Shumate, *A San Francisco Scandal: The California of George Gordon, Forty-niner, Pioneer, and Builder of South Park in San Francisco* (San Francisco, California:

The California Historical Society, and Spokane, Washington: The Arthur H. Clark Company, 1994), 95.

4 Ibid., 103.

5 Ibid., 120–4.

6 Ibid., 130.

7 Ibid., 148. From *Hutchings' Illustrated California Magazine* (April 1857).

8 Ibid., 181.

9 Phillip Ross May, *Origins of Hydraulic Mining in California* (Oakland, California: The Holmes Book Company, 1970), 12.

10 J. F. Clark, *The Society in Search of Truth or Stock Gambling in San Francisco, a Novel* (San Francisco, California, 1878), *passim.*

11 Joseph L. King, *History of the San Francisco Stock and Exchange Board* (San Francisco, California: Jos. L. King, 1910), 3. Lists of stock trades, 23–7.

12 Ibid., 4–5. The San Francisco Stock and Bond Exchange and the Los Angeles Oil Exchange, formed in 1889, merged to create the Pacific Coast Stock Exchange in 1957. It existed until 2003, became digital, then was merged into the New York Stock Exchange. A "Pacific Coast Stock Exchange," started in the 1860s, merged into The San Francisco Stock and Currency Exchange.

13 Ibid., 54.

14 Ibid., 34, 39–40.

15 Ibid., 80.

16 Ibid., 78.

17 Ibid., 117.

18 Ibid., 174.

19 Ibid., 259.

20 James Joseph Hunter, *Partners in Progress, 1864–1950: A Brief History of the Bank of California N.A. & of the Region It Has Served for 85 Years* (New York: Newcomen Society in North America, 1950), 13–29.

21 George D. Lyman, *Ralston's Ring: California Plunders the Comstock Lode* (New York: Scribner's, 1937), 56.

22 Lynne Pierson Doti and Larry Schweikart, *California Bankers 1848–1993* (Needham Heights, Massachusetts: Ginn Press, 1994), 36.

23 Ibid., 29–45.

24 Ira Cross, *Financing an Empire: History of Banking in California* vol. I, (Chicago, Illinois: S. J. Clarke, 1927), 412.

25 Doti and Schweikart, *California Bankers 1848-1993*, 220–1.

26 Ibid., 45.

27 Oscar Lewis, *Silver Kings: The Lives and Times of Mackay, Fair, Flood and O'Brien, Lords of the Nevada Comstock Lode* (Reno, Nevada: University of Nevada Press, 1986) [Reprint. Originally published: New York: A. A. Knopf, 1947], 41.

28 Ibid., 42–3.

29 Ibid., 135–7.

30 Ibid., 4.

31 Ibid., 220–1.

32 Ben[jamin] Cooper Wright, *Banking in California, 1849–1910* (New York: Arno Press, 1980), 51.

33 Lynne Pierson Doti, *Banking in an Unregulated Environment: California, 1878-1905* (New York: Garland, 1995), 35.

34 Cross, vol. I, 436.

35 King, 174.
36 Robert W. Fogel, *Railroads and American Economic Growth: Essays in Econometric History* (Baltimore, Maryland: Johns Hopkins Press, 1964).
37 The difficulties involved in overland travel was reaffirmed recently by two brothers who attempted to follow the Oregon Trail using a wagon pulled by three mules. In spite of the fact that in modern times they were greeted enthusiastically by Park Rangers, ranch owners and people in the small towns, who replaced the former hostile Native American population along the route, it was a difficult journey. This 2,000-mile trip became the basis of the book: Rinker Buck, *The Oregon Trail: A New American Journey* (New York: Simon and Schuster, 2015).
38 Economists call this "correcting for positive externalities."
39 W. W. Robinson, *Land in California: The Story of Mission Lands, Ranchos, Squatters, Mining Claims, Railroad Grants, Land Scrip, Homesteads* (Berkeley, California: University of California Press, 1948), 149.
40 They met in Utah, after an inattentive Congress let them by-pass each other for about 400 miles.
41 Robinson, 151.
42 Richard Orsi, *Sunset Limited: The Southern Pacific Railroad and the Development of the American West 1850–1930* (Berkeley, California: University of California Press, 2005), 80.
43 Ibid., 37.
44 Ibid., 56.
45 Robinson, 155.
46 Frank Norris, *The Octopus: A Story of California* (New York: Penguin Books, 1994 [1901]).
47 Robinson, 161.
48 Ibid., 157.
49 David Vaught, *After the Gold Rush: Tarnished Dreams in the Sacramento Valley* (Baltimore, Maryland: The Johns Hopkins University Press, 2007), 19.
50 George Phillips, *Vineyards and Vaqueros: Indian Labor and the Economic Expansion of Southern California, 1771–1877* (Norman, Oklahoma: The University of Oklahoma Press, 2010), 57.
51 Brian McGinty, *Strong Wine: The Life and Legend of Agoston Haraszthy* (Palo Alto, California: Stanford University Press, 1998), 304–305.
52 *From Desert Land to Fairy Land: San Bernardino Valley Centennial Edition of the Evening Index* (City of San Bernardino Historical and Pioneer Society, January 2007). Pamphlet compiled by Steve Shaw from a June 1910 series in a newspaper, the *Evening Index*. Available online at www.ci.sanbernardino.ca.us/about/history/ sesquicentennial/s_4_yields_exciting_moments.asp.
53 Burr Belden, *San Bernardino Sesquicentennial: 1810–May 20th 1960* (San Bernardino, California: The Sun Telegram, May 20 1960), S2 to S7. Available online at www.ci.san-bernardino.ca.us/about/history/sesquicentennial/s_1_sesquicentennial_cover.asp.
54 Alice Grimshaw, "History of Early Anaheim," Orange County History Series, vol. 1 (Orange County, California: Orange County Historical Society, 1931). Available online at www.orangecountyhistory.org/history/grimshaw-anaheim.html.
55 Walter Bean, *California: An Interpretive History* (New York: McGraw Hill, 1968), 205.

4   The Southern California land boom
1881–1919

Like the rest of America during the 1880s and early 1890s, California grew at a phenomenal rate. For the nation, manufacturing, particularly steel production, played a large role in this growth, but for California, the full development of agricultural production occurred with the expansion of railroads throughout the state. The transcontinental railroad also encouraged tourism, especially when a rate war developed after the Santa Fe railroad reached Los Angeles through a southern route to compete with the Central Pacific. Speculators bought land once deemed nearly worthless, then subdivided it, and sold it to create small towns and farms.

The federal government's role in land development

It wasn't only the railroads that brought federal financing into the state of California. The 1862 Federal Homestead Act made official the practice of granting land ownership to those who settled and improved the land. The federal government gave any settler a 160-acre plot, as long as it was not previously "appropriated," settled or owned. The conditions to obtain full title changed over time, but the land could be gained from for free if it was occupied and improved. The 1862 Act required five years of residence and cultivation to earn, or "prove," full title to 160 acres. Alternatively, the land could be purchased at $1.25 to $2 an acre. In California there was an advantage of outright purchase, of government land or Mexican land grants, to accumulate larger pieces of land necessary for grazing in the arid climate.

The early 160-acre plots were unmanageably large for most parts of the country that were being settled in the 1860s. On the other hand, even the 640 acres allowed in the timber-and-stone provision of the Act, which provided land to settlers who maintained forests or mines not suited for cultivation, was not enough to sustain a herd of cattle on unirrigated ground in Southern California. Speculators often bought the land, then consolidated parcels, and sold the larger property to ranchers. Desert land laws of 1877 allowed grants, or purchases at twenty-five cents an acre, of 640 acres to irrigate and farm. This land was sometimes proved, then abandoned, but the provisions did encourage experiments with irrigation. In spite of some drawbacks, California settlers made extensive use of the homestead laws, and the federal government's contribution to financing land acquisition was extensive.

Promotion of southern California

San Francisco, with its thriving trade, natural port, and rail links to the east coast and the rest of California, was already one of the great cities of the world by 1880, but the southern part of the state remained rural. Los Angeles County had 8,329 people in 1850. During the Gold Rush, the southern cattle ranchers supplied meat to the northern part of the state. The population of Los Angeles remained largely Hispanic and Native American, mostly vaqueros. In 1868, Abel Stearns was one of the first rancheros in the south to sell his ranch. The Mexican government had granted him and his Mexican wife, Arcadia Bandini, almost 200,000 acres. Stearns' huge herds of cattle and sheep supplied the rising population during the silver boom. When demand for his meat dropped, he sold 177,000 acres to a San Francisco syndicate on credit to re-sell as smaller lots. By getting a portion of the funds whenever a lot sold, Stearns paid his debts, retained a block of downtown Los Angeles, and remained influential until he died.[1] Other rancheros did not end so well. In the 1860s and the 1870s, the area was hit repeatedly with years of drought, devastating the cattle industry. Many ranchers borrowed in the good years, but could not pay their loans and lost their land. The near-total lack of rain from 1875 to 1876 brought an end to almost all of the remaining large, free-range cattle ranches.[2] Title changed hands, mostly from the land grant recipients to investors from San Francisco, who often had no more luck with cattle ranching than the earlier owners. But once the railroad made the area accessible to tourists, the idea of selling the sunny climate to visitors, in the form of farms, became popular. The large land grants were broken down into tracts of small farms, minimally developed, and heavily advertised. Banks funded the purchase of the tracts.[3] Savings banks and B&Ls expanded, financing purchases by the eventual occupant. In the 1880s, the southern part of the state experienced a furious land boom from all the land sales to tourists.

The financial system grew along with the state. State-chartered institutions grew the most, as the nationally chartered banks were still not allowed to lend against real estate. Banks became the main source of funding for real estate development, and savings banks and B&Ls supported individual home ownership. Banking resources went from roughly $100 million in 1870 to around $135 million in 1880; $268 million in 1890; $384 million in 1900, $970 million in 1910, and $2.5 million in 1920. Their real estate lending also rose (see Graph 4.1).[4]

As the financial system and the economy matured, the bankers sought regulation to protect their reputations and avoid competition. The new constitution in 1879, the bank examination requirements initiated in 1878 and a comprehensive financial bill passed in 1905 formalized banking laws, but still left state-chartered institutions far more freedom than those under the National Banking System, particularly in regard to real estate lending and branch banking. In 1913, the Federal Reserve System created new restrictions on nationally-chartered banks.

The three Bank Commissioners appointed under the 1878 act reported complete income statements and balance sheets of every state-chartered bank or

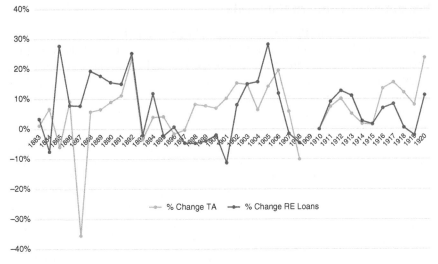

*No bank reports were published for 1878, 1882, 1909, and 1910

Graph 4.1 Percentage change in total assets and real estate loans of financial institutions in California, 1883–1920.

Source: Compiled from the Board of Bank Commissioners *Annual Reports* (Sacramento, California: Office of the Board of Bank Commissioners, 1878–1920), and Board of Commissioners of the Building and Loan Associations of the State of California *Annual Reports* (Sacramento, California: California State Printing Office, 1891–1920).

savings bank they examined. They noted that the distinctions between commercial and savings banks were not clear. Traditionally, commercial banks lent on business ventures, including buying land for resale. Savings banks focused on keeping your money safe, and making loans to individuals. At this time, in California, both made the same types of loans, including loans on real estate, although it is worth noting that they loaned on income-producing land, not homes. The 1878 California Banking Act put some extra restrictions on savings banks. At least 50 percent of their loans on real estate had to be secured by first mortgages, and be for less than 60 percent of the market value of the property. Savings banks were not permitted to participate in the popular sport of investing in mining stocks, nor to loan funds to people for that purpose. These provisions were not enforced.[5]

In 1880, the Commissioner noted that San Francisco commercial banks did not usually pay interest on deposits. Outside San Francisco, two-thirds of the commercial banks paid interest on deposits, but mostly on time deposits that limited withdrawals. The Commissioner's opinion was that the commercial banks should not pay interest on deposits and he wanted more differentiation between commercial and savings banks, but this differentiation never occurred at the state level.[6] Savings banks (occasionally called savings and loan associations) were often mutual societies requiring membership. Opening a deposit account conferred membership and allowed a customer to apply for a loan. There was no expectation that capital existed to provide an extra cushion between deposits and loans, as was normal for commercial banks. Therefore, the policies needed to be more cautious for a savings bank than a commercial bank, where depositors and borrowers are not the same individuals, and deposits and loan payoffs are more predictable. However, in the early days, the name of a financial institution was not always a reliable guide to an institution's characteristic activities. Some savings banks were commercial banks, and vice-versa.[7]

In 1880, the bank Commissioner called attention to the advisability of limits on large deposits by one party at an institution. The large deposit was perceived to be a particular danger for California, since the twenty largest banks had twenty depositors with over a $1 million total. The average value of these large deposits was over $50,000. Large loans to one individual were also a destabilizing factor which the Commissioner thought should be eliminated. The Commissioner recommended that commercial banks loan no more than 15 percent of its paid-up capital to one borrower, and savings banks loan no more than 5 percent of assets to one borrower. All institutions should limit dividends to their earnings, and savings banks should not be allowed to do commercial business. However, banks that opened mostly to serve the needs of a few owners were a tradition that started with the silver era, and that was hard to change. In spite of knowledgeable recommendations, the institutions would remain intertwined into the 1930s, when federal law changed.[8]

The 1880 economy still did not show any signs of recovery. Banks had taken more real estate, repossessed for non-payment of loans.[9] Deposits were also down dramatically from previous years. The state bank examiners expressed the hope that bankers would be less tolerant if the interest on a loan was not paid, as it was probably an indicator that the principal would also not be paid. They argued that savings banks should make less unsecured loans, but noted most of these loans occurred in savings banks that were run jointly with commercial banks.[10]

The recommendations of 1880, so forcefully made, were ignored. In fact, the reports themselves seem to have been largely ignored by the legislators and the state Governors who received them. The state legislature did not even fund printing the 1881 report. This lack of interest on behalf of the Legislature was a constant problem in the early years. In the report of the Board of Bank Commissioners for August 10 1886, for example, the Commissioner complained that the Board continued to make recommendations that were completely ignored by the Governor and the Legislature, "Yet, so far, not the least notice has been taken of their reports, or of any suggestion made in those reports, by the Executive of the state, or by the Legislature to which the reports were submitted," the Commissioner stated.

> We will not in this report name in detail the legislation needed, as the Commissioners have done in so many former annual reports, for to do so might be idle; but we respectfully suggest that a select committee be appointed on "Banks and Banking" in each branch of the Legislature ... With this suggestion we leave it with the honorable the Legislature to decide whether they

> will again ignore the existence of the Commission, or to take up this our report and give it that careful consideration we think the subject demands.[11]

Perhaps because of the petulant tone that prevailed throughout the document, the legislators discounted its warnings. For example, one report stated: "We will not here discuss the matter, and only say that if the opportunity we ask or is given to appear before a legislative committee, we will there give our views."[12] This laissez-faire attitude to the activities of banks by the legislature certainly contributed to the next real estate boom.

Southern California bubble

With the transcontinental railroad complete and the Central Pacific branch line to Los Angeles finished in 1876, the southern part of California took on more importance. By 1887, when the "Silver Kings" bank, Nevada National Bank in San Francisco, nearly failed, the management asked I. W. Hellman of Los Angeles to come and restore the institution, rather than asking a San Francisco banker.

Isaias W. Hellman had come to Los Angeles in 1859 from Bavaria, with his brother and cousins.[13] His first job was as a clerk in a retail store owned by the family. The dry goods store he bought in 1865 featured a safe, allowing him to diversify into banking activities. His was not credited as the first bank in Los Angeles—James A. Hayward and John G. Downey incorporated their bank in 1868—but Hellman quickly developed a reputation as one of the most solid businessmen in the Los Angeles region.[14] In 1871, he merged his bank with Downey's, bringing in twenty-three other local business and agricultural leaders as investors, to form the Farmers and Merchants Bank of Los Angeles. In 1876, Hellman replaced Downey as president after a panic in the city. The Farmers and Merchants Bank quickly prospered under his leadership, and Hellman's business interests extended throughout the state. Even by 1867, when he was twenty-one, he had purchased several lots in what would become part of downtown Los Angeles, at prices ranging from $50 to $180 each. In fact, he bought his first parcel of land in 1863. A neighbor's cook had purchased it on speculation and she offered it to Hellman for $200. "It was far out of the city and I could not take the time to look at it, so I hunted it up on the map and decided it would be worth more someday and bought it."[15]

Later, he bought land to the west of the city, thinking growth would be in that direction. These were larger parcels which he subdivided. Even later, he bought ranches in other areas of California, including the 37,500-acre Nacimiento Ranch in Monterey and San Luis Obispo counties.[16] In 1879, Hellman was developing a large subdivision southwest of downtown Los Angeles. He and his partners donated 308 of the lots for the founding of a university, the University of Southern California (USC). And then they built a trolley to link it to the city.[17]

While Hellman focused on developing Southern California, he was not the only one purchasing the old Mexican land grants to subdivide for development. James Irvine, who lived in San Francisco, was one member of a syndicate which bought several large land grants in Los Angeles County and what would become Orange County. The syndicate, composed of Irvine, Thomas and Benjamin Flint, and Llewellyn Bixby, substituted sheep for cattle, as they believed the sheep could survive with less water. The venture was not a success. Although the owners leased and sold a few parcels for ranches, they soon abandoned the project. Irvine bought out the partners, and shifted his focus back to San Francisco. Irvine's son, James Irvine II, inherited all his father's businesses when he was twenty-three years old. In spite of his youth, he quickly became known for his business acumen, and served on the boards of railroads, sugar refineries, and power companies. He managed the 100,000 acres of Southern California land so well that the Irvine Company was still managing most of the land in 2015.[18] His success came from attacking the water problem. He intercepted the winter rainfall that drained from the hills, and built dams to store the water for summer and dry spells. Canals directed the water to flat farming areas he was able to lease. The resulting farms grew beans, grains, fruit, and vegetables. On the land that could not be irrigated, he continued to graze cattle and sheep. However, even with all the developments, Los Angeles in 1875 still did not look like San Francisco.

The city had a population of about 7,000, but J. A. Graves, a lawyer who came to Los Angeles in that year, remarked that about half really lived on horseback. There were three banks: the Farmers and Merchants, the Los Angeles County Bank, and the Temple and Workman Bank (the last of which failed in 1875). The name of the Los Angeles County Bank changed later to the Bank of America, but it, too, soon liquidated. None of the streets in the "downtown" area had paving, but there were gas lights in a small portion of the business section. Sewage was dumped into an orchard near the corner of Tenth and Main streets, to use as fertilizer. A street car ran from the Pico House (hotel) along Main Street to Spring Street, down Spring Street to Sixth, and out Sixth to Figueroa Street.[19]

Infrastructure improvements that had occurred before the 1880s were focused on trading cattle products to passing ships and to the fortunes of San Francisco. A rail line connected Los Angeles to a primitive harbor in Wilmington by the late 1860s, and there was a serviceable wharf south of that, built by the Anaheim grape growers in 1857. In 1876, the Southern Pacific linked Los Angeles to the San Francisco Bay area, which, through the transcontinental railroad and the ports, linked it to the rest of the nation. The effect on Los Angeles was minimal until the Santa Fe Railroad came through to the city from the southern route in 1885. This prompted a rate war with the Southern Pacific, which in turn brought a tourism boom.[20] Notoriously, on March 6 1887 the price of a train ticket from Kansas City to Los Angeles dropped to $1. Of course this price did not last, but the normal $100 ticket brought four trainloads of people a day. People came as tourists, but stayed or returned for the opportunities. This tourism boom prompted a demand to buy land in California, and speculators to promote and sell land for small farms. A real estate bubble began to form. Twenty-five acres were offered for sale in Los Angeles in 1886 for $11,000. A year later, the plot sold for $80,000. Speculators laid out twenty-five new towns along a thirty-six-mile stretch of the Santa Fe rail lines from Los Angeles to San Bernardino in less than two years.[21]

The town of Orange was a typical boom town. A prominent Los Angeles attorney, Andrew Glassell, and his partner, Alfred Chapman, developed the sub-division south of Los Angeles from land they had received in payment from a lawsuit. The land was once a tiny part of the huge Spanish land grants to pioneers Jose Yorba and Luis Peralta. By adding sections to what they received in the settlement, in 1870 Chapman and Glassell owned about 5,400 acres. It seemed like a good location for a town: the nearby Santa Ana River provided water, the soil was rich, and a stage road ran nearby. Chapman hired a surveyor to divide the land into tracts of 40, 80, and 120 acres, and began selling the lots.[22] Glassell's brother laid out a downtown area. He created a circular plaza surrounded by commercial lots and twenty-five by fifty-feet town lots, then built a canal to bring water from the Santa Ana River to the farms. By 1873, there was a store, a church, and a school, as well as about a dozen residents clustered nearby. Small farms formed a ring around the town center. Some could be reached by a horse-drawn trolley, which extended east and west from the town center, allowing farming to become a part-time occupation for some owners. Forty-acre farms further from the downtown supplied the neighboring towns of Anaheim and Santa Ana with grapes, barley, oats, wheat corn, and rye. By then, orange groves were becoming the preferred commercial crop. In 1883, Southern California had 12,000 acres in orange trees, and rail cars transported the production all the way to the east coast.[23]

When the Santa Fe arrived and railroad rate wars started, Orange land-owners and civic leaders financed and sent promotional flyers across the country, and built three hotels in the downtown area. From the older farms, additional subdivisions were created and offered for sale. The first public library was opened in 1885. Asphalt sidewalks and gas streetlights were added to the downtown, and two streetcar lines began operating. The town's first bank, the Bank of Orange, was organized in 1886.[24] In short, Orange became a community within a few years, one whose growth was planned and directed. This type of planned community became popular in the 1880s in the vicinity of Los Angeles. A developer or a syndicate would buy a ranch, designate a center for commercial activity, and subdivide small town lots, reserving spaces for churches and schools. Often a trolley or streetcar would stretch through this town center. Outside this area were larger lots where small farms could provide fruit and vegetables, milk, eggs, and some meat locally. Even further out would be large plots designed to grow regional crops such as citrus, grains, and less perishable produce for export. The trend produced an agricultural landscape dotted with small, but growing, towns.

By 1884, land speculation in Southern California had reached a fevered pitch. Advertisements sent throughout the United States provided testimonials of the weather, the pure air, the low living expenses, and the beauty of the orange groves. Train excursions from the East Coast flourished. Promoters greeted tourists at the rail stations in Los Angeles, San Bernardino or San Diego. The prospective purchasers were loaded into wagons and taken along carefully selected routes to the development, where they were treated to entertainment, a picnic lunch, and a glorified picture of the future aspects of the barren land they stood on. Land prices soared. One property in downtown Los Angeles, purchased for $12,000 in 1883, sold for $40,000 in 1887. Los Angeles' population increased from around 11,000 to 80,000 when, between 1886 and 1888, there were 1,770 tract maps, subdivisions, and revisions of maps filed in Los Angeles County. In the month of April 1887 over $7 million-worth of land changed hands in Los Angeles County alone.[25] Riverside, San Bernardino, and San Diego counties developed as quickly.

William Spurgeon took another approach in developing his land. He persuaded the San Diego stage line to locate a station there, by providing good roads. The Southern Pacific Railroad followed with a spur from Anaheim to the town, called Santa Ana, and Spurgeon was able to sell lots. A boom was well underway by the end of 1886, and a thriving community developed to serve the neighboring farms.[26] Santa Ana became the capital of Orange County when it split from Los Angeles County in 1889, just as the land boom was cooling.

Commercial banks funded the acquisition of land and turning it into subdivisions, but they did not grant individual loans to the acquirers of small plots designed for residences. In the 1880s land boom, B&Ls became an important financing method for property owners. These associations were started as mutual associations of people who wanted to build a house for themselves. Members would pay in a certain amount each month. When the society had sufficient funds, a qualifying member received the money to build their house. The payments continued, with interest paid to the depositor who did not owe for a house, and those with a home paying interest into the fund plus extra to reduce the amount of the loan (amortizing the balance). The first B&L in California was the California Building and Loan Society of San Francisco, established February 9 1865, with an authorized capital of $250,000. It was gone by 1891, when the first Building and Loan Society Commissioner's reports were filed. By then, there seemed to be 126 associations, with assets of $12 million. Sixty-four were in San Francisco and nine were in Los Angeles. Bank Commissioners completed examinations of these institutions from 1891 to 1893, and then the Board of Commissioners of the Building and Loan Association formed and began making reports to the Governor on May 31 1894.[27] This form of financial institution grew in assets through the early part of the twentieth century, then gradually switched their charters to Savings and Loan Associations in the 1950s.

The statewide capital market

The funds for development, preparing large properties for sale as smaller lots, came mostly from commercial banks who actively competed for the loans. In fact, many bankers were the developers of property subdivisions. Commercial banks grew as quickly as the communities in this period. In addition, capital flowed freely from Los Angeles and San Francisco to the more rural areas. Even by the first examinations of banks in 1878, there were only three banks of the eighty-eight commercial banks licensed by the state which did not have loans on real estate on their books. San Francisco bankers seem to have been particularly aggressive in real estate lending. The Bank of California, healthy again, had over 10 percent of their assets in loans on real estate. The savings banks were even more involved. German Savings and Loan had 92 percent of their assets and Hibernia Savings Bank had about 85 percent of their assets invested in real estate loans. While some once thought local banks had a monopoly on local loans, by the end of the nineteenth century California was part of an efficient US capital market that moved funds quickly to areas where credit was less available. In 1880, San Francisco banks had 23 percent of all their property loans on land outside the city. The German Savings Bank loaned in eight counties in 1878 and in thirty-eight counties in 1908.[28] Los Angeles was developing banks to loan on local real estate too. It had an increase in the number of banks after 1884, when there were only three state-chartered banks, to nineteen in 1889 and twenty-four in 1894.[29]

In the early years of the reports to the state Bank Commissioners, banks reported the location of the property upon which the banks had made loans. It seems likely that the funds pooled in the larger cities and towns, and loans came from more metropolitan banks as an area first developed. In fact, this is supported by the reports. San Francisco property was financed almost entirely from loans from San Francisco banks. Los Angeles land was financed from banks outside the county area for 42 percent of the loans in 1878 and 64 percent of the loans in the peak year of 1889. As shown in Table 4.1, most of the lending on real estate from banks in California was from banks outside the county where the real estate was located.[30]

This lending was not all from San Francisco, still the financial center of the state (and indeed, the entire western United States). Table 4.2 shows that most banks loaned on real estate outside the county in which they were located.[31]

In spite of the growth of local banks, the capital market seemed to be very competitive. Of the fifty-seven counties in the state, few did not have sources of loans outside the county.[32] In fact, the fastest-growing counties of the southern part of the state often received the most from banks in other counties, as the growth in real estate lending seemed to outpace the formation of banks. Los Angeles remained below the average for the entire period, reflecting the fact that Los Angeles banks loaned for new developments in southern counties. San Bernardino had consistently much higher averages. In fact, in 1878 all of the loans came from other counties, in spite of the fact that San Bernardino was one of the largest counties in area and had some of the oldest settlements.

Table 4.1 Average percentage of real estate loan funds from banks outside the county where the property was located, 1878–1905

	Year					
	1878	*1884*	*1889*	*1894*	*1899*	*1905*
Percentage (%)	68.1	59.9	57.6	61.9	66.2	49.9

Source: Compiled from the Board of Bank Commissioners *Annual Reports* (Sacramento, California: Office of the Board of Bank Commissioners, 1878–1920).

Table 4.2 Percentage of banks reporting loans in one county, 1878–1905

	Year					
	1878	1884	1889	1894	1898	1905
Percentage (%)	33.0	32.0	48.0	37.0	34.0	46.0

Source: Compiled from the Board of Bank Commissioners *Annual Reports* (Sacramento, California: Office of the Board of Bank Commissioners, 1878–1920).

The capital markets of the late 1800s seem to have been remarkably fluid. Estimates of interest paid on all types of loans indicate that, even when comparing commercial and savings banks in San Francisco with banks in southern California for five-year intervals from 1879 to 1905, interest rates did not differ significantly. Comparing interest rate estimates between various parts of the state, and between urban and rural areas, indicates little difference in interest charged on loans.[33] In other words, competitive lenders ensured that if interest rates rose in more rural areas, borrowers had access to funds from urban areas.

As Southern California developed, interest rates appear to have increased there, but this soon attracted new funds into the area. The increased demand for capital created by new developments allowed any bankers in the area to charge higher interest rates. Bankers in other parts of the state and nation would make funds available, so they too could receive the higher interest rates. This would lead to scarcer capital in the older areas and interest rates would rise there, while this new capital would bring interest rates in the developing areas down. Interest rates in different locations would tend to equalize. Until 1905, California had no barriers to entry which would have slowed the flow of capital. Unlike in many parts of the United States, any entrepreneur could open a new bank, branch, or lend on property far from the existing institutions. Therefore, lending in this period responded quickly to changes in demand.[34]

Collapse in 1887

As often happens, when the bubble is growing at an amazing rate, it is ready to burst. Isaias Hellman himself had a role in the downturn of 1887. He became nervous about the growth rate, and ordered that Farmers and Merchants Bank cut back on lending. The percentage of the bank's loans in real estate dropped from a peak of 80 percent of assets in 1885 to 50 percent in July 1887, and to 25 percent by the end of that year. In October, Hellman announced that no new real estate loans would be issued by the bank. A statement by the town's most influential banker could not be ignored by the other bankers.[35] J. A Graves, who would become the president of Farmers and Merchants Bank, recalls the sudden slowing in his memoirs.[36] The bubble burst as fast as it had risen. Unfortunately, the real estate development would be sluggish for some time. Financing for real estate fell, only rising in 1902.

Nationally, 1893 was a year of financial panic. There seems to have been a lag before the financial disruptions hit California. In 1891, the Bank Commissioner's report bragged that the financial storms that raged in the rest of the world created hardly a ripple in California.[37] However, by the July 1 1893 report, his tone had changed and the problems were evident. The report described a panic which started with the closure of the Riverside Banking Company on June 14. In a few days banks had closed their doors in San Francisco, San Bernardino, Los Angeles, San Diego, and in other towns. Twenty-five banks in the state closed temporarily. All but seven reopened in a few days, while four did not reopen at all.[38]

The panic may have more decisively ended the boom of the 1880s in Southern California, but growth in small family farms continued at a slower pace. The trend of subdividing large ranches continued. Towns continued to be planned, to serve the surrounding farms. The continued growth of the real estate market was well supported by the banking system. While lending dropped, in 1894, only 6 percent of the state-chartered commercial banks in California did not have real estate loans on their books. The percentage rose to 12 in 1899, and 18 in 1905, but this is still generous support of the real estate market, considering that nationally chartered banks still could not lend on real estate at all.[39]

Increased bank regulation

The 1878 Banking Act was suspended in 1903 and quickly replaced with a very similar law, which was amended extensively in 1905. The 1905 act initiated a minimum reserve requirement for commercial banks to back deposits. Capital requirements of $25,000 to $100,000 to start a commercial bank depended on the size of the city where the bank was located. Although this was struck down by the state court, a new capital requirement of 10 percent of total liabilities with a $25,000 minimum and a $100,000 maximum was decreed.[40]

These new rules did not seem to affect the banks. In fact, their assets jumped 20 percent and continued to grow until the Panic of 1907. This crisis manifested itself as a New York stock market crash in October. Again, negative effects on the California financial community tended to lag behind the national trends, as the land-obsessed financial institutions still experienced growth in 1907 and 1908. Then growth became negative (see Graph 4.1). Unfortunately, by the time California experienced difficulties, they were so severe that the Bank Commissioner did not even file reports for 1909. It wasn't until the growth of financial institutions resumed in 1911 that the extent of the problems was revealed. Growth rates resumed and continued until World War I began. One more land boom would occur before the war.

Developing Imperial Valley

The Imperial Valley lies near the center of California by the southern border. Coastal and inland ranges mark the ancient boundaries of a lake fed by the Colorado River, but by 1900 the area was indisputably a desert. The California legislature granted around 16,000 square miles of it to a developer, Oliver Wozencraft, who, in 1859, thought he could bring water and make the desert suitable for farming. The area was forgotten through the Civil War. In 1869, John Wesley Powell redis-covered the Colorado River's Grand Canyon, entering from upstream. While he found the water in the river unsuited to reliable transportation, his discovery reac-tivated interest in irrigating the desert. Wozencraft renewed his claim on his grant, but never was able to proceed on his planned development, and he died in 1887.[41]

John Beatty was the next developer to plan to irrigate the Imperial Valley. In 1890, he hired engineer Charles Rockwood to survey a part of the desert in Mexico that he claimed to own. Rockwood declared Beatty's plan to irrigate this desert to be impossible, but thought that, if a ridge of sand dunes could be cut through, there was land further north that could be irrigated.[42] Even though he did not own that land, Beatty nevertheless used that information to promote his company. One of his major investors, William Heffernan, apparently eventually spotted Bailey's fraud, and he and Rockwood drove Beatty off and reorganized the project as the California Development Company (CDC).[43] In 1899 a new investor joined CDC, George Chaffey. Chaffey was a well-known land developer who came from Ontario, Canada, and founded Ontario, California. He had devel-oped sophisticated irrigation systems, and subdivided and sold the resulting 1,400 acres of productive farmland near Riverside. Chaffey surveyed the desert area and agreed that a cut in the sand dunes and the use of a dry streambed in Mexico could route water to the area.[44] Three families came to homestead the land in 1901. Instead of farming, as they had planned, they served as a labor team to begin a canal. Soon, water was flowing to their farms. Settlers continued to arrive, and to be shocked at the heat and desolation of the desert they encountered. In spite of the reaction, by the end of 1902 there were about 2,000 people farming, and nearly four times that many by one year later. By 1905, the Southern Pacific Railroad branch line ran through one of the seven towns and 800 miles of canals that fed 120,000 acres under cultivation. Unfortunately, this did not save the CDC from its deteriorating financial situation. Debt had accumulated much faster than income. Heffernan essentially bought out Chaffey.[45]

Dredging the canals created constant expense. It is still often said that the Colorado River is "too thick to drink and too thin to plough." It is also prone to massive flooding, as it collects most of the runoff from melting snow in the Rocky Mountains. Elaborate filtering devices meant to reduce the sediment in the river often washed out in the spring deluge. Unable to keep the water flow-ing, Rockwood cut another canal in 1904 to temporarily divert the main branch of the river while the riverbed was re-dredged. Before the repairs were complete, four floods in the spring of 1905 destroyed much of the canal system and forced Rockwood to divert water into the Salton Sink, a prehistoric depression just north of the farming area. Farmers were left with insufficient water, and, as the river flowed into the sink, a lake began to form in the desert.[46]

The disaster in the spring planting season forced Rockwood to seek help. He went to the Southern Pacific Railroad. Since the produce of the valley had no local market, and most of it was shipped to Los Angeles, the railroad bought

51 percent of CDC's stock. The Standard Pacific Company then appointed Epes Randolph president of the company. By June, most of the river's water was running its old natural course to the Gulf of Mexico, but the diversion was still open to the Salton Sink and had eaten into the Colorado River banks. The sand of the banks flowed into the "New River," until it was 150 feet wide, and the Salton Sink was becoming the Salton Sea. The sea spread to threaten settled areas. Repairs began, but too late. The biggest flood since 1891 overwhelmed the repairs and erased several miles of railroad track near Yuma, Arizona. The river into the Salton Sea was now a quarter-of-a-mile wide, but Rockwood developed plans for two new head gates to guide the water back to the canals.[47] By April 1906 one floodgate was finished, but Rockwood was out of funds. Randolph went north, to E. H. Harriman, then head of the Southern Pacific Railroad, to elicit $250,000.[48] The timing was unfortunate. The great San Francisco earthquake and fire had just occurred.

Randolph, without the extra funding needed, managed to engage a new engineer, Harold Cory. He noted that the Salton Sea was rising seven inches a day, and the diversion had cut the canal waters to a trickle. However, a month later, the New River began to cut deeper into the land, and threatened to drain the entire canal system and completely flood the valley.[49] Cory decided to redirect the New River into a new channel, and succeeded by October 10, with the help of local Native Americans, from at least six tribes, recruited for the job. The new channel lasted only a day before the Colorado undercut its walls and turned back to feeding the Salton Sea. Again Cory built a new channel and diverted the river. That attempt lasted a month. Meanwhile, the Southern Pacific Railroad, its funds frighteningly depleted by the recent San Francisco disaster, had already spent $1.6 million on the Imperial Valley, and felt it should spend no more.[50] The Railroad sought aid from President Theodore Roosevelt, a big thinker and an ardent nationalist to whom the notion of saving the Imperial Valley proved appealing. He vaguely agreed to reimburse the Southern Pacific if the problem could be solved. Backed by this hopeful message, Harriman assured Cory of all the resources he needed. Cory took him at his word, commandeering 1,200 miles of track, 300 railcars and an "army of workers."[51] He absorbed so many of the railroad's resources that rail service was affected. Between December and February he built trestles into the wayward river and relentlessly dumped rocks into the water. On February 10, the Colorado flowed back toward the Gulf of California and into the canal system.[52] Some $3.2 million had been spent, and eighteen months of labor needed, to make that a reality.[53] Roosevelt took credit, even before the final success, telling Congress the federal government had made the desert productive, and that as much as 700,000 acres could come under cultivation by a broadened system of irrigation.[54] Imperial Valley did quickly grow into a major producer of citrus and vegetables. The Salton Sea had become the largest lake in California, at 500 square miles, although, after losing its water source, it immediately began to shrink and grow increasingly brackish. It was briefly the source of a land boom in the mid-1900s, before the vacation home owners noticed their beaches were invariably growing in size. This was one of the last major areas of development in the state.

Notes

1 Frances Dinkelspiel, *Towers of Gold: How one Jewish Immigrant named Isaias Hellman Created California* (New York: St Martin's Press, 2008), 49.

2 Kevin Starr, *Inventing the Dream: California Through the Progressive Era* (New York: Oxford University Press, 1985), 15.

3 The interest rate appears to have been about 1 percent per month. James Lynch, "Banking in the Transition Period," *Financial California: An Historical Review of the Beginnings and Progress of Banking in the State,* edited by Leroy Armstrong and J. O. Denny (1916. Reprint. New York: Arno Press, 1980), 129–46, 132.

4 These numbers include commercial and savings banks. The numbers are partly the author's own estimates and partly from Leroy Armstrong and J. O. Denny, *Financial California.* They are very rough estimates for 1870 and rough estimates for 1880. Beginning in 1879, numbers for total assets and real estate loans have been computed from the Annual Reports of the Board of Bank Commissioners of the State of California, the Annual Reports of the Superintendent of Banks of the State of California, FDIC Historical Statistics, the Board of Governors of the Federal Reserve System: All Bank Statistics, and the California Building and Loan Commissioner.

5 Ira Cross, *Financing an Empire: History of Banking in California* vol. I. (Chicago, Illinois: S. J. Clarke, 1927), 437. Also see Larry Schweikart and Lynne Pierson Doti, *California Bankers 1848–1993* (Needham Heights, Massachusetts: Ginn Press, 1994), 228–30.

6 Board of Bank Commissioners, *Annual Report* (Sacramento, California: Office of the Board of Bank Commissioners, January 7 1880), 12–13.

7 Ibid., 18.

8 Ibid., 12–25.

9 Rising OREO (other real estate owned) is an indicator that foreclosures occurred. The bank premises, when owned, are not in this category.

10 Board of Bank Commissioners, *Annual Report* (Sacramento, California: Office of the Board of Bank Commissioners, January 7 1880), 9–10.

11 Board of Bank Commissioners, *Annual Report* (Sacramento, California: Office of the Board of Bank Commissioners, August 10 1886), 3.

12 Ibid., 7.

13 Robert Cleland and Frank Putnam, *Isaias Hellman and the Farmers and Merchants Bank* (San Marino, California: Huntington Library, 1965); and Michael Konig, "Isaias W. Hellman," *Encyclopedia of American Business History: Banking and Finance to 1913,* edited by Larry Schweikart, 249–60 (New York: Facts on File, 1990), 9.

14 Cleland and Putnam, 13.

15 Dinkelspiel, 49.

16 Cleland and Putnam, 11.

17 Ibid., 46.

18 J. E. Pleasants, *History of Orange County California* vol. II (Los Angeles, California: J. R. Finnell & Sons Publishing Co., 1931), 8. The Irvine Company lost its last ties to the family in 1996.

19 J. A. Graves, *My Seventy Years in California: 1857–1927* (Los Angeles, California: The Times-Mirror Press, 1927), 96–7.

20 Starr, 40.

21 Dinkelspiel, 131.

22 "History of Orange," *City of Orange, CA.* Available online at www.cityoforange.org/about/history.asp.

23 Glenn Dumke, "The Boom of the 1880s in Southern California," *Southern California Quarterly* 76, no.1 (San Marino, California: Huntington Library, Spring 1994), 101.

24 "History of Orange." Available online at www.cityoforange.org/about/history.asp.

25 Dumke, 101–5.

26 Ibid., 115.

27 Board of Commissioners of the Building and Loan Associations of the State of California, *Annual Report* (Sacramento, California: California State Printing Office, 1950), 12.

28 Lynne Pierson Doti, *Banking in an Unregulated Environment: California 1878-1905* (New York: Garland Publishing, 1995), 88–9.

29 Ibid., 123.

30 Ibid., 99–101.

31 Ibid., Appendix Table 37.

32 Ibid., 94.

33 Ibid., 139–40.

34 Ibid., 87.

35 Dinkelspiel, 133–4.

36 Graves, 99.

37 Board of Bank Commissioners, *Annual Report* (Sacramento, California: Office of the Board of Bank Commissioners, July 1 1891), 5.

38 Board of Bank Commissioners, *Annual Report* (Sacramento, California: Office of the Board of Bank Commissioners, July 1 1893), 3.

39 Doti, 87.

40 Ibid., 36.

41 Michael Hiltzik, *Colossus: Hoover Dam and the Making of the American Century* (New York: Free Press, 2010), 17.

42 Ibid., 21.

43 Ibid., 23.

44 Ibid., 26–7.

45 Ibid., 33–5.

46 Ibid., 39–40.

47 Ibid., 40–3.

48 Harriman had fought Henry Huntington, James Hill and Theodore Roosevelt to gain control of the Union Pacific and the Southern Pacific only a few years before. See Larry Haeg, *Harriman vs. Hill: Wall Street's Great Railroad War* (Minneapolis, Minnesota: University of Minnesota Press, 2013), *passim.*

49 Hiltzik, 47.

50 Ibid., 49.

51 Ibid.; Maury Klein, *The Life and Legend of E. H. Harriman* (Chapel Hill, North Carolina: University of North Carolina Press, 2000), 383.

52 Hiltzik, 49.

53 Ibid., 42.

54 Ibid., 51.

5 Farming, oil, movies, and branch banking

1920–1932

While the New York stock market boom dominated the history of the 1920s, California had three other booms: real estate, oil and the movies. Los Angeles was the center of all three booms. The oil and the movie booms did not generate large numbers of jobs, nor much demand for real estate. Agriculture in California was still growing, more slowly, but steadily, after the late 1800s and early 1900s land booms. However, the oil discoveries and the growing motion picture industry boosted awareness of the area. By 1920, the Los Angeles County population was larger than San Francisco's, and began to grow at an amazing pace. From 1920 to 1930, two million Americans moved to California. Of these, 1.5 million ended up in the southern part of the state, mostly in Los Angeles County.[1]

Post-World War I housing bubble

The arid climate was, and is, always an impediment to the development of Southern California. The Owens Valley Project brought extra water to Los Angeles in 1913 via an aqueduct from east of the Sierra Nevada mountains, allowing for more growth. Los Angeles began the decade with about 600,000 residents. By 1930, 1.4 million people lived there, making it the fifth-largest city in the nation.[2] Building followed, as shown by the increase in building permits for the decade (Graph 5.1). It is clear that most of the growth came in the early part of the twenties.[3] Developers started 3,233 new subdivisions in Los Angeles with a total of 246,612 building lots encompassing 49,608 acres.[4]

Fewer showy promoters existed in the post-World War I boom than in the 1880s, and many of the subdivisions of the 1920s resulted in streets, water pipes, and electricity for small lots where homes were built. Many of the homes were full-time residences, and some were "cabins" for hunting or escaping to the beach when the hot, smoggy summer months made Los Angeles uncomfortable. No one alive today would regret any of these purchases if their ancestor had been able to hold onto them through the Depression. Santa Monica beachfront, Brentwood Canyon, and the Wilshire district were all developed in this time, and were among the most expensive areas in the world by the late 1900s.

Edward Garner Lewis started one of the successful developments, Palos Verdes.[5] In 1913, he bought a 23,000-acre ranch midway between San Francisco

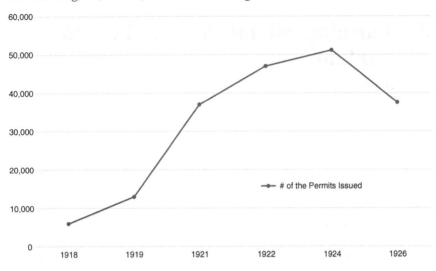

Graph 5.1 Number of housing permits issued in Los Angeles, 1917–1927.

Source: Kevin Starr, *Material Dreams: Southern California through the 1920s* (New York and Oxford: Oxford University Press, 1990), 69–70.

and Los Angeles, with a down payment of $500, supposedly borrowed. The area, later called Atascadero, was put into a trust, for which Lewis sold "beneficial shares." Presumably Lewis realized that the inaccessibility of the area would slow development, so he also bought 3,200 acres of land close to the Los Angeles shipping port. This was a 16,000-acre ocean-side hill formerly owned by Frank A. Vanderlip, a prominent financier, once president of National City Bank of New York. With the close proximity of this property to population centers, Lewis could replicate the methods of 1880s promoters: meet trains as they arrived from the east, offer a free trip to the property, and throw in lunch and some extra amusements. In this case, the extras included music, Spanish dancing, stunt flying, athletic contests, aquaplaning, and yacht racing.[6]

Lewis sold lots, built roads on the hill, landscaped 800 acres of park, and built apartments. But in 1923, problems with his financing on the Atascadero property interfered with his promotions. In the end, Lewis lost the land back to Vanderlip, who put it into a new trust managed by the Bank of America of Los Angeles, a new bank organized by Orra Monnette with the backing of Charles C. Chapman. In 1927, this bank was purchased by Liberty Bank, one of the banks owned by A. P. Giannini, and the trust was placed into the Bank of Italy trust department. The bank loaned the trust the funds to pay taxes, but ended up repossessing the lots backing the loans.[7] In spite of this poor start, Palos Verdes became a highly coveted location by the 1960s.

When the Bank of Italy, Giannini's flagship bank, in one of its many acquisitions, absorbed the Merchants National Bank in 1928, auditors found many subdivision loans on the books. One of Bank of Italy's managers said of the portfolio, "I am inclined to believe that we have quite a serious situation in these subdivision loans, and it is going to take a lot of skillful, careful handling to work the bank out without material loss."[8] Similar sentiments were expressed when the entire town of San Clemente, midway between Los Angeles and San Diego, showed up in Merchants National's assets.[9]

Charles R. Bell was a vice-president of Merchants National Bank and owned 136 acres located in the path of Wilshire Boulevard, which was already destined to be one of the major thoroughfares of Los Angeles. He planned the west side of the city to be independent of the downtown area, with shopping centers and a theatre to rival the famous Grauman's Chinese Theatre. The residential lots sold easily, and new owners erected homes on them, but the "Cathay Theatre" ended up in the holdings of Merchants National when it was acquired by Bank of Italy. The bank discovered there were many repossessed properties in subdivisions near San Francisco, too. When Giannini took over Oakland Bank, there were $4 million in outstanding loans on twelve subdivisions. These loans were all worked out by lot sales, except one, called Piedmont Pines, located on the hills above Oakland.[10]

Perhaps because of these bad experiences, Giannini was generally not interested in financing subdivisions. When William Randolph Hearst, Irving Hellman, and two other prominent citizens of Los Angeles tried to get financing for buying the foreclosed mortgage of a large ranch near Los Angeles, Giannini declined. In fact, Giannini was interested in a different goal: becoming the largest branch banking system in the world.

Branching and the structure of California financial institutions

The typical California bank of the 1920s had three departments: savings, commercial and trust. Each had its own allocated capital and surplus; each operated under its own laws. In effect, the "departmental bank" consisted of three separate institutions under the same roof. In 1920, the state Superintendent of Banks said

> The theory has been that in thus allocating the duties of a bank to several separate departments … we have thrown about savings deposits safeguards that could not be set up were those deposits intermingled with commercial assets; we have given the commercial activities of the bank additional freedom and opportunity through relieving them of responsibility for the savings deposit; we have held the sacred trust obligations free from the diverting influences of any other activity of the bank.[11]

After the Federal Reserve System ("the Fed") started in 1913, many banks became members. However, commercial and savings banks could still have either a federal or a state charter. In the early 1920s, the most common bank situation would be a commercial department with a federal charter and a savings bank operated under a state charter, even when the two shared a building. The attraction of the federal charter was the ability to issue nationally recognized Federal Reserve notes, and access to the services the Fed provided. The disadvantages of federal charters for California banks were the inability to establish branches, and the limit on real estate loans, a restriction left over from the National Banking Act of the Civil War period.

There would be considerable shuffling between state and federal charters in the 1920s. One reason was the branching war. Giannini started the Bank of Italy in San Francisco in 1905. The 1906 earthquake and resulting fire, which closed most banks, made it clear that multiple locations were desirable. In 1907, he opened his first branch. Other banks also began to branch, so that in 1910 there were thirty branch banks in the state. Giannini embarked on a plan to establish as many branches as possible. By the 1920s, his bank had twenty-six branches.[12] Joseph Sartori (a former real estate developer) began to aggressively establish branches of his Security National Bank, based in Los Angeles.[13] He was anxious to keep Giannini out of the southern part of the state. There were times that the reigning state Superintendent, in sympathy with Sartori and in spite of the lack of laws restricting branching, opposed Giannini's ambitions. To avoid conflict with the Superintendent, Giannini sometimes established separately chartered banks to expand his empire without branching.[14] The debate ended with the McFadden Act (1927), which allowed federally chartered banks to branch within their own state, as long as no state law prohibited it. This was the case in California, and Giannini re-chartered the Bank of Italy under federal law, then combined almost all of his banks to create the massive Bank of America, with 275 branches, in 1930.[15]

The growth of Giannini's banking empire was encouraged by the healthy economy of California, and in turn helped to quickly develop growing parts of the state. Funds deposited in one area could quickly be loaned through branches in other neighborhoods. Giannini started his Bank of Italy with the innovative idea that banking services would be accessible to all people, not just the rich, and he stuck with this vision, opening branches in the most remote parts of the state, encouraging small saving accounts and making home loans easily available. While most commercial banks made only short-term loans to developers, or to investors who bought mortgages, Giannini made loans directly to homeowners. While these were usually also short-term, five years or so, they were renewable. As Giannini's goals became national and even international, he became a threat to more traditional bankers, who did not serve small depositors or support home loans. Bringing his Bank of Italy into the Federal Reserve System drew national attention. When Giannini bought the Bank of America of New York in 1928, one of the city's oldest banks, he changed the Bank of Italy name to Bank of America. While his bank had more branches than any other, and was one of the world's largest, Giannini was not embraced by the financial establishment.[16]

For California, the McFadden Act relieved the branch banking systems that were state-chartered from the necessity of supplying $25,000 in capital for each of their branches by joining the federal system. It also allowed banks to commingle the funds from the savings department with the commercial department. With a California charter, the savings departments could only invest in in real estate, state-approved bonds, or high-grade securities. The McFadden Act still made real estate lending harder for federally chartered banks. They could invest up to 25 percent of their capital in real estate. However, the loan could only be for up to 50 percent of the value of the property, instead of the 60 percent allowed for banks chartered under California law.

Other financial institutions also financed the expansion of real estate. Life insurance companies provided a further source for financing real estate. This was probably true in California even from the Gold Rush era. At the national level, they provided substantial amounts of real estate financing. A sampling of their balance sheets for 1920 reveals that most of their assets were in mortgages, with another substantial amount in real estate owned.[17] This is also true for 1925, although in 1930 stocks and bonds were often the biggest part of their assets.[18] As their real estate lending was not defined by location of the property, further study would be required to determine the extent to which this lending affected the California markets. It is clearly possible that they could have provided an important conduit to direct funds from other states when California growth was greatest. B&Ls continued to provide a modest additional source of real estate financing. By 1920, the societies operated as not-for-profit institutions providing for savings deposits and real estate loans to homeowners. While they required membership, the depositors and borrowers now could be different people.

A novel source of funds took advantage of the investment frenzy of the 1920s. Real estate bonds appeared in 1901 when the Royal Trust Company of Chicago floated bonds to finance mortgages on apartment buildings. These and many other early bond issues defaulted, although in the 1920s, when real estate values rose, this system of financing became popular all over the United States.[19] Their popularity in the 1920s was an early step in separation of the lender and the borrower that eventually resulted in collateralized mortgage securities and other mortgage-based derivatives.

The expansion of suburban development

It was not until after World War I that purely residential real estate ownership became important in the US. Prior to that, real estate ownership by occupants was mainly confined to farms. While very wealthy individuals bought lots and built elaborate homes on them, city dwellers mostly rented. With rising consumer wealth in the 1920s, more people wanted to own their homes. With the increased demand for housing, developers faced some new issues. Because of frequent earthquakes in California, the size of the cities had been constrained vertically. In spite of this, the water surrounding San Francisco tempted land-owners to build upward. On the other hand, Los Angeles and San Diego had abundant unoccupied land around, leading to sprawl. In the suburbs, town lots were often twenty to fifty feet wide on the front, to minimize the walk to shops and businesses.

Starting just before World War I, transportation innovation changed the configuration of towns and suburbs. In the late 1800s, urban trolleys ran to the edges of town and defined the limit of convenient housing. When the trolleys ran out of town it was to a specific suburban development, often forming a "hub and spoke" pattern. In many places, to use the trolley to get from one suburban location to another one had to go back to town and out again. By the end of the war, the popularity of the automobile began to rapidly expand these suburbs. Transportation by Model T was available in any direction (the Ford Model T was designed to function well "off-road"). With an automobile, a family could more easily buy a home out of town, adding living space and cleaner air to their lives.[20] A house was still a big investment, however. Unlike a farm, there was no income generated by ownership of a home. The 1920s homeowner was dependent on income from a job to pay the cost of a home and therefore it was difficult to get a loan for this purpose.

By 1921, the supply of land was augmented by the fact that the small farmers on the edge of town were selling their farms. Like the rest of the nation, the farming sector suffered after the expansion of the post-World War I boom. The damage done to European agriculture by World War I temporarily increased prices for most agricultural crops. The increased profits just after World War I encouraged farmers to expand, often with borrowed funds. When, in 1921, agricultural prices dropped, farmers nationwide found they were overextended. The California State Superintendent of Banks, Charles Stern, noted the effect on California in 1920.

> From each quarter comes the story of falling prices, of markets that are not absorbing the normal quotas, of buyers holding aloof in expectation of lower prices. Whether it be rice in the Sacramento Valley, cotton in Imperial Valley, wool in the northern counties or beans or barley on the south coast, the general situation seems largely common to all.[21]

The supervisor worried that the failure to sell crops would result in the inability of the farmers to liquidate the loans that allowed the raising of these crops. He urged financial institutions to insist the farmers sell their products at any price possible.[22] Inevitably, some farmers had to sell their farms. This made land available that could be subdivided into plots suitable for country homes or suburban developments. Developers and realtors quickly realized the need for financing. However, the result of the farm problems, according to the Superintendent of Banking, was that "there has been a very large [re]payment of real estate loans and great care in the granting of new ones."[23] In 1914, 64 percent of the resources of savings banks were invested in mortgages; in 1920 only 47 percent was so invested.[24]

Even in 1921, the residential market was growing. Housing was in great demand, especially in Los Angeles. There was a shortage in spite of what the *Los Angeles Times* called "one of the greatest building booms in their history."[25] Already Los Angeles was absorbing twice the building and loan societies' fast-growing funds as the rest of the state combined.[26] Los Angeles County dominated as the location of the societies and the location of the bulk of the loans through the decade.[27] For all B&Ls in 1921, assets, virtually all invested in real estate loans, increased 14 percent, while the number of new building loans increased

15 percent.[28] Business in southern California was dominated by the building industry. In Los Angeles County, construction by value in 1921 was as much as nine average California counties.[29] In 1921, B&L assets in Los Angeles County grew $3.8 million, while the next-largest growth was $1.6 million in Santa Clara. No other county grew more than $500,000.[30]

The real estate boom and also oil speculation were fuelled, according to Robert Cleland, by the following situation: "Money was available in unheard-of quantities, much of it brought into the state by new arrivals that had not yet had opportunity to invest it in more substantial ways."[31] This is observable in the population increase, but bank deposits grew in the entire nation during the 1920s. The subdivision concept was again taking off, this time for housing. An individual or a group would buy a larger parcel of land, usually a farm or ranch, and sell plots for small residential properties. Financing was provided by the original owners, who themselves raised money to buy the land through investment pools and banks. All types of financial institutions loaned for this purpose. For the years 1923 to 1927, there is ample evidence of growth in lending (see Graph 5.2). State regulators' reports show that combined state and federally chartered bank assets climbed 12 percent in 1923 and 13 percent in 1924, but real estate lending for state-chartered banks grew 21 percent in 1922, 16 percent in 1923, and 32 percent in 1924. Growth in both total assets and state bank real estate lending dropped in 1925, but growth in bank assets was still nearly 7 percent.

The slowed growth of real estate lending for 1925 may have been due to several factors. The deflation of the even more spectacular Florida land boom and the failure of its banks may have frightened lenders. However, since the full collapse

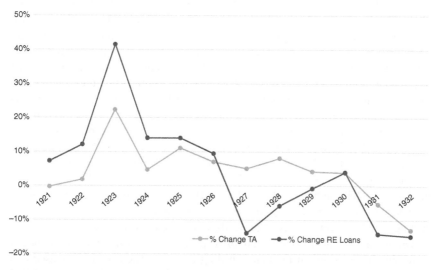

Graph 5.2 Change in total assets and real estate loans of financial institutions in California, 1921–1932.

Sources: Compiled from Annual Reports of the Superintendent of Banks of the State of California *Annual Reports*, California Building and Loan Commissioner, *Annual Report*.

in Florida did not really occur until 1926, this explanation seems unlikely.[32] The decline was not limited to California. A nationwide slowing of the real estate boom occurred in 1925, and in 1926 foreclosure rates rose.[33] Looking inside the state for problems, the only depressive event seemed to be an outbreak of hoof-and-mouth disease among the beef stock. Yet the *Wall Street Journal* reported that "the banking brakes were some time ago applied to the sub-division of suburban property as it [had] been developed in the Los Angeles area." In spite of the slowed lending, they reported, there was not yet any apparent decline in values. Banks "will not loan for speculative building." In spite of that, they said, building has been increasing since 1923.[34]

The oil bubble

Oil was discovered in the state in earlier years, but became important in the 1920s, when one of the largest oil deposits in the country, the Wilmington Field, was discovered along the shore from Huntington Beach to Santa Barbara.[35] Some of the land belonged to the state, which blocked drilling along the beaches. The oil drillers struck back, going to the California Supreme Court to get an order to allow them access to the oil. Drilling on private land could access the oil from state-owned lands. The amount of oil they found made the issue important. A battle over coastal drilling became part of California politics virtually forever. But in the 1920s, homeowners were happy to have a well producing in their backyard, and many of them still moved into developments where oil was being pumped from under them.

In 1890, as the oil industry began, there was only one field in California, Pico Canyon in Ventura, California.[36] Edward Doheny bought a lot east of downtown Los Angeles in the 1890s, sensing that the tar there was a promise of oil. Digging a well and drilling with a makeshift wooden drill, he found oil pooling in the bottom of the shaft at 460 feet. A land boom followed in the area, and drilling started to produce modest amounts. Bigger discoveries in 1900 shifted the center of the industry nearer to the center of the state, in Kern County.[37] But the oil discoveries that made California a major oil producer occurred in 1920 and 1921, in the southern part of the state. Huntington Beach, a sleepy beach resort south of Los Angeles, had early wells on Reservoir Hill that produced forty barrels a day. In 1920, a well at the edge of Gospel Swamp boomed forth and produced 20,000 barrels a day.[38] The city was soon blanketed with oil derricks, which dominated until the 1950s brought a residential boom. By the 1970s, the city became known as "surf city" for its pioneering role and US Championship competitions in board surfing, but there were plenty of oil wells still tucked in backyards.

On Signal Hill, near Long Beach, on a spring night in 1921, the ground began to rumble beneath one of the many drilling derricks. The rumble increased and a crowd gathered to watch a 114-feet geyser of oil shoot into the air. Signal Hill would reveal itself to be one of the largest deposits of oil in the world. In October 1921, another discovery occurred on a large farm in Santa Fe springs, southeast of Los Angeles. Former tennis star and wealthy heir Alphonzo Bell was at his well nearby when a similar big discovery saturated him.[39] Santa Fe, like many oil discoveries, occurred on land already subdivided by previous development. The oil didn't respect property lines, so the first to drill could drain oil from far away. This made for chaos, and another land boom, as prospective drillers sought to be the first to acquire property and mineral rights in promising areas. As in most booms, corruption entered the scene and spread to the banking system. The oil boom was a particular type of real estate boom. As the surface area needed to pump oil from underground was small, the boom was in buying "mineral rights" to property. Some of the techniques of the oil companies resembled the techniques of land developers. The C. C. Julian oil swindle illustrates this.

Chauncey C. Julian started Julian Petroleum Corporation in 1922.[40] At the time, Julian was in his early forties, with a past in the Texas oil industry and in oil fields in Los Angeles, Santa Fe Springs and Signal Hill. His business consisted of leasing oil rights on property and then selling shares to the public. Advertising in newspapers quickly brought customers. Within months of starting, Julian had collected $11 million. He used the funds to obtain leases on already-producing land, and acquired additional land. He set up tank farms to store oil, bought drilling machinery and tools, put employees in office buildings, and had thirty-five service stations. After about a year, Julian Petroleum became a corporation with a Delaware charter and issued 600,000 shares of stock at $50 par value and another 600,000 shares of no-par common stock. The company was audited by Price, Waterhouse & Co., a nationally known public accounting firm, which gave the company mixed reviews.[41]

In 1922, Julian bought land in Santa Fe and established a "common law trust," in which investors put their money into a trust fund held by a bank. The owners of "units" had fewer rights than corporate shareholders, but were led to believe that they had limited liability and certain income.[42] Before Julian's well yielded oil, a neighboring property struck oil. Julian used this to write effective advertisements soliciting funds. As in earlier booms, bringing investors to the land was important. Instead of fake oranges tied to scarce trees, various devices produced flows of black liquid to show busloads of potential investors. In five months, Julian sold over $350,000-worth of shares, and had two wells producing at modest levels.[43] His fundraising, however, was assisted by the discoveries made by others drilling near his land. Wells were producing at a 3,500-feet depth when Standard Oil drilled to 4,644 feet and a week later was producing 6,345 barrels every day. Three weeks later, a small company nearby also reached the deeper reservoir and yielded 8,000 barrels a day. This was national news. None of Julian's four wells in the areas were producing large amounts. He acquired more leases. One piece of land was $80,000, plus 50 percent of the oil yield paid to the previous owner. Three of his wells did produce well, and Julian used this success, his neighbor's success, and some exaggeration, to raise over $2.5 million from investors in his first year of operation.[44]

In 1924, Julian sold his company, and the buyers laid the foundations of a banking scandal. Henry Robinson founded Pacific Southwest Trust and Savings. Earlier, he had been a corporate attorney who assisted in mergers and the founding of corporations. When, in 1906, he moved to Pasadena, near Los Angeles, he quickly became involved in a variety of business activities.[45] In May 1924, Robinson reorganized Pacific Southwest Trust and Savings, naming former State Superintendent Charles Stern as Chairman of the bank. The same year, C. C. Julian sold his company to S. C. Lewis, a former Texas lawyer, and Jack Berman (also known as Bennett). The new owners would take the Julian Petroleum Company, and Pacific Southwest Trust and Savings, into scandal and prolonged litigation.[46] When S. C. Lewis moved the offices of Julian Petroleum into the Pacific Southwest Building in 1926, he immediately set to winning the friendship of Stern, the Flint brothers, and the other bank directors. Julian Petroleum needed more financing. Pacific Southwest Trust and Savings arranged for short-term loans, and introduced them to the venerable Anglo & London-Paris Bank of San Francisco. The loans were secured by a deed of trust on virtually all of Julian Petroleum's physical assets and stock.[47]

Will Wood, as the Superintendent of Banking, reported on the Pacific Southwest Bank situation in 1927. He contended that Pacific Southwest was not involved in any illegal or dangerous way with the Julian Company. Loans made to Julian Petroleum Co. were secured with real property.[48] However, the Julian Company and the Pacific Southwest Bank began to collapse in February 1927, as investors realized the likelihood of an over-issue of shares.[49] The state banking department wrestled for years afterward with the resulting bankruptcy of Pacific Southwest Bank.[50]

Movie industry in Los Angeles

In spite of the swindles and the scandals, the oil industry brought people and money into the state. So did films. The "moving picture" industry took off in the 1920s and production promptly centred itself in Southern California. There was an abundance of natural sets in the mountains, deserts and beaches; the sun provided the needed bright light, and there was also available financing.

A. P. Giannini's brother, A. H. ("Doc") Giannini, was one of the first bankers to offer financing to the newly emerging film industry. In 1909, he loaned $500 to Sol Lesser, a part-owner of a theatre in San Francisco. Seven years later, Lesser became the head of All Features Distributors, which had a regular line of credit with the bank.[51] In 1918, there was an outstanding loan of $50,000 to the Famous Players-Lasky Company, a film producer.[52] Doc went to New York in 1919 to take charge of the East River National Bank and brought his knowledge of the movie industry. East River financed *The Kid*, with Charles Chaplin in the lead, and reported that it was a better investment than government bonds. By 1923, film-maker Cecil B. DeMille was named to the advisory board of one of the Los Angeles branches of the Bank of Italy. He even served as president of Commercial and Saving Bank of Culver City, which was a part of Giannini's collection of banks.[53]

Motley Flint and his brother Frank were bankers who became movie directors. They organized Metropolitan Bank and Trust Company in 1905. In 1906, Frank became a US senator and Motley became president of the bank. Los Angeles Trust and Savings absorbed Metropolitan, and Motley became a vice-president and director of the acquiring bank. Frank retired from the Senate in 1911, and Los Angeles Trust and Savings merged with First National Bank that year. Both brothers then became movie directors. Motley organized the Cinema Finance Company in 1917, which made First National a leading financier for the Hollywood movie industry. After divorcing his wife, he joined the glamorous Hollywood social crowd. He was good friends with Jack Warner and convinced First National Bank to bail out Warner Brothers Corporation when they ran into trouble in 1920.

Frank Flint was also active in real estate development. He developed Flintridge, an exclusive residential community built on a hillside to resemble a Greek village. For financing, Flintridge included a mansion for Motley. Motley had organized an investment pool backed by Julian Petroleum stock. When Julian Company failed, Motley was devastated by the accusations that the large investors had manipulated the results, stealing all of the company's assets so that other investors lost everything. He left Los Angeles and moved to France. When he returned to Los Angeles, just to testify in a lawsuit David Selznick brought against First National Bank, he was shot and killed by a person who had lost money with Julian Co. (and presumably with other stock, as it was July 1930).[54]

There may have been scandals in the oil industry and slowing fervor in the real estate industry in the late 1920s, but, otherwise, there seemed to be few hints of the disastrous changes in the economy so soon to arrive. In 1927, Will C. Wood became State Superintendent of Banks and complained of current bank problems. Chief among these he includes the threat to the advantages the state banking system supplied over the federal system. The McFadden-Pepper Bill in Congress would allow federally chartered banks to branch in states where it was legal. That would include California. A. P. Giannini controlled Bank of Italy, Liberty Bank, and other banks. When they combined in early 1927, they had 276 branches, making Bank of Italy the biggest branch banking system in the country.[55] As feared, when the Act passed, Bank of Italy combined with other Giannini-owned banks and joined the federal system.

The other problem Wood saw in 1927 as a cause of reduced lending was the "overproduction" of agricultural products. Agriculture was still the biggest industry in the state. In the cases of grapes and peaches, Wood notes, "the less productive orchards are gradually exhausting the resources of their owners and, as they are not salable at present, are deteriorating and will subsequently be abandoned or converted to other uses." Examiners from the banking department were having trouble deciding what the land underlying mortgages was worth. The individual reports of banks showed large amounts of "frozen" agricultural real estate loans, where owners were not making any payments on the principal. There were also larger amounts of foreclosed land held by banks.[56]

In 1928, the bank Superintendent reported that 1927 building activity had been quieter than in the last five years. In spite of that, he said "while there are certain areas and industries in California that present difficult problems of readjustment, the state, taken as a whole, has had a satisfactory year." Employment, manufacturing output, wholesale trade, retail sales, and auto distribution numbers were all up. However, agriculture had continuing problems.[57]

In fact, 1928 was just a temporary reprieve. Assets of deposit institutions were up slightly after a 3.4 percent decline in 1927. B&Ls continued to grow until 1930, and then declined at a modest pace, but the assets for state and national commercial banks, savings banks, and trust associations virtually crashed. The total dropped from $4 billion in 1928 to $2.4 billion in 1929. Strangely, the asset total recovered in 1930, dropped slightly in 1931, and dropped again in 1932 (see Graph 5.2).

Real estate lending by California state-chartered banks tells a different story. The period of acceleration ended by 1924 (Graph 5.2). In 1925, growth dropped into negative numbers. The uptick in loans in 1927 resulted in negative growth, and real estate loans continued to drop in subsequent years. The decrease in the value of the loans is undoubtedly more dramatic than the numbers show, as the loans are still on the books at the loan's balance. Many of these loans would never be paid back.

Steven Gjerstad and Vernon Smith have recently contended that real estate boom and bust periods have preceded periods of deterioration in the US economy. In one article, they review the US boom and bust in real estate that preceded the Great Depression.[58] Their study shows the peak year of real estate investment in the United States is 1925. The financial pattern in California in the 1920s seems to support this (Graph 5.2). As in their national figures, California growth in real estate appears to first falter in 1925. Gjerstad and Smith's graph of real estate investment shows the decline slowed in 1928, and the California estimates indicate recovery that year also.[59] However, as also indicated in the national figures, real estate in California plummeted in 1929. The methods used to estimate the strength of the real estate market are quite different, but the picture of boom and bust seems quite compatible. There clearly was an expansion in the real estate market in the early 1920s that started in 1921. Nationally, there was a marked dip between 1924 and 1926, then a brief recovery before the decline in the real estate market in 1929. In California, the dip also occurred, but, even as bank assets fell after 1932, real estate loans stayed fairly strong.

Notes

1 Los Angeles County includes much more acreage than San Francisco.
2 Kevin Starr, *Material Dreams: Southern California Through the 1920s* (New York: Oxford University Press, 1990), 69.
3 W. W. Robinson, "The Real Estate Boom of the Twenties," *Quarterly Journal of the Los Angeles Historical Society* 24, no. 1 (March 1 1942), 25.
4 Marquis James and Bessie R. James, *Biography of a Bank: the Story of Bank of America NT & SA* (New York: Harper & Row, 1954), 236.
5 Ibid.
6 W. W. Robinson, "The Southern California Real Estate Boom of the 'Twenties'," *Historical Society of Southern California Quarterly* (March 1942), 26.
7 James and James, 239.
8 Ibid.
9 Ibid., 240.

10 Ibid.
11 Superintendent of Banks of the State of California, *Annual Report* (Sacramento: State Printing Office, 1920), 10.
12 Lynne Pierson Doti, "Banking in California: The First Branching Era," *Journal of the West*, XXII, no. 2 (April 1984), 66.
13 Lynne Pierson Doti and Larry Schweikart, *California Bankers 1848–1993* (Needham Heights, Massachusetts: Ginn Press, 1994), 69.
14 It was legal for a bank to acquire banks that had been in existence for three years or more, and then make them branches. It seems likely Giannini had a branch breeding program.
15 Doti and Schweikart, *California Bankers*, 75–95, esp. 69.
16 Will Wood Papers on Branching in the 1920s and Bank of Italy. Copies at UC Berkeley. Original at California State Library.
17 Insurance Commissioner of the State of California, *Annual Report* vol. 2, *passim* (Sacramento, California: Department of Insurance, 1920). The 1920s reports show assets and liabilities for companies selling insurance in California. In the case of real estate owned by insurance companies, this amount was an investment; it did not reflect repossessed property.
18 Insurance Commissioner of the State of California, *Annual Report* vol. 2, *passim* (Sacramento, California: Department of Insurance, 1925); Insurance Commissioner of the State of California, *Annual Report* vol. 2, *passim* (Sacramento, California: Department of Insurance, 1930).
19 Louis K. Boysen, President, Chicago Mortgage Bankers, speech, "A History of Real Estate Bonds," presented in Chicago, Illinois, 1933.
20 For more specific details about development in Los Angeles, see Mark S. Foster, "The Model-T, the Hard Sell, and Los Angeles's Urban Growth: The Decentralization of Los Angeles during the 1920s," *The Pacific Historical Review* 44, no. 4 (University of California Press, November 1975), 459–84. Available online at www.jstor.org/stable/3638066.
21 Superintendent of Banks of the State of California, *Annual Report* (Sacramento: State Printing Office, 1920), 4.
22 Ibid., 5.
23 Ibid., 6.
24 Ibid., 12.
25 No author, "Great Projects Under Way," *The Los Angeles Times* (1886-current file, November 5 1920); ProQuest Historical Newspapers *Los Angeles Times* (1881-1986), II-4.
26 Building and Loan Commissioner of the State of California, *Annual Report* (Sacramento, California: California State Printing Office, August 30 1920), 4.
27 Building and Loan Commissioner of the State of California, *Annual Report* (Sacramento, California: California State Printing Office, various dates).
28 Building and Loan Commissioner of the State of California, *Annual Report* (Sacramento, California: California State Printing Office, August 31 1922), 6.
29 No author, "Leads World In Agriculture," *Los Angeles Times* (1886-current file, July 31 1921); ProQuest Historical Newspapers *Los Angeles Times* (1881-1986), II-1.
30 Building and Loan Associations of the State of California, *Annual Report* (Sacramento, California: State Printing Office, September 15 1921), 5.
31 Robert Glass Cleland, *California in Our Time (1900-1940)* (New York: Alfred A. Knopf, 1947), 132.

32 Raymond Vickers, *Panic in Paradise: Florida's Banking Crash of 1926* (Tuscaloosa, Alabama: University of Alabama Press, 1994) is one story of the boom and bust in the southeastern United States.

33 Leo Grebler, David M. Blank and Louis Winnick, *Capital Formation in Residential Real Estate: Trends and Prospects* (Princeton, New Jersey: National Bureau of Economic Research and Princeton University Press, 1956), 350; Historical Statistics of the United States Millennial Edition Online, tables Dc826, Dc827 and Dc828. Available online at www2.census.gov/prod2/statcomp/documents/HistoricalStatisticsoftheUnitedStates 1789_1945.

34 No author, "California Leans to Conservatism," *The Wall Street Journal* (1889-current file, April 18 1924); ProQuest Historical Newspapers *The Wall Street Journal* (1889-1992), 11.

35 Paul Sabin, "Beaches versus Oil in Greater Los Angeles," *Land of Sunshine: An Environmental History of Metropolitan Los Angeles*, edited by William Deverell and Greg Hise (Pittsburgh, Pennsylvania: University of Pittsburgh Press, 2005), 95–114.

36 Jules Tygiel, *The Great Los Angeles Swindle: Oil, Stocks, and Scandal During the Roaring Twenties* (New York: Oxford University Press, 1994), 20.

37 Ibid., 21.

38 Ibid., 14.

39 Ibid., 15, 16.

40 Guy W. Finney, *The Great Los Angeles Bubble: A Present-Day Story of Colossal Financial Jugglery and of Penalties Paid* (No Place: Guy W. Finney, 1929), 27.

41 Finney, 28–32.

42 Tygiel, 33.

43 Ibid., 50.

44 By June 1922. Tygiel, *The Great Los Angeles Swindle*, 54.

45 Tygiel, 169.

46 Finney, 35.

47 Tygiel, 172.

48 Will Wood Letter to Chas. Wesley Reed, July 14 1927. Copy at UC Berkeley. Original at California State Library.

49 Tygiel, 196.

50 James and James, 244.

51 Ibid., 245.

52 Ibid.

53 Ibid., 247.

54 Tygiel, 4–7.

55 James and James, 198.

56 Superintendent of Banks of the State of California, *Annual Report* (Sacramento: State Printing Office, 1927), xxxiv, xxxii, xxxiii.

57 Superintendent of Banks of the State of California, *Annual Report* (Sacramento: State Printing Office, 1928) 5.

58 Steven Gjerstad, and Vernon L. Smith, "Consumption and Investment Booms in the Twenties and Their Collapse in 1930," Chapter 3 in National Bureau of Economic Research series "Housing and Mortgage Markets in Historical Perspective." Available online at www.nber.org/chapters/c12794.pdf.

59 Compiled by the author from Reports of the National Banks and California *Report of State Banking Commissioner* for years 1915 to 1934.

6 Depression and war
1930–1945

During the Great Depression and the years of World War II, the increase in the federal government's role in financial institution regulation and in the housing market increased dramatically. At first, the financial institutions coped with bank panics and focused on simply surviving. Then they faced an onslaught of burdensome regulations during the New Deal. These dual blows resulted in a complete retreat from real estate lending into purchase of government-issued securities, creating a general decrease in the housing supply and extreme shortages in areas that experienced population growth. California was one such area, with farmers coming from the devastated Midwest during the Depression and then workers arriving to take the many available jobs in the defense industry.

Housing in the Depression

After the brief contraction of 1926, loans for real estate by commercial banks, savings banks, and B&Ls rose in 1928. Then, as in the rest of the nation, bank runs severely depleted deposits and assets of lending institutions from 1930 to 1932, while the Federal Reserve System ("the Fed") at the same time continued its constricting monetary policy. After 1934 there was a long, slow increase in financial institutions' assets. Even real estate loans increased in California from 1934 until the Fed tightened regulations in 1937. As in the years 1929 to 1932, when they had allowed a precipitous drop in the money supply, the Fed's 1937 actions caused a sharp contraction in the US economy, which California shared.[1] As the economy recovered from this recession-within-a-depression, funds flowed back to financial institutions. But lingering fear kept the lending low. It was only when the war in Europe stimulated purchases from airplane- and ship-builders in California that bankers began lending more freely on real estate (Graph 6.1).

Commercial and savings banks continued to be regulated by the State Superintendent of Banks, who reported on their condition annually. Now both types of banks lent on real estate development and construction. Financing individual mortgages on farms and residential housing was common. B&Ls continued to be the most important source of financing for individual home mortgages, and were regulated by the Building and Loan Commissioner, who did annual reports on their assets.

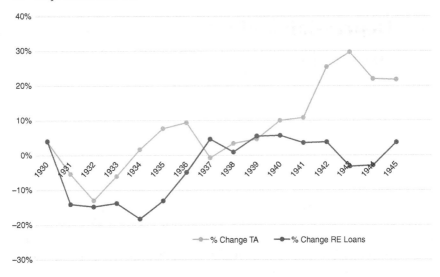

Graph 6.1 Change in total assets and real estate loans of financial institutions in California, 1930–1945.

Source: Compiled from the Annual Report of the California State Superintendent of Banks and the Annual Reports of the Building and Loan Commissioner, State of California.

Review of the data on commercial banks, savings banks, and B&Ls makes it abundantly clear that the financial institutions had money during the Great Depression, but did not lend it. Saving account deposits rose steadily. However, financial institutions moved away from lending and instead shifted their assets into investments in state and local bonds. Fear of failure, or the regulators' strict examinations, produced this reluctance to lend. Both the cash (currency and accounts at other banks) and government bonds increased by leaps and bounds every year of the Depression. Government borrowing and lending had pretty much replaced private real estate financing in California by the end of the Depression. President Hoover tried to bolster the financial system through the Reconstruction Finance Corporation (RFC), which invested in newly issued preferred stock of the banks (a solution they also tried in the 2008 crisis), but this only weakened the banks further as public law required that any bank receiving RFC funds had to be identified publicly, which set off new rounds of withdrawals. Congress also started programs to assist farmers and residential property owners who were not meeting their mortgage obligations.

During the Great Depression, in spite of efforts to revive economic activity, the housing market died. Except for transient camps and other temporary buildings, the property subdividers, the promoters and the home-builders had no work. Construction was not listed in the employment data of the 1930s, and cannot be detected in any of the other listed employment categories.[2] David Lavender contended that the California economy was affected by the Depression mostly because of a complete lack of tourism and the collapse of the real estate market.[3] In spite of the lack of added housing, immigration into the state was high—1.2 million people during the decade. Many were the farmers from Oklahoma, Arkansas, Missouri, and North Texas, who worked as migrant farm labor or settled more permanently in the San Joaquin Valley.[4] The Imperial Valley also grew with the help of new federally funded irrigation projects.

Transient labor camps for the immigrants would shape the future of housing in the United States, by the use of uniform mass-produced homes. At first, privately run auto or trailer camps supplied the migrant workers coming to the state in overloaded vehicles in response to the possibility of jobs. Often a camp simply supplied water and sanitary facilities to families familiar with sleeping in the open. Common facilities varied widely, starting with barns, chicken sheds or other old buildings, converted for shared use as sanitary or cooking spots. When people devised their own shelters, the name "Hooverville" was most often applied. However, Californians had their own derisive term: "Little Oklahomas."[5] In 1935, a Little Oklahoma developed outside Modesto. In this development, local farmers subdivided their land into plots which they sold for $125, on terms of $10 down and $5 a month. By the summer of 1938, more than 200 families—about 1,000 people—resided on these premises, in shelters of their own devising.[6]

A Berkeley Professor, Paul Taylor, proposed the establishment of a network of federally supported migrant labour camps. He had intimate knowledge of their needs from two sources. First, from 1927 to 1929, he had studied the society and culture of Mexican farm laborers. Then, in the 1930s, he researched migrant agricultural laborers in California in the company of his later wife, Dorothea Lange. Lange's photographs would later make her the more famous half of the couple, but Taylor's study resulted in a federal program to build camps for the migrant laborers. The first two federal camps were at Marysville in Yuba County and at Arvin in Kern County. Eventually the federal housing program housed about a fifth of the state's migrants.[7]

The model for transient or labor camps was close at hand. Six Companies, the unoriginal name of the combined companies who together won the bid for Hoover Dam, found ample numbers of workers willing to bear demanding work in punishing heat. In January 1931, thousands of hopeful laborers, families in tow, headed for the remote desert site.[8] At first the only housing the workers could find was in caves along the Colorado River. As the numbers increased, a Hooverville-type camp developed at a bend in the river known as Hemenway Wash. By spring, perhaps 1,500 people lived there.[9] Thousands more poured in to the nearest town, a hamlet known as Las Vegas, quadrupling the estimated population. The Salvation Army, the Red Cross, and local people tried to help the newcomers with food, but the long distance to any population center meant people still went hungry that winter. By April, Six Companies started building Boulder City. It started with a water tank at Hememway Wash, high on the sloping bank. Saco Rienk DeBoer, a famous urban planner, began plotting a modern oasis. He created zones for commercial, industrial, and residential uses, and even an area for worship.[10] In the residential area, V-shaped blocks of cottages would share an open space in lieu of backyards. In clear violation of the nature of the desert, he added a forest.

In practice, a $2 million grant from the Bureau of Reclamation for housing went for a much more pragmatic arrangement. The company headquarters ended up at the top of the slope, most likely to benefit from any breeze, and was surrounded by executive residences. Solidly built stucco homes spread slightly lower on the hill. Then Six Companies built nearly 1,000 homes within a few months. Each was a drafty wooden box.[11] The resulting effect was neatly uniform and supremely efficient, if not aesthetic or even comfortable. The mass-produced housing of the federal and private labor camps would share many of these features of Boulder City.

Clearly there was a demand for housing in California during the Depression from the rising population. The Modesto project shows that developers could still sell land. Lack of financing was the restricting factor. The bank run of 1930 left the surviving banks with limited funds and deep fear of lending. However, after people took their money out of the banks (the "run") and buried it in the back yard (the "hoarding"), most had second thoughts. The funds trickled back into the financial system, but did not go out to mortgages.

The financial institutions flee to bonds

Ed Rainey became Superintendent of Banks in time to write the 1931 *Annual Report*. In spite of the fact that the United States was entering the worst economic period in history, he reported that commercial and savings banks were more stable than the year before. He said:

> Increasing evidence of the stability of banking in California has been manifest during the past year and satisfactory progress has been made. The June 30, 1931 statements of the banks show an even greater liquidity than was shown last year. Primary and secondary reserves have increased from 45 percent of the total deposit liability of the banks on June 30, 1930 to 52 percent on June 30, 1931. At no time in the past have depositors been offered greater security and more ample protection for their funds.[12]

Of course, this was precisely what was happening in the entire United States, since the banks built up reserves to reassure their customers, and themselves, of the safety of the deposits. The high reserves were also a reaction to the increased regulation and supervision of the banking system, which made banks reluctant to loan in general. Rainey confirms this in his subsequent remarks: "The amount of cash, cash resources and investments held by the banks constitute their primary and secondary reserves." This would include funds due from other banks, clearing house balances and investments in bonds approved by the state banking department, usually municipal or local government and assessment district issues.

> This [ratio] compares very favorably with the similarly derived ratio of 39 percent based on the statement of a year ago and is greatly in excess of the 25 to 30 percent which is usually assumed to be a safe margin. The present

high ratio has resulted from a further contraction in the amount of commercial financing carried on by the banks.[13]

When a financial institution has a deposit, it incurs cost. While, in the thirties, banks kept an unusually liquid position, with plenty of cash, they had to earn interest to stay in business. The solution for the banks was to invest its funds in bonds. While for most privately issued bonds prices dropped, the public (government) issues stayed high because of their perceived safety.[14] Commercial banks usually held about half of the funds that were invested in United States government, state and local government, school, and other public agencies or districts bonds. In 1931, commercial banks held 60 percent and the savings banks held from 75 to 80 percent of their total investments in these bonds.[15]

During the Depression, while public bonds seemed to be the most favored investment for banks, and even many of them were defaulting, the market for privately issued real estate bonds was dying. The vigorous expansion of bond financing for real estate construction of the 1920s, concentrated in loans for hotels, furnished apartment buildings and special purpose buildings, was over. By 1933, the president of the Chicago Mortgage Bankers Association noted, "it is generally reported that our real estate bond situation is one of the blackest spots in our present financial situation."[16] In the United States, there were $400 million in real estate bonds in foreclosure. Losses ranged from 25 to 70 percent when the real estate backing the bonds was sold. New real estate bonds were non-existent as the construction industry died.[17]

The fact that the state-chartered banks seemed to be retreating to safe investments is not surprising, as there were many that were unable to survive the national whirlwind of problems that faced the nations' banks and savings banks. Twenty-two state banks with eleven branch offices were closed by the Superintendent during 1931. The assets of the closed banks constituted less than 1 percent of the total assets for all the state banks, but the Superintendent approved no new requests for charters during the year. California commercial banks still seemed to be doing relatively well when the Superintendent made the 1932 *Annual Report*. "The soundness of California's banking law has been demonstrated under most unfavorable conditions," he said.[18] However, in the magazine *The California Banker*, definite signs of the Depression were apparent: one article complained of the current quality of bank presidents, another article expressed concern about an obvious surplus of citrus, several industries reportedly had difficulties because of the high American tariffs; and, due to obvious surpluses for many commodities and labor, it reported that prices and wages were falling. Even worse, one article urged bankers to "face their problems."[19] Later in 1932, Superintendent Rainey addressed a gathering of California bankers. He mentioned that he was still turning down all applications for new bank charters, "even with the number of applications made to the Department." He also denied a good many of the bonds issues for which certification was requested (certification allowed savings banks to buy them). He warned about lending on real estate, mentioning that trying to set a value on real estate was difficult without an active market.[20]

The nationwide problem of hoarding also bothered California banks. Customers heard of bank failures, withdrew their deposits, and put them in cash. Then they hid the cash, according to popular stories, under their mattress or buried on their property.[21] An article appeared on preventing withdrawals and hoarding by offering customers a "home saving bank." This item seemed to be a mechanical bank, but one that could only be opened by the banking institution.[22] Another anti-hoarding scheme was described: a giant check that was just endorsed and passed along. Later it would be recalled by the bank. Oversized, the check would hold many endorsements, illustrating the effect of improving circulation of money instead of hoarding it.[23] This clever economic illustration impressed the bankers, who gave it plenty of publicity. Obviously, none of these ideas prevented the bank run that was gathering momentum. By the end of 1932, the financial system was collapsing.

The bank holiday and financial collapse

The governor of California closed all the state's banks on Thursday, March 2 1933, after bank deposits dropped dramatically in February. Bank of America lost $22 million in deposits that month, and considered itself lucky.[24] When Franklin Roosevelt took office in March 1933, most of the banks in the country were already closed. Roosevelt was inaugurated on Saturday, and closed all the banks in the nation on Monday, March 6. He gave them a pass to avoid withdrawals by declaring a bank holiday, which in Britain still means "a vacation." In this case, it was for three days, or until a bank could be inspected and declared to have adequate reserves. The idea was to instill confidence that banks were safe, so deposits would return.

The process inevitably turned political. As the Federal bank holiday was to end on Thursday, March 9, A. P. Giannini, who had recently come out of retirement to regain control of Bank of America, telegraphed to Washington for permission to open, but he was told that reopening was up to the Federal Reserve District bank. Since he had had trouble before with the San Francisco (district bank) Governor, John Calkins, Giannini was concerned. He asked the California senators to watch over his application. They sent him reassuring letters.[25] A. P and others thought that the bank closures would cause a crisis in the money supply, and bankers suggested that scrip be issued, which would be backed by mortgage loans.[26] In fact, none of the western district banks received approval to open until March 13.

On Friday, March 10, a major earthquake, centered near Long Beach, interrupted all local focus on the bank holiday. Over 100 people were killed and 4,000 injured. There was particular concern over the schools. The earthquake occurred earlier than the school day started, but many of the masonry school buildings were heavily damaged. Rebuilding these schools would be one of the public works of the following years, and would bring new construction standards to state schools.

Late Sunday night, Roosevelt gave his first "fireside chat." As with many politicians before and after him, he blamed the banking situation on the bankers:

"Some of our bankers had shown themselves either incompetent or dishonest in their handling of the people's funds ..."[27] Knowing that he had few political friends among the Democrats, Giannini was deeply disturbed at the implications of Roosevelt's charge. He spent the rest of Sunday night calling every friend he had, including publisher William Randolph Hearst. In the end, with the Secretary of the Treasury's tacit approval, the Bank of America, with all its branches throughout the state, opened on March 13 to receive over a million dollars more in deposits than in withdrawals.[28]

By 1933, the effort to maintain the air of optimism became obviously strained. In the *Proceedings* of the California Bankers Association annual meetings, topics included "Will faith in Municipal bonds be Justified?" and "Problems of farm taxation, agriculture and banker and farmer relationships."[29] In 1934, the new Superintendent, Friend William Richardson, assessed the state's position: "For the state chartered banks, after making adjustments for those banks which left the state system to join the Federal Reserve System, loans in real estate declined $31 million, while OREO [which consisted of repossessed property] increased $7 million. Real estate lending was down and foreclosures were up. However, banks added $48 million to investments, mostly in government bonds, roughly matching the $49 million the Federal Government had infused by purchasing preferred stock and capital notes of banks in California. Commercial deposits and savings accounts were both increased from the previous year."[30] There was one major shadow still darkening the scene: applications for really bankable loans were "comparatively few in number."[31]

The Superintendent worried that government's attempts to help the general financial situation favored borrowers over depositors. The Superintendent was concerned that the borrowers seemed to have more political clout than the depositors whose money was at risk. In his 1935 report he said, "A large part of the assets of the banks in liquidation consist of loans secured by real estate or real estate acquired through foreclosure .... Legislative moratoria, both national and state [on foreclosures], have slackened payments of borrowers ..."[32] Typically, as the government made life easier for borrowers, borrowing increased. In 1936, both commercial and saving bank business steadily increased. Deposits continued to increase. The institutions were still holding unusually large amounts of cash, but the Superintendent noted "one of the most encouraging aspects of last year's business was the heavy increase in commercial loans."[33]

This good news for the economy did not help the real estate market. Commercial loans generally consisted of short-term loans for inventory purchases or for funds to pay bills while the company waited for payment for sales already made. Mortgages for individuals still came mostly from B&Ls. Louis Drapeau was the Building and Loan Commissioner for California during the "emergency period," which lasted from 1933 to 1937. The office did not issue any reports during this period, but, at the end of 1937, Drapeau said:

> All associations are now paying out freely on withdrawals, except in a few instances, in accordance with the permanent provisions of the Building and

Loan Associations Act. Only a few associations had found it necessary to restrict withdrawals under the emergency legislation.[34]

In fact, the B&L industry, once the main provider of individual mortgages, would decline in importance until well after World War II, when the institutions morphed into savings and loan associations.

Still, in the Building and Loan Commissioner's 1937 report, it was clear that the real estate market improved somewhat after 1933. Aggregate loans had increased by almost $7 million, and real estate owned (through foreclosure) decreased $5.8 million. The real estate sold by the B&Ls allowed granting new loans. However, the Commissioner mentioned that associations found it difficult to find "safe" new loans, so many were not accepting new members. In spite of that, they made 4,717 new construction loans, plus 11,848 other loans on real estate. It is apparent that many building and loan societies were remaking themselves into savings banks or S&Ls. Forty-one of the 124 associations were insured by the Federal Savings & Loan Insurance Corporation (FSLIC, established in 1934 to insure deposits at savings banks).[35] The 1937 contraction reversed this progress. By 1939, the number of California B&Ls dropped to 106; eight had ceased operations in 1939, with foreclosed real estate overwhelming them. Every institution that failed had let their OREO account get beyond their ability to sell it. The Building and Loan Commissioner's office took this real estate and tried to sell the assets. The 1939 *Report* states: "This means that the disposal of real estate is the principal activity of our liquidation department. Our policy has been to sell the properties as rapidly as fair prices can be obtained for them."[36] (See Graph 6.2.)

Pacific States Savings and Loan Company of San Francisco was one of the most problematic institutions in the state. The Commission seized their assets in

Graph 6.2 Other real estate owned (OREO) by financial institutions in California, 1929–1940.

Source: Compiled from the Superintendent of Banks of the State of California, *Annual Reports*; Commissioner of Building & Loan Societies, *Annual Reports*. Covers all Commercial and Savings Banks and B&L Societies.

1939, citing unsafe practices and impaired capital. Seventy-two percent of their assets were in real estate loans. The 591 parcels included hotels, apartments, commercial property, and farms and ranches in California and adjoining states.[37] The Commissioner defended the takeover:

> It has been obvious that the Pacific States situation has been a constant threat to the stability of the entire building and loan structure of this state for years, and we are confident that its elimination will have a healthy effect upon the attitude of the public toward all.[38]

Other institutions also were limited by the amount of real estate they had acquired through foreclosure. In the 1939 report, the Superintendent of Banks expressed concern about the large amounts in the OREO accounts held by commercial banks:

> It is my opinion that a bank should not be in the real estate business and that the property is worth more to others than it is to the bank. Consequently I have insisted that each bank formulate a program for disposing of its other real estate, particularly that which has been carried for many years.[39]

George J. Knox became Superintendent of Banks for the state in February 1940. His first report on all of the commercial and most of the savings banks in the state was optimistic:

> While the banks of this state have much available cash on hand and in banks, yet it is apparent to me that all of them stand ready, willing and anxious to make proper investments in the form of loans to legitimate enterprises and to individuals where such loans can be justified under the law. There is a marked increase in loans by banks during the past year and the volume of increase is greater than that reported for the previous year. In a survey recently made by the ABA [American Bankers Association], it is shown that there is a definite expansion of bank credit in the field of new loans. It is apparent from the survey that California banks compare favorably with those of other states throughout the nation in the matter of the extension of credit. As evidence of this there is a notable increase in automobile, personal, home loans and open lines of credit extended to business.[40]

The B&Ls also showed some improvement in 1940. Only two disappeared in the previous year, one voluntarily and the other forced into liquidation. In the remaining 104, "there has been very definite improvement in the condition of the active associations." In fact, there seemed to be active competition for new real estate loans.[41]

Most bankers had mixed feelings about the federal government's 1930s involvement in the banking system. San Diego Trust and Savings Bank, for example, though rich with marketable securities, borrowed from the RFC in 1931, and then advertised the availability of funds for home remodeling and construction, as well as business loans. On the other hand, the bank's president, Joseph Sefton, vigorously protested the forced closing of his bank during the bank holiday. Subsequent Federal actions were equally unpopular with Sefton. His son, Tom, recalled his reaction to the Federal Deposit Insurance Plan (FDIC): "My father felt very strongly about the FDIC. He thought it was terribly bad. [He] believed that the introduction of deposit insurance would cause people to become careless in choosing banks."[42]

Sefton felt more positive toward another federal program. When the Federal Housing Administration started to provide government guarantees for housing loans in 1934, through Home Owners Loan Corporation (HOLC), San Diego Trust and Savings moved quickly. It was the first bank in San Diego to offer the loans, and soon was writing up to thirty of the loans a day.[43] Created in June 1933 as a federally owned corporation, HOLC refinanced roughly one-fifth of all the nation's non-farm home mortgages during the Depression. The federal government guaranteed the bonds that were issued by HOLC. HOLC then used the funds from the bond sale to replace the original loan to a homeowner in the financial institution with their own bonds, so the lending institution received an HOLC bond valued at or near the amount owed by a delinquent homeowner. HOLC also established the definition of "single-family" as a building containing one to four living units, at least one of which was occupied by the borrower.[44]

The homeowner had to apply to get their bank loan replaced, and the HOLC accepted applications from May 1933 to November 1934, and May to June 1935. The loans granted to the homeowner carried a rate of 5 percent regardless of the original loan's terms, which were usually higher interest. Maturity dates on HOLC bonds ranged from 1949 to 1951. The bonds paid 4 percent after Congress offered to guarantee repayment in 1934.[45] HOLC shut down in 1951 after it paid its last bond due, having made over one million loans worth a total of three billion dollars to homeowners. It foreclosed on 19 percent of these loans.[46]

HOLC loans could be considered very creative for the times. Most loans for home purchase in the 1920s and 1930s were for 50–60 percent or less of equity, and were short-term, often five years, with balloon payments. The lender usually allowed them to be renewed.[47] But HOLC instruments allowed payment of interest only for a few years, with higher payments later. However, even their standard loan was unusual for the era. It was fully amortized over fifteen years on 80 percent of property value.[48]

Public works projects

Today, the accepted economic wisdom is to increase government spending in a depression when no other spending is available. At the beginning of the Great Depression these "Keynesian" ideas were just being disseminated. Federally funded projects were an important boost to the generally depressed California economy, and there is some indication that the state received a good share of federal spending. This may have been one of the reasons that California suffered less than other states. Economist Frank Kidner found that per capita income in California in 1929 was 1.45 times per capita income in the United States in the same year, and that by 1937 this ratio had increased to 1.53.[49] In addition to providing extra employment during the Depression, many of these public projects were essential preconditions to the post-war housing boom. Rebuilding Long Beach after the March 1933 earthquake, for example, required federal assistance to replace the many schools that were destroyed. Without these newer schools in place, it is unlikely that this city would have experienced the growth it did after World War II.

For California, available water and electric power limited population growth, especially in the south. Hoover Dam would remedy this problem for many years into the future. The $165 million projected cost made it the largest single Congressional appropriation ever. The dam truly was a Colossus: It was twice as high as any dam ever built.[50] While seven states claimed interest in the Colorado River, when Congress approved the project to dam it, California received an allotment of a little over 58 percent of the water. This allotment was later contested, but when the Hoover Dam was finished, not only did Los Angeles get 36 percent of the power generated by the dam (plus any power refused by Arizona and Nevada), federal funds helped build another dam to divert the water to the aqueduct which channeled the water to Los Angeles.[51]

San Francisco also benefited from federal government spending. The Golden Gate Bridge dramatically improved access to the downtown area, and also allowed the completion of a west coast highway near the ocean. Planners had dreamed for decades of a bridge between San Francisco and the hills of Marin County to the north. The bridge would span the "Golden Gate," a lovely name for the viciously narrow drain to the Pacific Ocean for most of the water in Central California. In 1923, a Golden Gate Bridge District formed, with banker Frank Doyle as a member. The District issued bonds to pay the anticipated cost. The bonds would be retired with revenue from tolls, a plan which, surprisingly, worked. Marin already was a popular area for housing, with growth of over 50 percent in the 1920s (commuters travelled to the city by ferry before the bridge—and still do). Groundbreaking for the bridge was on February 26 1933, and it opened in 1937. Frank Doyle helped sell the bonds issued to pay for the bridge, and claimed he had the privilege of driving across it two months before the completion.[52]

While the real estate market was nearly inactive during the Depression, in spite of population growth, the government investment in schools, dams, roads, bridges and even parks provided a foundation to support the housing boom that would occur after the war. In fact, during the war there would be a boom in housing.

World War II housing shortage

"As no other single event in the history of the West, the war stimulated economic growth," according to Gerald Nash.[53] While this may be an overstatement, the war certainly stimulated the state's economy, attracting federal spending and jobs, bringing additional population directly, and exposing temporary workers and military personnel to its charms. The population increased from 6.9 million in 1940 to 10.5 million in 1950. During the war, the federal government provided about 90 percent of the new investment capital that flowed into the West.[54] California was the most important manufacturing state in the West. Its production of petroleum products, leisure clothes, auto assembly and small machinery made it eighth in the national ranking of manufacturing states on the eve of the war.[55] Now the government added war materials construction.

As the manufacturing came to California, so did people. As there was virtually no private residential construction during the war, housing had to be provided by government or companies. The lack of housing was a major impediment to the recruitment of war workers. Donald Douglas, the president of Douglas Aircraft Company, stated that the biggest obstacle to increased production at his plants was the housing shortage. At the Salinas Army Air Base, civilian mechanics could not be hired because there was "absolutely no housing in the area."[56] Even if shelter was provided, one government official noted, the lack of recreational opportunities, shopping and other facilities caused many of the workers to decamp for other more attractive locations. Congress approved a Coordinator of Defense Housing to solve the problems. A committee headed by California Senator Sheridan Downey felt the Coordinator failed miserably. He charged that "many thousands of workers ... are living under conditions that must be characterized as abominable."[57] In 1943, Senator Harry Truman criticized the Coordinator for building 750 inadequate dormitory units for aircraft workers in San Diego. Amazingly, forty-four of the units were occupied in spite of the flimsy construction and the fact that absolutely no furniture was provided.[58]

Henry Kranz, the Regional Director of the US Civil Service Commission, felt that private industry had handled the housing problem much better than he could. Henry Kaiser provided an example. Kaiser, an important cement supplier for Hoover Dam, became famous for building "Liberty ships." His first shipyard was in Richmond, California, across the bay from San Francisco. Funded by British loans, the yard's construction started in December 1940. By April 1941, the keel of the first ship was finished.[59] By the time the war started for the United States, Kaiser was finishing one Liberty ship a week. He famously built one in less than five days. Seven hundred and forty-seven ships eventually came from Kaiser's Richmond Shipyard.[60]

At the end of 1943, almost 100,000 men and women worked at the Richmond Shipyard, in a town that had a population of 23,000 before the war.[61] By 1942, the lack of housing for these workers became a crisis. In nearby Oakland a series of articles depicted the lives of the homeless people with jobs at the shipyards. They showed families living out of their car, eating in restaurants, and washing in service station restrooms. Men worked night shifts and slept on park lawns all day. The local marina, the owner said, was a "floating hotel."[62] Kaiser added home-building to his businesses, throwing up 24,000 utilitarian housing units for those workers.[63] Congress authorized the FHA to offer financing to private builders. Several builders, including D. D. Bohannon, R. H. Chamberlain and Ellie Stoneman, applied prefabrication and pre-assembly to quickly create subdivisions of simple housing in the bay area. Bohannon and Chamberlain created a nicer neighborhood, called Rollingwood, in nearby San Pablo in 1943. The three-bedroom houses there had a separate entrance to accommodate the likely boarders or visiting relatives. Another development, Brookfield Village, had 1,200 homes. Workers could buy the homes outright, or lease them for the duration of the war, with an option to buy.

Since discrimination was still rampant, the black shipyard workers could find housing only in the previously black neighborhoods of west Oakland and north Richmond. By 1950, 56 percent of the households in north Richmond were judged to be overcrowded by the census bureau. Maya Angelou's family moved from Arkansas to west Oakland during the war. Angelou, later one of the nation's most famous poets, lived with her mother, two uncles, and her brother in an apartment that had a bathtub in the kitchen and was next to a railroad track.[64]

The federal government and local governments built some temporary housing for war workers. Congress shifted all the funds from the NHA, designed for slum clearance, into temporary housing for war workers. Government projects filled in roughly sixteen miles of San Francisco Bayfront with migrant neighborhoods. In all, the federal government created more than 30,000 public housing units in the East Bay, holding an estimated 90,000 people.[65]

California's economy received an unusual boost from federal spending during the war. Half of the $70 billion Congress earmarked for war material production in the West was earmarked for California. In fact, according to Nash, the state secured a tenth of all federal monies expended during World War II.[66] The RFC granted various subsidies to finance manufacturing in the West. The Defense Plant Corporation (DPC) financed the development of new rubber factories, aluminum, magnesium, steel, and aircraft plants. In addition to the warships, California produced airplanes in factories that employed over 200,000 people in the Los Angeles area alone. In addition, smaller companies provided parts and materials to the large factories of Douglas, Lockheed, North American Aviation, Northrup, and Hughes. Fortunately, Los Angeles Supervisors expedited building permits and allowed the building of 160,000 housing units during the war. Vacancy rates still remained near zero.[67]

The farms of the state contributed to agricultural needs during the war. California was now a major source of fruit, nuts, grain, and fiber. Again lack of housing hindered efforts to increase production. Already in 1942, the citrus-growers claimed they lost half of their crop because there were insufficient workers to harvest it.[68] A government plan to grow guayule in California and other parts of the arid west, to replace rubber, proved to be a futile effort. 40,000 acres were planted in Salinas, but in less than a year synthetic rubber replaced guayule.[69]

By the end of the war, in spite of the government limits on building, new small, flimsy, rectangular houses in neat rows provided homes to forcibly relocated ethnic Japanese, ship-builders attracted from the southern states, and farm workers in the central and Imperial valleys. Also new to the landscape were large neighborhoods of bungalows owned by middle-income earners.[70] These more permanent neighborhoods would preview the direction post-war private developers would take.

Financial institutions bunkered

As the war approached, deposits at commercial banks, savings banks, and B&Ls rose. The Depression taught workers to be cautious about spending, plus the priority put on defense production left little for consumers to buy. After the war started, this phenomenon was even more marked. Yet as deposits rose, the financial institutions continued to be cautious. Most of the funds still went into bonds, and cash balances at banks remained high. Even by 1941, the Superintendent of Banks happily stated that banks had reduced their holdings of foreclosed real estate by about 20 percent. They had also reduced their holdings of substandard bond issues, particularly in the area of railroads and utility bonds. He expressed optimism about the future because of improved prices for agricultural products and larger payrolls due to defense programs. The 1942 report noted an increase in cash and investments in US federal government securities. Deposits were rising rapidly. Other real estate holdings continued to drop. He still had a warning, however. He advised the banks to build up their reserves for post-war adjustments, reflecting a widespread attitude that the Depression would return at the end of the war.[71] The next year, a new Superintendent expressed similar concerns:

> It will be the policy of this department to urge banks to conserve their earnings during the present emergency and to build up reserves as a further protection to their depositors and a cushion against the shock of post-war adjustments.
>
> Many banks are following the conservative policy of adding to their capital and surplus from earnings during the present period and the department feels that this policy is a wise one on the part of the banks.[72]

Shifts in the state's population were apparent even in 1942, as people moved toward the military bases and the jobs producing war materials. Californians were used to such a high number of bank branches per person that it seemed to amount to a branch on every corner.[73] The Superintendent noted the need to find a fast way to approve branches to serve the armed forces and defense areas.[74] San Diego was one of many California communities that grew and prospered during World War II, due to the presence of a major naval base. The population doubled during the war, as did San Diego Trust & Savings Bank assets. Most of these funds went into war bonds and cash, rather than real estate.[75] The federal government not only limited the construction of private housing, they instituted price ceilings to preserve lumber, concrete, tar, and other vital materials for the war effort. In 1942, banks made just 2,500 construction loans, compared to 6,400 the previous year.[76]

During World War II, the state's banks gained 19.5 percent in demand deposits compared to a United States gain of 7 percent.[77] Loans rose slightly, and most of the extra growth was invested in US government obligations. Even near the end of the war, holdings of US government securities were up 23.8 percent for the nation, but up 35.5 percent for California state banks.[78] When the war ended, loans immediately began to show a strong upward trend. In 1946 state banks' total loans increased 25.7 percent, but the Superintendent warned bankers again of a possible recession:

> Loans based on present market values may prove troublesome later. It is suggested that bankers should resurvey their loaning policies and use increasing discretion in extending credit to individuals or firms that are vulnerable in case of a sharp or continued recession in values.[79]

However, the banks were more optimistic, and, as war bonds matured, the banks shifted the funds to loans.

Loans on real estate began to increase (Graph 6.1). By 1945, the Building and Loan Commissioner noted that there was "marked inflation in the selling prices of real estate, particularly homes, both old and new."[80] The real estate market was ready for a remarkably long period of growth.

Notes

1 The Fed raised the reserve requirements for banks. This loss of a cushion against failure nearly halted their lending until they could build up their reserves.

2 Frank Kidner, *California Business Cycles* (Berkeley, California: University of California Press, 1946). See graphs and data *passim,* esp. 37.

3 David Lavender, *California* (New York: W. W. Norton and Co., Inc., 1976).

4 Lynne Pierson Doti and Larry Schweikart, *California Bankers 1848–1993* (Needham Heights, Massachusetts: Ginn Press, 1994), 97.

5 Kevin Starr, *Endangered Dreams: The Great Depression in California* (New York: Oxford University Press, 1996), 229.

6 Ibid.

7 Ibid., 234–5.

8 The dam straddles Arizona and Nevada not far from the border with California. First it was named Hoover Dam, then the government renamed it Boulder Dam. Since 1947 it has been Hoover Dam again.

9 Michael Hiltzik, *Colossus: Hoover Dam and the Making of the American Century* (New York: Free Press, 2010), 181.

10 Ibid., 253.

11 Ibid., 255–7.

12 Superintendent of Banks of the State of California, *Annual Report* (Sacramento: State Printing Office, 1931), 7.

13 Superintendent of Banks of the State of California, *Annual Report* (Sacramento: State Printing Office, 1932), 10. Also see Schweikart and Doti, *California Bankers*, 98.

14 The government can raise taxes if necessary to repay the bonds.

15 Superintendent of Banks of the State of California, *Annual Report* (Sacramento: State Printing Office, 1932), 10.

16 Louis K. Boysen, President, Chicago Mortgage Bankers, speech, "A History of Real Estate Bonds," presented in Chicago, Illinois, 1933.

17 Ibid.

18 Superintendent of Banks of the State of California, *Annual Report* (Sacramento: State Printing Office, 1932), 10–11.

19 California Bankers Association, *The California Banker* (San Fransisco, California: 1932), *passim*.

20 California Bankers Association, *Proceedings of the 42nd Annual Convention*, The Huntington, Pasadena, California, May 24 1932, 17–25.

21 In February 2014, a couple walking their dog found $11 million worth of gold coins that had been buried on their property. The coins had dates from the late 1800s, but it is speculated that the owner of the property buried them during the 1930s when it became illegal for private citizens to hold gold (although collectors were exempted).

22 California Bankers Association, *The California Banker* (San Fransisco, California: 1932), 127.

23 Ibid., 139.

24 Marquis James and Bessie James, *Biography of a Bank: The Story of Bank of America, NT& SA* (New York: Harper & Brothers, 1954), 366.

25 Ibid., 369.

26 Ibid., 368. It should be noted that Bank of America was one of the largest holders of mortgage loans in the country.

27 James and James, 371.

28 Ibid., 374.

29 California Bankers Association, *Proceedings of the California Bankers Association* (May 1933).

30 Superintendent of Banks of the State of California, *Annual Report* (Sacramento: State Printing Office, 1934), 15–16.

31 Ibid., 129.

32 Superintendent of Banks of the State of California, *Annual Report* (Sacramento: State Printing Office, 1935), 15.

33 Superintendent of Banks of the State of California, *Annual Report* (Sacramento: State Printing Office, 1936), 11.

34 Building and Loan Commissioner of the State of California, *Annual Report* (Sacramento, California: California State Printing Office, 1937), 3.

35 Ibid., 3–5.

36 Ibid.

37 Building and Loan Commissioner of the State of California, *Annual Report* (Sacramento, California: California State Printing Office, 1939), 4.

38 Ibid.

39 Superintendent of Banks of the State of California, *Annual Report* (Sacramento: State Printing Office, 1939), 12.

40 Superintendent of Banks of the State of California, *Annual Report* (Sacramento: State Printing Office, 1940), 11.

41 Building and Loan Commissioner of the State of California, *Annual Report* (Sacramento, California: California State Printing Office, 1939), 5–6.

42 Theodore Davie, *San Diego Trust & Savings Bank 1889-1989: A Centennial Book* (no place: San Diego Trust & Savings Bank 1989), 30–2.

43 Davie, 33.

44 Price Fishback, Jonathan Rose and Kenneth Snowden, *Well Worth Saving: How the New Deal Safeguarded Home Ownership* (Chicago, Illinois: The University of Chicago Press, 2013), ix-8, 32, 48–54.

45 Ibid., 48, 50–2.

46 Ibid., 127.

47 Ibid., 13.

48 Ibid., 100.
49 Kidner, 37.
50 Hiltzik, 119–20.
51 Ibid., 155.
52 Santa Rosa Exchange Bank, *History of a Partnership*, (no publisher, circa 1980), 7.
53 Gerald Nash, *The American West Transformed: The Impact of the Second World War* (Lincoln, Nebraska: University of Nebraska Press, 1985), 17.
54 Ibid., 19.
55 Ibid., 7.
56 Ibid., 42.
57 Ibid., 45.
58 Ibid., 46.
59 Mark Foster, *Henry J. Kaiser: Builder in the Modern American West* (Austin, Texas: University of Texas Press, 1989), 71.
60 Larry Schweikart and Lynne Doti, *American Entrepreneur: The Fascinating Stories of the People Who Defined Business in the United States* (New York: Amacom, 2010), 318; Foster, 71.
61 Foster, 71–2.
62 Marilynn Johnson, *The Second Gold Rush: Oakland and the East Bay in World War II* (Berkeley, California: University of California Press, 1993), 91.
63 Foster, 73.
64 Johnson, 91–3.
65 Ibid., 99.
66 Nash,19.
67 Ibid., 63.
68 Ibid., 46.
69 Ibid., 22.
70 Kevin Starr, *Embattled Dreams: California in War and Peace 1940–1950* (Oxford, England: Oxford University Press, 2002), 152.
71 Superintendent of Banks of the State of California, *Annual Report* (Sacramento: State Printing Office, 1942), 9–10.
72 Superintendent of Banks of the State of California, *Annual Report* (Sacramento: State Printing Office, 1943), 13.
73 Doti and Schweikart, *California Bankers 1848-1993*, 111.
74 Superintendent of Banks of the State of California, *Annual Report* (Sacramento: State Printing Office, 1942), 11.
75 Theodore Davie, *San Diego Trust & Savings Bank 1889-1989: A Centennial Book*, (no place: San Diego Trust & Savings Bank, 1989), 36.
76 Superintendent of Banks of the State of California, *Annual Report* (Sacramento: State Printing Office, 1942), 3.
77 Superintendent of Banks of the State of California, *Annual Report* (Sacramento: State Printing Office, 1944), 14.
78 Superintendent of Banks of the State of California, *Annual Report* (Sacramento: State Printing Office, 1945), 11.
79 Superintendent of Banks of the State of California, *Annual Report* (Sacramento: State Printing Office, 1946), 12–13.
80 Building and Loan Commissioner of the State of California, *Annual Report* (Sacramento, California: California State Printing Office, 1945), 4.

7   Post-war housing boom part I
1946–1965

After World War II, the housing market exploded nationwide. In addition to the family formation known as the "baby boom," interest rates were very low, and the 1930s housing programs and the new home loans available to veterans made home ownership more accessible than it had ever been before. In-migration to California dramatically added to the demand for housing. The growth in California real estate relative to the rest of the nation was so rapid that moving funds from outside the area into real estate development, construction, and mortgages became the major challenge to the financial industry.

This real estate boom would completely change the structure of the state's financial system. At first, commercial banks, building and loan societies, savings banks, and insurance companies all played a role in massive flow of funds into real estate. However, the balance between sources of funds shifted. During this period, the savings and loan industry became the main provider of home mortgages. Building & Loan Societies (B&Ls) continued to change their charters to savings banks or to savings and loan associations, and commercial banks increasingly focused their lending on business and consumer loans. Life insurance companies played an important role in channeling funds from other states to developers and homeowners in California via mortgage banks. The government continued its assistance, leaving in place programs that started in the 1930s and adding new programs to encourage home ownership.[1]

Early part of the boom 1945–1956

As the war ended, new housing was in such demand that it was restricted to war workers and veterans. But not everyone was optimistic that the real estate market would stay strong. In 1946, Frank C. Mortimer, the Building and Loan Commissioner of the State of California, provided a caution against the real estate boom, which many thought had started. He felt that the home prices were artificially inflated because of shortages of building materials:

> With regard to new construction, many people have decided to postpone their intentions to build in the hope that later on they may obtain places to live at lower costs ... Equities, as figured today, may shrink or disappear. When

building materials are more freely available at lower prices, and other costs of construction, including builders' profits, are brought down to a figure within the range of the buyers' capacity to pay, we may expect a greater volume of new building.[2]

He also warned of another situation:

> When the applicant is a veteran who desires to finance a home under the GI Bill of Rights, with partial government guarantee, the financial ability of the veteran to carry out his obligation is reviewed in detail by the lending officers. In some instances, it is disclosed that the veteran is not in a position to meet his proposed total financial commitments. He may be buying an automobile on installments; he will need equipment for his prospective home, washing machine, refrigerator, and other appliances. There may be an unpaid doctor's bill or one in the offing. These debts, present and proposed, are added up and matched with the veteran's income. Sometimes it is found that the veteran cannot meet all the contemplated debts. Should a loan be granted by an association in the fact of these conditions, it would be tantamount to assisting the applicant toward financial embarrassment. Sympathetic explanation is made and the loan is wisely declined.[3]

Undoubtedly, his warning made sense, but there was a factor he overlooked.

The military activity in California during the war brought large numbers of Americans to the state. California was a major departure point, staging area, arsenal, and training ground for the Pacific campaign. Perhaps the military personnel working in, or passing through, these facilities glimpsed something they liked and its memory lingered pleasantly in their minds, drawing them back after the war. Whatever the reason, growth in population from 1940 to 1950 was 53 percent; in the 1950s, growth was another 50 percent. Demand for housing would grow as it never had before. As before, it was relatively easy to meet the demand. Already, in 1946, Hubert Scudder, the state's Real Estate Commissioner, noted that several thousand acres of California's best farmland, used for growing tree crops and "truck crops," was being lost to housing. Land prices were rising rapidly, and most of the complaints about realtors were that they had allowed clients to move too slowly, which resulted in their properties being lost to someone else. Scudder noted that, "the subdivision market is rapidly approaching a speculative stage."[4] In March 1946, there were 140 new tracts (parts of subdivisions) for sale in the state, as compared to 52 in 1945. Even though people bought these lots with only the promise of streets and utilities to come, tracts sometimes sold out in a matter of days.[5]

Unfortunately, the improvements and the home-building were often delayed, disappointing buyers. Homebuilding materials such as cement and lumber were price-controlled in 1946, and often scarce. In the early years after the war, construction was limited by federal policy to housing for veterans only.[6] Although these factors sometimes caused sales of the lots to lag, the developers (in this period called "merchant builders") still filed requests for new subdivisions.[7] In March 1946, developers requested 140 subdivisions. In April 1946 the number was 161, but the number stayed in the 140 per month range into 1947.[8] Building was not stopped completely. In 1947, the State Real Estate Commissioner estimated that over one million homes had been built since the end of the war. In January 1948, he estimated that 160,000 housing units were constructed in California during 1947 in spite of the lack of materials.[9]

The demand for houses exceeded the supply, and this would change the nature of the homes. In April 1948, R. S. Davis, the Assistant State Real Estate Commissioner, reported that:

> leading realtors hold forth little hope for sharp reductions in homebuilding costs, particularly for individually styled homes. Families desiring new homes, who have determined to wait until costs drop, will probably not build in the near future. Intensive studies were made of ways to reduce small home construction cost. One logical plan consists of complete standardization of materials. Some mass production home-builders are delaying completion of the home until it is sold, to give the purchasers some choice in the finishing.[10]

The post-war developer no longer provided lots in sizes large enough for farming, even for a "gentleman farmer," who used his land to supplement another income. People wanted homes within driving distance of the factories or office buildings where they worked. Developers realized the solution to providing this type of home was the same as it had been in the 1920s: buy a farm and subdivide it into buildable lots. But, very quickly, developers realized that mass production could speed building and produce economies of scale, just as it had for ships and airplanes. Indeed, Liberty ship builder, Henry Kaiser, had used prefabricated construction during the war to provide low-cost housing for the thousands of new employees in his shipyards, but many builders expanded on this idea to build nicer family homes after the war. Kaiser himself, with the war now over, turned to other mass production industries including cars and housing. He and Fritz Burns became homebuilders in 1945, using partly prefabricated porches and roofs, pre-made interior panels and plumbing fixtures made in their own factories. In 1946, they sold homes for $7,000 to $9,000 for a house of 730 to 1,086 square feet. The partnership produced less than 10,000 homes in California, but, in addition to his home-building, Kaiser supplied cement, gypsum, sand, gravel, and later, aluminum, steel, and appliances to other builders.[11]

The typical low-cost family house of the early post-war period was a two-bedroom square structure on a "slab" (of concrete) instead of the basement common in most parts of the country. Basements were a luxury in California due to the extra construction and materials needed to keep them intact during earthquakes. This typical house was a 1,200 square-feet wood-framed square building, notched in one corner for a tiny "porch" and a front door.[12] The exterior would be stucco, with perhaps a few decorative siding boards or stone facade near the ground. Inside, the walls would have been plastered for the kitchen, living/dining room, two bedrooms, and the bathroom. The family auto was left to the elements. This type of house could be built quickly and inexpensively. "Trailers" were also popular housing. Post-war, they were manufactured to be permanent homes, albeit on wheels. Financing was available, so people usually purchased them and placed them in trailer parks, which rented space and provided electricity and telephone service to the trailer residences. As trailers had to be mobile, they had a maximum width of eight feet and maximum length of fifty feet, which was more than the length of the "The Long, Long Trailer" made famous by Lucille Ball and Desi Arnaz in a 1953 movie.[13]

By 1950, the year he was on the cover of *Time* magazine, most people had heard of William Levitt and his mass production of homes on the east coast.[14] In California, builders had used mass production for housing during the war. For example, Louis H. Boyar had started developing land in 1939. Through the FHA, he secured huge loans to build homes for war workers. By 1950, he had progressed to building a town. He bought 3,375 acres of farmland for $8.8 million in 1950, and laid out a community of 17,000 homes designed for a population of 70,000 people in what he called Lakewood Park, near Los Angeles. He used the latest technology to get the project done quickly: power diggers made a foundation trench for each house in fifteen minutes, lumber was delivered precut to each home site, and conveyor belts loaded shingles to a roof and then were moved to the next house to load the shingles on that roof. Carpenters, plumbers, and electricians completed a task at one house, and then moved to the next to repeat the job.[15] By the end of the first two years, 10,000 homes existed in Lakewood Park. They were quickly occupied, most often sold before completion.[16]

The post-war boom finds its path

The market would change in 1949 as the Veterans Administration (VA) loans became available. The VA loans gave veterans a chance to buy a home at low interest without a down payment. These loans also covered necessary appliances, as did FHA loans, so builders began to include flooring, stoves, and refrigerators with the homes. By 1950, the typical house had grown to include three or four bedrooms, one to two bathrooms, a garage, and choices from a handful of styles and floor plans. Joseph Eichler had an even more glorious vision. His family briefly rented a house designed by Frank Lloyd Wright, in the very upscale Hillsborough neighborhood near San Francisco. Eichler decided that excellent architecture should be available to the average person, and hired prominent architects to design distinctive small, modern houses.[17] Starting in 1949, he built and sold 11,000 homes in the bay area, Sacramento, and in Southern California. Most of the homes still exist and are highly coveted. A couple that bought a new "Eichler" in 1963 recreated it in Palm Springs in 2015, spending a million dollars to do it.[18]

The market paused briefly in 1949, but the Korean War brought a new wave of military personnel through California. Again, many returned when the war was over. This time, developers were ready for the influx. By the mid-fifties, the developers had learned how to get the houses built. Carl Schroeder of First National Bank of Orange County recalled, "All along Tustin [Avenue, in Orange] where there were 10 acre farms, we'd take off from the road, run two streets through, and divide the land into lots for home sites."[19] The bank hired a firm to create the subdivision and provided financing for the building cost. Payments would be made to the contractors as they completed portions of their jobs. Final payment of the loan was to the builder as he completed the construction of the homes and began to sell them. When the individual buyers picked out their finished home, they obtained mortgages, most often from savings banks, and the builder began repaying the loan.

Not all home-building was for primary residences. By the 1950s, there are persistent notes of "resort property" selling briskly. Ample evidence indicates this is mountain property. The construction of the summer cottages (some quite impressive) of Lake Tahoe, Big Bear, and Arrowhead began in the 1920s, and, like many trends, picked up again in the late 1940s. Skiing, although still primitive in California mountains, became popular in the 1950s, further increasing interest in mountain resorts. Palm Springs developed in the Coachella Valley desert in the 1950s, and became a popular winter resort for actors. Elvis Presley, Frank Sinatra, Bob Hope, and Desi Arnaz and Lucille Ball were among those whose publicity shots showed them at their winter homes there. A few beach areas in Malibu, Laguna Beach, Newport Beach, and San Diego were also included in this vacation home boom.[20] The Irvine property, now in the ownership of the third generation, included eight miles of ocean frontage from Laguna to Newport Beach, and Myford Irvine subdivided a large number of tracts of homes. Each development included community amenities such as tennis courts and swimming pools or beach clubs. He leased, rather than sold, much of the underlying land, and maintained architectural and maintenance standards. Owners paid rent on the land and monthly fees for maintenance of the common property. This cooperative type of ownership did not become popular in California until the 1970s.[21]

Shifts in financing sources

Even before the end of World War II, financial institutions had the funds available to finance the housing boom. Americans accumulated savings during the war, as incomes rose and most consumer goods remained unavailable. After the war, pent-up demand absorbed almost every product as soon as it was made. Assets of financial institutions did not grow much until 1950 (Graph 7.1). It wasn't until 1953 that savings accounts began to rise dramatically. In the United States that year, more was added to consumer savings than in any year since World War II. The savings rate was 7.3 percent of after-tax income.[22] Savings deposits at commercial banks were the highest in California of any state. However, from 1945, S&Ls started registering the largest relative gain in savings. While the greatest dollar amount of savings in S&Ls was in Ohio, California was second in the post-war period.[23]

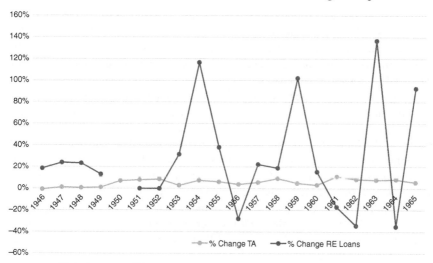

*No bank reports on RE loans were reported for 1950 or 1951

Graph 7.1 Change in total assets and real estate loans of financial institutions in California, 1946–1965.

Source: Calculated from Board of Governors of the Federal Reserve System "All Bank Statistics"; Board of Bank Commissioners of the State of California *Annual Reports* (Sacramento, California: Office of the Board of Bank Commissioners, 1946–1965; Superintendent of Banks of the State of California *Annual Reports* (Sacramento: State Printing Office, 1946–1965) and Federal Deposit Insurance Corporation *Annual Reports* (Washington, DC: 1946–1965).

In the early part of the post-war boom, commercial banks kept pace with the growth of the housing market with their loans on real estate. From 1946 to 1950, commercial banks held over half of all the institutionally held mortgage debt in the state.[24] Most of the real estate held by commercial banks was in insured loans such as FHA or VA, which were backed by federally insured bonds. Federal statutes allowed a national bank to loan up to 60 percent of its savings deposits on real estate, but government-insured loans were not counted in the percentage. Even though California laws put no limits on real estate loans, state-chartered commercial banks collectively never even approached the federal limits on their real estate loans. They increased mortgages as a percentage of assets from 6.9 percent in 1945 to 20.7 percent in 1956. The remainder of their increasing deposits was channeled into supporting the infrastructure of the growing economy. Commercial banks invested in school, utility, road-building, or other state and local bonds. As the production of consumer goods resumed, they moved toward more lucrative financing of business expansion and consumer spending for household goods, especially autos. In 1963, real estate loans as a percentage of assets of commercial banks remained at about 20 percent.[25]

Several of the state's largest banks did pursue the growth in the real estate market. The most prominent was, not surprisingly, Bank of America.[26] In 1948,

Bank of America held $600 million in VA loans—10 percent of all the VA loans in the nation.[27] While Bank of America had been an early, enthusiastic lender on individual mortgages in the 1920s, they had resisted funding developers. In this boom, Bank of America funded several major developers, including Paul Trousdale. Trousdale, who had started his sales career with chewing gum, then, wanting something "larger," switched to houses, received up to $8 million dollars in loans from Bank of America when he was building "two houses a day, seven days a week" for war-industry employees.[28] As soon as the war ended, he began building tract homes and communities, complete with churches and shopping centers, including many in minority areas in Long Beach, Wilmington, Compton, and the San Fernando Valley. "I built community centers in those projects," he proudly recalled, "and a community swimming pool, play yards and a clubhouse in each." At one point, his company had so many outstanding loans with Bank of America that the bank founder, A. P. Giannini, personally popped into Trousdale's office in Westwood Hills to quiz him on how much he was paying for nails and concrete.[29]

When Henry Kaiser applied his mass production techniques to home-building in southern California, the Bank of America extended about $50 million for a single development with 6,000 homes. The Bank of America had loyally supported his building ships, steel, aluminum, household appliances, and even his unsuccessful auto company. Henry Doelger, who started by producing homes near San Francisco in the 1930s, received a $75 million loan from Bank of America after the war for a development west of Los Angeles, known as the Sunset district.[30]

However, most of the commercial banks in California did not keep pace with the growth in mortgage lending. It wasn't that they didn't have plenty of money to loan. Funds flowed into the California commercial banks rapidly from 1946 to the 1960s. Nationwide, deposits increased dramatically from 1946 to 1960, but deposits also grew more rapidly in California than in the rest of the nation after 1950. There is evidence that California banks were receiving funds from outside the state. Although some of the capital inflows came with the migrating labour force, deposits did not all come by this method.[31] Hyman Minsky speculated on the source of the funds. He said funds came to California in part as a result of an excess of federal spending in California over the taxes collected there, in effect reallocating funds from other areas. These surplus funds amounted to $225 million in 1952, $1.982 billion in 1958 and $2.54 billion in 1960.[32] But Minsky also noted that for individual investors, "out-of-state funds [loomed] large in the financing of mortgages on property."[33] He estimated that 37.5 percent of the funds invested in non-farm mortgages by private investors at the end of 1960 came from outside the state. In the nine years from 1951 to 1960, California mortgages held by out-of-state investors grew at an annual rate of 14.3 percent.[34] This, in fact, may be the reason that real estate lending was shifting from commercial banks to other institutions that were easier conduits for out-of-state funding. At any rate, although commercial banks may have imported funds from out of state, they did not appear to import funds for the mortgage market.[35]

California commercial bankers were trying to keep up with the service needs of the growing suburban communities. They were adding branches at an amazing rate in the 1950s, trying to service the new customers appearing in the growing suburbs.[36] The Superintendent of Banks may have been a hindrance. In 1948, he reported that:

> the shortage of housing in established communities has led to the development of new business and residence districts outside of the densely populated areas. Many of these communities are far enough away from presently established banking facilities to be inconvenienced thereby. Consequently there have been numerous requests made to this department and to the Comptroller of the Currency for permission to establish new banks or branches in these rapidly growing communities. Many of these requests have been denied as obviously premature. Investigation in many cases has shown that, while banking facilities are lacking in certain communities, these communities are not yet able to support an independent bank or furnish sufficient business to enable a branch bank to operate profitably.[37]

While Bank of America continued to set the pace for new branches in the 1950s, other commercial banks similarly expanded their branch systems. And if the Superintendent was not enthusiastic about new branches, he did not block the acquisition of banks. California Bank had been started by the pioneer Chaffey family, and had a long branching history. In the Depression the bank consolidated, going from fifty-seven branches in 1939 to thirty-nine in 1943. As World War II ended, the bank began adding ten to twelve branches a year and also bought as many banks as possible. Under president Frank King, California Bank bought forty-three other banks in the first decade after the war.[38] California Bank was most interested in loans to business and industry, but participated in the real estate market by acquiring mortgage companies.[39]

Commercial banks financed state and local bond issues because of the tax-free interest they paid, the safety and liquidity of the investment, and for the community goodwill necessary to move into new neighborhoods. Commercial banks participated less in the long-term mortgage market; increasing their construction lending, home improvement loans, and other short-term real estate-related lending versus their longer-term loans.[40] There may have been other reasons for commercial banks to reduce the share of real estate loans in their portfolios that foreshadowed changes that would occur in the 1960s. Commercial banks could not legally offer terms as generous as those offered by the saving banks on longer-term deposits. Congress mandated a 0.25 to 0.5 percent higher deposit interest rate for savings institutions over banks throughout this period. For their savings deposits, the public began to accept the savings banks as close substitutes for banks, and this made it harder for commercial banks to attract long-term deposits.[41]

Insurance companies, savings banks, and mutual savings banks were supporting their faster growth in the mortgage market by importing even more funds from other states than were commercial banks (see Table 7.1).[42]

Table 7.1 Non-farm California mortgages: holdings of six major sources of funds, 1951–1961

Type of institution	Annual growth %	Estimated average % funds from outside California
Insured savings and loan associations in California	23.0	18.5
Mutual savings banks	55.0	100.0
Life insurance companies	9.9	77.0
Commercial banks	6.8	0.0
Federal National Mortgage Association (FNMA)	14.0	95.0
Cal-Vet	27.5	51.9
Total	14.3	38.5

Sources: Estimated from Hyman P. Minsky, "Commercial Banking and Rapid Economic Growth in California," in Minsky, editor, *California Banking in a Growing Economy, 1946–1975* (Berkeley, California: University of California Press, 1965), 121. Estimates of the contributions of FNMA and Cal-Vet contributions are based on the assumptions that Californians held 5 percent and 50 percent of the bonds issued by those programs. Estimate of out-of-state funds is from J. Gilles and T. Grebler, "Financing of Nonfarm Housing in CA," in *Appendix to the Report on Housing in California*, Governor's Advisory Commission on Housing Problems (Sacramento, California: 1963), 379–80.

With these funds they were making FHA and VA loans. Albert Schaaf presents a possible cause for the fact that commercial banks increasingly allowed other financial institutions to outpace their growth in mortgage lending:

> Faced with so much competition in the mortgage market and enjoying certain shelters in their position in various nonmortgage lending areas, it is understandable that commercial banks would increase their relative activity in the lucrative fields of business and consumer lending and regard mortgage investment as more of a residual.[43]

This does not explain why in most other states the commercial banks increased their real estate loans more in proportion to the real estate development.[44]

By 1960, non-farm real estate in California was increasingly financed by the B&Ls, savings banks, insurance companies, and S&Ls. The S&Ls increasingly opened, or converted from B&Ls, as stock-issuing corporations which allowed capital to come from a wide geographic area. Congress regulated these corporations as to the minimum percentage of assets invested in mortgages. Most of their mortgage loans had to be on single-family and small (up to four-unit) multi-family buildings. The B&Ls, saving banks, and S&Ls also competed aggressively in real estate lending, but did not make consumer and business loans. To consumers there did not seem to be a difference between the various types of financial institutions when they were considering deposits or mortgages.

Albert Schaaf summed up the changing scene:

> California commercial banks traditionally have been among the most active in the nation in permanent mortgage lending. The absence of mutual savings banks, the widespread use of branch banking, the importance of time deposits, and the relative intensity of the demand for mortgage credit have contributed to this result. In the post-World War II period, the importance of mortgages to California commercial banks has lessened; the degree to which California banks differ from the average nationwide picture has diminished; and the decline in the relative importance of commercial banks in the provision of long-term credit to California real estate markets has been profound.[45]

Building and loan societies change to savings and loan associations

In spite of a short post-war surge, B&Ls practically disappeared during the post-war period, and were replaced by S&Ls. They failed or reincorporated as S&Ls and, in 1956, their state representation became the California Savings and Loan League. At the end of 1945, there were 106 associations, with $331 million in assets, an increase of 25 percent from the year before. Like all financial institutions, they had moved into US government bonds during the war and now were shifting back to home loans. In 1945, bonds in their asset portfolio decreased 16 percent. Loans on real estate increased 29 percent. In 1949, with anticipation of war in Korea, the regulators again worried that loans to veterans would prove to be a heavy burden, and that building costs would continue to keep housing prices too high. By 1950, the warnings became prophecy. There were 190 foreclosures in 1949 among the B&Ls, and their holdings of real estate owned increased 22 percent over the previous year. Loans, however, still increased 19 percent.[46]

The fast growth of the savings institutions in California could have been a reaction to one 1946 California law that gave the B&Ls and S&Ls a new power. The provisions of the law would be little used in the early post-war period, but in the 1950s and 1960s would help make California B&Ls and S&Ls the most coveted financial institutions in the nation. The law was Section 9.02a, *Real Property for Sale or Income*.

> An association may invest in real property and such investment may include subdividing and developing real property and building thereon homes and other buildings principally for residential use by veterans; and an association may own, rent, manage, and operate the same for income or may sell the same; provided that no association shall have investments, under this Section 9.02a, aggregating at any one time more than whichever of the following is the lesser: (a) 5 percent of its total assets or (b) an amount equal to the sum of its capital, surplus, undivided profits, loan reserve and federal insurance reserve, and such other reserves as the commissioner may prescribe.

No investment pursuant to this Section shall be held by an association more than five years, except with the approval of the commissioner.[47]

Obviously this law was very restrictive, but it opened the door to financial institutions developing and owning real estate rather than merely making loans on it.

In 1951, the B&Ls experienced greater growth than in any year in history. There were 117 associations with thirty-three branches in the state system, with assets of $755 million of which $634 million was in loans on real estate. Their new lending was about equally divided between new construction and existing homes. However, a shift that started in the 1930s was accelerating. Six B&Ls changed their names to "Savings and Loan Association (S&L)."[48] This trend continued at about this pace over the next decade. The total assets of the California chartered S&Ls grew through the 1950s at annual rates of near 30 percent. Loans on real estate exceeded $1 billion for the first time in 1952. In 1954, there were 139 S&Ls with 63 branches, but 14 were either new or conversions from B&Ls. On the other hand, existing S&Ls were aggressively buying up other institutions.[49] By 1956, the real estate owned by California S&Ls had increased to $15 million. The State Commissioner stated that, "most of the 686 parcels represented in that total amount evidence purchases by associations of real property for subdividing and development principally for residential use by veterans in accordance with permissive statutes."[50]

Howard Ahmanson was one of the early developers who recognized the opportunity in also being a banker. In 1947, he bought Home Building and Loan. He liked the name and its qualifications to make loans for real estate development in an unlimited geographic area. After he bought the institution, he started its rapid growth.[51] Known for his creative cost-cutting, he realized that if a housing project was pre-approved as fitting FHA/VA building guidelines, he did not have to review the individual homes, as they were sold before offering mortgage terms.[52] He also saved by avoiding face-to-face contact with the customers, both by offering standardized loans and by accepting payments on those loans only at remote locations.[53] By 1950, Home Savings and Loan financed over 500 housing tracts. Then he started buying other S&Ls, so that, by 1951, he owned the nineteenth-largest S&L in the country. By 1953, Home Savings and Loan was the fifth-largest, and the next year it was the largest S&L in the United States.[54]

In 1957, the total assets of $3.3 billion in California S&Ls exceeded the total in any other state. Growth that year was slower, but still 21.5 percent among the 165 associations. Demand was pushing the prices of homes higher, and the state increased the loan limit from $15,000 to $20,000 per unit in 1958. However, the average loan was only just over $11,000 in 1958. On single family homes the loan could equal no more than 80 percent of the market value. The state increased the term from twenty to twenty-five years on all residential property. By 1960, the average loan was $13,500, but the Commissioner found the average percentage of those loans was only 68.8 percent of the appraised value of the property. California S&Ls remained the fastest growing among states, with total assets now increasing at 20 to 25 percent annually.[55] The larger

Table 7.2 Growth in savings and loan association deposits, 1945–1961

Year	Deposits ($ million)	Percentage change (%)
1945	503	–
1946	587	17
1947	691	18
1948	820	19
1949	992	21
1950	1,159	17
1951	1,386	20
1952	1,744	26
1953	2,210	27
1954	2,743	24
1955	3,405	24
1956	4,203	23
1957	4,982	19
1958	6,096	22
1959	7,353	21
1960	8,905	21
1961	10,794	21

Source: Minsky, "Commercial Banking and Rapid Economic Growth in California," in Minsky, editor, *California in a Growing Economy 1946–1975* (Berkeley, California: University of California Press, 1965), 121. No bank reports were published for 1945.

S&Ls continued to buy smaller ones, but five to ten new associations started each year. While S&Ls experienced phenomenal growth, the much larger assets of commercial banks meant that they still held twice the total loan amount of mortgages held by commercial banks (see Table 7.2).[56]

The aerospace lull

Between 1960 and 1965, growth in the entire economy slowed, but California had some particular problems. Defense was a major industry in the southern half of the state. The aircraft and related industries that supplied the support for World War II (and even World War I) remained active for some years after the war ended. The companies built aircraft for civilian use and helped the military catch up with the new technology developed during the war. Passenger travel increased dramatically and the Cold War fuelled demand for the latest military equipment. When the Soviets put up the Sputnik satellite in 1957 and President Kennedy started the space race, a brief slow-down occurred. Contracts for new equipment were granted to companies in other states, and many of California's technical employees moved to follow the jobs. North American, a large company in Los Angeles, lost a contract in 1957 and laid off 15,600 workers. As the industry lost government jobs, other subcontracted orders were cancelled, and private companies failed. This trend continued through the early 1960s. In 1965, one defense contractor in Santa Monica laid off 40,000 workers.[57] In 1961, the aircraft manufacturer Glenn L. Martin merged with the American-Marietta Corporation, a large sand- and gravel-mining company. Jack Northrup, another pioneer in aviation construction, had already sold his company to Donald Douglas. Douglas Aircraft, which built the DC-3, the world's most popular passenger airline vehicle, merged with McDonnell aircraft in 1967, as jets replaced their propeller plane. All of these companies were located near Los Angeles. The aerospace slow-down created pockets of foreclosures, often in upscale neighborhoods, where very specialized engineers made their homes.

Fortunately, these losses were soon reversed. California received about 40 percent of all aerospace contracts from 1962 to 1978, most in the Los Angeles area.[58] Lockheed, Rocketdyne, Convair, Hughes, and many other aerospace manufacturers had major production facilities in the Los Angeles area, and high-tech jobs returned. By the mid-1960s, the California housing market resumed its growth again and funding was still moving into the state's economy. In the mid-1960s growth spurt, California was able to attract funds from outside of the region even more easily than it had before.[59] The large financial institutions in California, including banks, insurance companies, and S&Ls, took on a more national aspect, because now the financial institutions had recognizable names. This allowed them to sell bonds to raise funds nationally and even internationally. They were able to generate more mortgages because branching allowed them to be more flexible about location of the real estate than institutions in most states. The RFC, FHA, and VA contributed to making home loans a national asset by increased purchases of mortgages from financial institutions.[60] In 1963, S&Ls still dominated the mortgage market in California. Banks originated only 15.6 percent of the mortgage lending, while S&Ls originated 52.8 percent. Additionally, individuals provided 13.3 percent, insurance companies 2.3 percent, and other sources 16.1 percent.[61]

The state and local governments also contributed to the funds brought into California. Between 1950 and 1960 the bonded debt of the state grew at an annual rate of 23 percent. During the same period, the city and county debt grew at an annual rate of 14.2 percent. The debt instruments issued by these governments entered the national financial markets.[62]

The real estate boom took a short pause in the early 1960s, but would quickly revive. By the middle of the decade, the financing of real estate was in the second part of the long boom.

Notes

1 Lynne Pierson Doti and Larry Schweikart, "Financing the Postwar Housing Boom in Phoenix and Los Angeles, 1945–1960," *Pacific Historical Review* (1989), 173–94.
2 Building and Loan Commissioner of the State of California, *Annual Report* (Sacramento, California: California State Printing Office, 1946), 6–7.
3 Ibid., 7.
4 California Department of Investment, Division of Real Estate, *Report for Governor's Council*, (Sacramento: State of California, 1946), 2.
5 Ibid., 1–2. Subdivisions would be divided into multiple "tracts." Developers paid lower tax rates for undeveloped land, so they would develop one tract at a time. The "tract

house" was also the nomenclature for a group of homes built by one builder, rather than "custom" homes individually commissioned by the homeowner.

6 Ibid., 4.

7 Ned Eichler, *The Merchant Builders* (Cambridge, Massachusetts: The MIT Press, 1982), 62–79.

8 California Department of Investment, Division of Real Estate, *Report for Governor's Council* (Sacramento: State of California, 1947), 2–3.

9 California Department of Investment, Division of Real Estate, *Report for Governor's Council* (Sacramento: State of California, 1948), 3.

10 Ibid., "Summary."

11 Mark Foster, *Henry J. Kaiser: Builder in the Modern American West* (Austin, Texas: University of Texas Press, 1989), 133–5.

12 Eichler, 81.

13 "I Love Lucy," *Hepcat Restorations*, "Vintage New Moon Trailers," posted February 6 2003. Available online at http://hepcatrestorations.com/2013/02/06/new-moon-trailers/. The author lived in a "New Moon" trailer as a child. It was eight by forty feet and contained two bedrooms. Professionals with large trucks always moved it when it changed locations. Lucy and Desi had a fictionalized version of a one-bedroom model of the same trailer. When the "I Love Lucy" model was created for sale by the Redman Company, after the movie came out, it was thirty-six feet long.

14 Larry Schweikart and Lynne Pierson Doti, *American Entrepreneur: The Fascinating Stories of the People Who Defined Business in the United States* (New York: Amacom, 2010), 328.

15 Eichler, 67.

16 Remi Nadeau, "Supersubdivider," *Los Angeles: Biography of a City*, edited by John Caughey and LaRee Caughey (Berkeley, California: University of California Press, 1977), 402.

17 Eichler, 86.

18 Susan Stamberg, "With Sunny, Modern Homes, Joseph Eichler Built The Suburbs In Style," *NPR* [National Public Radio], (March 16 2015). Available online at www.npr.org/2015/03/16/392561864/with-sunny-modern-homes-joseph-eichler-built-the-suburbs-in-style.

19 Lynne Pierson Doti and Larry Schweikart, *California Bankers, 1848–1993* (Needham Heights, Massachusetts: Ginn Press, 1994), 120.

20 California Department of Investment, Division of Real Estate, *Report for Governor's Council* (Sacramento: State of California,1946), 3.

21 Rob Kling, Spencer Olin and Mark Poster, editors, *Postsuburban California: The Transformation of Orange County since World War II* (Berkeley: University of California Press, 1991), 57.

22 Savings accounts were term deposits that required more than 30 days' notice to withdraw. *US Savings and Loan Fact Book* (Chicago: United States Savings and Loan League, 1954), 11.

23 Ibid., 7, 9.

24 Frederic Morrissey, "The Allocation of Funds by the Commercial Banks in the California Economy, 1946–1975," *California Banking in a Growing Economy, 1946–1975*, edited by Hyman P. Minsky (Berkeley: University of California Press, 1964), 249.

25 James Gilles and Clayton Curtis, *Institutional Residential Mortgage Lending in Los Angeles County, 1946–51: Six Significant Years of Mortgage Lending* (Los Angeles: Bureau of Business and Economic Research, University of California, 1956), 66.

26 John Cox, "Institutional Mortgage Lending in the Los Angeles Metropolitan Area, 1953–54 and 1957–58." Ph.D. dissertation, University of Southern California (1962), 44.

27 Marquis James and Bessie James, *Biography of a Bank: The Story of Bank of America NT & SA* (New York: Harper and Row, 1954), 490.

28 James and James, 470.

29 Myrna Oliver, "Paul Trousdale, Developer and Innovator, Dies," *Los Angeles Times* (April 12 1990). Available online at http://articles.latimes.com/1990-04-12/local/me-1607_1_trousdale-estates.

30 Doti and Schweikart, "Financing the Postwar Housing Boom in Phoenix and Los Angeles," 187.

31 Cash due from banks increased twice as fast in California as in the rest of the nation. This account consists mostly of checks in transit, in this case, funds transferred through the Federal Reserve System to make payments to California banks. Hyman P. Minsky, "Commercial Banking and Rapid Economic Growth in California," *California in a Growing Economy 1946–1975*, edited by Hyman P. Minsky (Berkeley: University of California Press, 1965), 79–134.

32 Minsky, calculated from information on page 116.

33 Ibid., 119.

34 Ibid.

35 Schaaf, Albert H., "The Savings Function and Mortgage Investment by California Banks and Financial Institutions," *California in a Growing Economy 1946–1975*, edited by Hyman P. Minsky (Berkeley: University of California Press, 1965), 250.

36 Superintendent of Banks of the State of California, *Annual Report* (Sacramento: State Printing Office, 1947), 12.

37 Superintendent of Banks of the State of California, *Annual Report* (Sacramento: State Printing Office, 1948), 12–13.

38 Daniel Kibbie, *Their Bank Our Bank the Quality Bank: A History of the First Interstate Bank of California* (Los Angeles: First Interstate Bank, no date, about 1982), 160.

39 Ibid., 171.

40 Schaaf, 250. In most other states, the pattern differed. Arizona commercial banks were more active in real estate lending. Valley Bank and several newly formed commercial banks actively sought funds from east coast sources to fund builders. Local real estate agents championed the state to their national insurance underwriters. See Doti and Schweikart, *Financing the Postwar Housing Boom in Phoenix and Los Angeles, 1945–1960*, 173–94. Pages referred to are 174–184.

41 Schaaf, 250.

42 Until 1956, there were only technical differences between mutual savings banks, savings banks, building and loan societies, and savings and loan associations. They all often required "membership," and "interest" paid was actually a share of profits. As noted, building and loan societies were changing to saving banks and often using the "savings and loan" designation. Savings banks also started using this name in the 1950s, and mutual savings banks eventually disappeared from California.

43 Schaaf, 250.

44 Ohio also experienced fast growth of the savings and loan associations, and lagging commercial banks. Doti and Schweikart, "Financing the Postwar Housing Boom in Phoenix and Los Angeles, 1945–1960," 173–94.

45 Schaaf, 252.

46 Building and Loan Commissioner of the State of California, *Annual Report* (Sacramento, California: California State Printing Office, 1950), 5.

47 Building and Loan Commissioner of the State of California, *Annual Report* (Sacramento, California: California State Printing Office, 1947), 11.

48 Building and Loan Commissioner of the State of California, *Annual Report* (Sacramento, California: California State Printing Office, 1951), 5–6.

49 Savings and Loan Commissioner of the State of California, *Annual Report* (Sacramento, California: California Department of Savings and Loans, 1954), 5–7.

50 Savings and Loan Commissioner of the State of California, *Annual Report* (Sacramento, California: California Department of Savings and Loans, 1956), 6.

51 Eric John Abrahamson, *Building Home: Howard F. Ahmanson and the Politics of the American Dream* (Berkeley: University of California Press, 2013), 87.

52 The FHA and VA provided specific criteria for houses on which they would buy mortgages. For example, homes must have carpet or other flooring throughout, heating, a closet by the entry for coats, and a long list of other things.

53 Abrahamson, 105.

54 Ibid., 92–5.

55 Savings and Loan Commissioner of the State of California, *Annual Report* (Sacramento, California: California Department of Savings and Loans, 1960), 6–11.

56 Schaaf, 256.

57 Carl N. A. Heuse, "The Aerospace / Defense Complex," *Challenge* 13, No. 5 (June 1965), 32–35. Available online at www.jstor.org/stable/40718924.

58 Allen J. Scott, "Interregional Subcontracting Patterns in the Aerospace Industry: The Southern California Nexus," *Economic Geography* 69, no. 2 (April 1993), 142–156. Available online at www.jstor.org/stable/143533.

59 Minsky, 100.

60 Ibid.

61 David A. Alhadeff, "California Banking and Competition," *California in a Growing Economy 1946–1975*, edited by Hyman P. Minsky (Berkeley: University of California Press, 1965), 165.

62 Minsky, 122; Earl Pomeroy, *The American Far West in the 20th Century* (New Haven, Connecticut: Yale University Press, 2009), addresses the topic of out-of-state financing of California growth.

8 Post-war boom part II
1965–1980

In February of 1970, rioters set the Isla Vista branch of Bank of America on fire. The rioters were mostly students at the nearby University of California, Santa Barbara, and the issue was the Vietnam War, but the targeting of Bank of America was symbolic to the students of America's big business powers. It is ironic that the Bank of America had once created its own revolution when A. P. Giannini created a state-wide system of branch banks to serve "the little guy." There were radical changes in society in the late 1960s and 1970s. Equally radical (and perhaps confused) changes occurred in the California financial system and real estate markets. Some of these changes contributed to the real estate bubble in the 1970s, to the demise of the S&L industry in the 1990s, and to destructive influences that led to the 2008 financial crisis.

The early post-war real estate boom continued until about 1960 in California. The loss of defense contracts was one of the impediments to continued growth. By then, the nation's economy was also experiencing slow growth, which led to the first deliberate test of Keynesian policy. President Kennedy called for higher spending and lower taxes, but when President Johnson assumed the office, it was clear that there were no guidelines regarding "how much" of each was needed to fix the economy. Starting in the mid-1960s, the entire US economy was affected by high and variable inflation, coupled with increasing market interest rates. Federal regulation of maximum interest paid on bank deposits squeezed all mortgage lenders. Lenders could charge high interest rates on new loans, but they could not attract the funds to loan because of low interest rates on deposits. In California, there were additional circumstances that contributed to the uncertainty and fluctuations of the 1970s, particularly a law limiting real estate taxes and a court ruling that made assuming home loans a right for a home-buyer. In addition, the state was a leader in the "consumerism" movement, which added cost to lenders, and the anti-growth movement, which added cost to real estate development.

Commercial banks throughout the 1970s increasingly complained of uneven regulations that seemed to favor the S&Ls, mutual funds, life insurance companies, and investment trusts. Because of their greater legal freedom, especially in California, these non-bank financial institutions were developing new products to compete directly with the commercial banks. One of the solutions was for banks to form holding companies. The holding companies owned a main commercial bank, but also owned some more profitable businesses like mortgage companies, leasing operations, and subsidiaries which handled computer support for the financial companies.

Real estate lending took on increased importance over the decade; however, two legislative changes unique to California occurred in the late 1970s. These changes were reflected in a marked increase in real estate lending by both commercial banks and S&Ls. The first was a landmark 1978 California Supreme Court decision (*Wellenkamp vs. Bank of America*), which decisively increased the borrowers' power in all real estate loans. In the same year, California voters passed an initiative, Proposition 13 ("Prop 13"), which increased the security of residential real estate values by limiting property tax increases. While owners held their property, the tax on it could not be increased. It could be increased based on a reassessment of value when sold, but the cap was 1.5 percent of assessed value. Certainty about future taxes added to the demand for real estate created by the rise of inflation in the 1970s.

Furthermore, the positions of homeowners were strengthened by new rules that restricted supply. New construction in California was limited by increased requirements for low density, higher fees from local building departments, requirements for environmental impact studies, and the 1976 Coastal Commission Act that limited building along the more than 800-mile coastline. With all of these new factors to consider, banks and S&Ls changed their business models and real estate lending practices in California. Real estate financing would be shaken in this decade, and undergo changes that became permanent.

How California's financial system changed in the 1970s

California had gained production and employment in the late 1960s through aerospace contracts and other federal government-fueled employment. Tourism was flourishing and there was substantial in-migration. By 1975, the situation had changed. California's unemployment soared to above 10 percent (but was still below the national rate). The entire US economy in the late 1960s moved into a "stagflation" of high unemployment and high inflation that blew out of control by the end of the 1970s. The only comfortable spot in this messy economy was a nice house.

At the beginning of the 1970s, commercial banking and S&Ls each had a well-established business model. Commercial banks offered mostly checking accounts to depositors, both businesses and consumers. By federal law, they were not permitted to pay interest on these deposits, but the ability to use checks, instead of currency, for payments was a valuable service for customers. "Demand deposits" or "checking accounts" were payable on demand with presentation of a check. These short-term deposits were used to fund banks' loans for business capital equipment, working capital, and for limited types of consumer goods, particularly autos. The S&Ls, on the other hand, focused on attracting savings deposits, which were not as easily accessed. The S&Ls were all required to loan on real estate, particularly for one to four residential unit buildings. At this time, 75 percent of their assets had to be on these properties. They were not allowed to make commercial or consumer loans. These institutions funded their real estate loans from their main product, savings deposits. Interest paid on the savings deposits was at rates set by Congress. A deposit at an S&L or a savings bank paid 0.25 to 0.5 percent above the interest rate on a savings deposit at a commercial bank. Congress set this differential as part of a deliberate policy that reflected the desire to make saving banks more profitable and to encourage home ownership. Even in the early 1970s, there were signs that these simple models would not continue through the decade.

Bankers have always had trouble with their public image, but, in 1971, the year the "Fair Credit Act" passed, the California State Superintendent of Banks said:

> The present image of banking during this fiscal year deteriorated to the lowest level it has been since the Great Depression. Banking is deeply distrusted by the now formidable consumer interests and those on Capitol Hill who identify with "consumerism".... The bankers are blamed, all too often, for pollution, the plight of minorities, and the plight of the poor.[1]

The Fair Credit Act, which required transparency by creditors, specified the method by which interest rates were quoted. It was a major movement by Congress to support the popular concept of "consumer rights." This was one of the features of the 1970s, and subsequently would shift the weight given the consumers of loans versus the providers. But this was not the only major change in the way banks operated that would occur in this period and create a volatile market for financial institution assets and real estate lending, as shown in Graph 8.1.

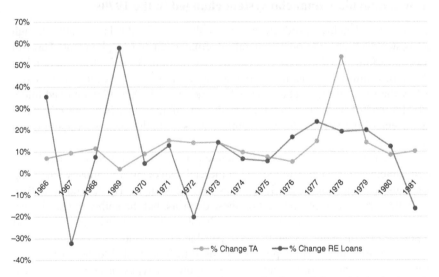

Graph 8.1 Change in total assets and real estate lending of financial institutions in California, 1966–1981.

Source: Calculated from Superintendent of Banks, State of California, *Annual Reports*; California S&L Commissioner, *Annual Reports*; FDIC Historical Statistics, https://www5.fdic.gov/hsob/.

Disintermediation

A flight of funds from depository financial intermediaries to direct investment became increasingly severe during the 1970s. Banks reacted by offering new products, and pushing to abolish the ceilings on interest paid on deposits imposed by Congress. The rates paid on deposits had been set by Congress since the 1930s, when the motivation had been to help banks to stay profitable by limiting their biggest expense, the cost of acquiring funds to lend. In December 1966, the Federal Reserve Board and Congress raised the discount rate (their own rate on loans) to discourage banks from borrowing from them, and simultaneously raised the allowable interest paid on time deposits (savings accounts). Interest rates in the economy began to rise, in response to this action and to a growing awareness of inflationary forces.

In late March 1967, most major banks increased the rate on larger deposits carrying longer than thirty-day maturities (certificates of deposit, or "CDs"),[2] while leaving the rate on short-term savings accounts unchanged: There was a shift of funds from the latter to the former. This is the first evidence of consumers becoming alert to the interest they earned on their savings. California S&Ls lost funds at this point, and mortgage lending tightened noticeably. As a result, the Federal Home Loan Bank Board (FHLBB) amended its regulations to let only California and Nevada S&Ls pay higher interest on regular passbook accounts. Later this ceiling was raised, and they were allowed to pay bonuses of 0.5 percent above the allowed amount on CDs.[3]

In 1968, the first step occurred in the deregulation of interest rates: the Fed permitted banks the discretion to pay higher interest rates on Negotiable Certificates of Deposit (NCDs), marketable deposits for over $100,000, which had penalties if funds were withdrawn before an agreed-upon time that the funds would remain on deposit. Although the deposit had to stay at the bank for at least thirty days, when the term ended the bank paid the bearer of the certificate, allowing the NCD to be bought and sold repeatedly during the time to maturity. This made it a very liquid asset. Banks hired brokers to sell NCDs in national markets, and these brokers often combined several smaller deposits to create the necessary $100,000 minimum amount.

The first major wave of disintermediation occurred in 1969. Consumers routed their potential savings deposits to more direct investments, such as stock and bond mutual funds. Soon, other mutual funds developed specifically to replace bank deposits. These funds, called "money market mutual funds" purchased short-term debt, particularly commercial paper. They even offered checking accounts based on these investments. Banks and S&Ls could not match the higher returns offered by these alternatives. By the late 1960s, virtually all institutions had to pay the maximum interest rate allowable as people became comfortable with the fact that their money was equally safe in any institution that had FDIC insurance. In California, particularly, there were such a large number of bank offices per person that competition for deposits was intense.[4] In 1969, savings deposits at state-licensed associations were down from the previous year.

At S&Ls, those deposit funds had been committed to long-term real estate loans. Because of this, S&Ls borrowed heavily from the Federal Home Loan Bank (FHLB), a high-cost type of borrowing.[5] The FHLB was charging 5.75 percent at the beginning of 1969, but it raised the rate to 7.25 percent by the end of the year. In comparison, the interest rate paid on deposits by S&Ls was limited to 6 percent.[6]

In contrast to the financial disintermediation (the outflow) experienced by California S&Ls during 1969, the year 1970 was a period of re-intermediation (inflow) of deposits. Savings balances increased, and S&Ls geared up their lending operations in order to channel funds into the real estate loan market.[7] There were several contributing factors to this. In January of 1970, associations were given the authority to issue a variety of new savings deposit instruments similar to NCDs, offering higher interest rates for a larger amount and a longer fixed-term deposit. At the beginning of the year, the "bonus rate" accounts, as they were called, represented 24 percent of deposits; by the end of the year they were 42 percent. Other factors slowing disintermediation included temporary suspension of the sale of selected government agency issues in denominations of less than $10,000, disenchantment of the small investor with the stock market, and increases in disposable personal income from the elimination of an income tax surcharge.[8]

In July 1970, the amount of real estate dollars loaned surpassed the same month in the previous year for the first time. At the time, 94.2 percent of the real estate loans were on residential property, while the required minimum was still 75 percent. Saving inflows increased dramatically. Only 4.2 percent in 1970, they were 20.2 percent in 1971. These savings flows were invested in real estate and repaid loans from the FHLB. According to the Savings and Loan Commissioner, "as 1972 progresses, it appears that associations will again have extensive sums of money for investment in real estate loans."[9] The Commissioner's forecast proved accurate. The next year, he reported: "California S&Ls experienced another exceptional year of growth and prosperity."[10] The S&Ls' management seemed equally optimistic. Extensive additions to their branching system were requested, and they began to add limited loan facilities in addition to full branches. In fact, 1972 was a good year for S&Ls. Savings flowed into the system, there was strong loan demand, and there was a comfortable spread between interest charged and interest paid on deposits. The gains in savings deposit levels that began in mid-1970 continued. S&Ls' loans on real estate rose 35.8 percent above those made in 1971. There was a decline in the "other real estate owned," property acquired in lieu of payment of loans during 1972.[11]

The growth of the financial industry continued throughout the early 1970s, but there were a few problems. While net savings inflows to California S&Ls increased, the new real estate loan volume in 1973 was 124.7 percent below 1972 activity. In 1974, there was another reduction in loan activity of 25 percent. State-licensed S&Ls increased their borrowings from the FHLB in order to fund withdrawals and to make real estate loans. Primarily as a result of these factors, net income declined, along with return on net worth from the previous year.

The S&Ls did not seem to be in trouble, however. Their total net worth was still higher than the 5 percent required by law.[12]

The year 1973 had some signs of slowing growth and declining profitability in the California commercial banking system as well. The failure of the venerable United States National Bank in San Diego, and the resultant sale to Crocker National Bank, came with revelations of blatant misbehavior by the president, C. Arnholdt Smith. Smith had set up a variety of corporations where he was part-owner, and made loans to them that, when aggregated, exceeded the limits on loans to one borrower.[13] There was an abrupt bankruptcy of Beverly Hills Bancorp, a one-bank holding company, with a regulator-forced sale of its bank to Wells Fargo. Failures had been almost non-existent, and these events weakened confidence in the system. Increased discussion followed of the possibility that one-bank holding companies were to blame. California and the United States as a whole soon increased regulations regarding transactions between the parent holding company and the banks or S&Ls they held.[14] Indeed, the holding company concept was clearly out of control. Great Western Bank in Los Angeles had as siblings a restaurant chain and an airline.

Savings flows to S&Ls improved substantially in the mid-1970s. Most associations reported record gains in savings balances for 1975.[15] This surge in saving deposits can be attributed mainly to money market developments, namely the Federal Reserve's increase in the money supply during 1975, but the rate of unemployment was still high, and that made consumers cautious about spending. As growth increased in the S&L industry, commercial banks moved more aggressively to compete with them in real estate lending. The prime mortgage rate was rising and approaching 9 percent.[16] Banks and S&Ls found real estate loans a very profitable use of their funds, given that they were still paying 4 to 5 percent interest on most deposits. The 1977 mortgage lending volume at the S&Ls showed an unprecedented increase of 44.2 percent over the record lending volume set in 1976. However, deposits rose even more when Congress allowed banks and S&Ls to increase the interest rate they paid on NCDs and other large, long-term deposits. The Savings and Loan Commissioner reported that, "during 1977, the California S&L industry realized an overall lower gain in savings deposits compared to 1976."[17] But treasury bills were back on the market, falling in price so their higher fixed-dollar interest, tax-free, was making them a competitor for savings deposits. As savings deposits lost their attraction, real estate prices were rising. This influenced the development of two new phenomena in the mortgage market. One was the variable rate mortgage, a change from the traditional twenty- to thirty-year fixed-rate, amortized loan that was usual for residential property. Under the variable rate mortgage, the interest rate paid by the buyer was recalibrated periodically against one of several interest rate indexes. A buyer could find his home mortgage payment skyrocketing if inflation surged, although most borrowers thought about the possibility of the payment decreasing if inflation slowed. The other development was the return of the mortgage banker. Popular in the 1920s, and in the 1960s used to channel insurance company money into the state, the mortgage banker started with borrowed funds from banks as a business loan, then made loans to individuals or investors on real estate.

New institutions and instruments in the real estate markets

Mortgage bankers as direct lenders for mortgages had undoubtedly always existed. Even in the 1880s rush, there must have been alternative sources of mortgage lending, since total assets of most commercial and savings banks and B&Ls were not large. Early in the post-World War II housing boom, mortgage banks formed specifically to channel funds from insurance companies into the California market. Mortgage banks became prominent in the 1970s, probably due to the difficulty of obtaining funds by banks and S&Ls, but the rise may also have been due to the increased comfort consumers had with direct investment. Mortgage bankers sold "pass-through" shares in the mortgage loans they made. In this type of investment, when payments on mortgages came to the company, it passed the funds (less a fee, of course) to investors. In one study of Sacramento, the author revealed that in 1976, 24 percent of all real estate loans in the city were issued by mortgage bankers, commercial banks issued 17 percent, S&Ls issued 27 percent, life insurance companies 9 percent and miscellaneous investors 23 percent.[18]

Most old mortgages paid fixed interest rates, possibly as low as 6 percent, while the interest paid on deposits grew to as much as 8 percent on long-term deposits. As a survival tactic, a number of state-licensed S&Ls began to issue more adjustable-rate mortgages (ARMS). For a number of years, only two small S&Ls offered mortgages with interest rates that changed when some specified index changed. In 1975, six large state-licensed associations introduced this type of loan. By the early months of 1977, nineteen of the 88 state-licensed S&Ls indicated that they were offering ARMS.[19]

Changes in the real estate market

As changes occurred among real estate lenders, they contributed to changes in the real estate market. A number of other direct and indirect factors affecting the California real estate market in the 1970s made the state market even more volatile than the national market. There were policy changes, stronger consideration of environmental and equality concerns, and a shift in consumer power, which added complications to building, lending and selling that had never been experienced before.

The median price of a home in California went from $88,700 in 1970 to $167,300 in 1980, an 89 percent increase. This far exceeded gains seen in the rest of the nation, where values increased 43 percent.[20] Yet GDP grew only 35 percent over the decade.[21] Even population grew only 11 percent nationally and 18 percent in California.[22] Clearly, there was a reallocation of expenditures toward real estate, and it was more dramatic in California than in the rest of the country.

The 1970–71 decline in the real estate market was evident in a number of trends. New home construction fell dramatically in 1969 and sales of existing homes also slowed in the middle of the year. In Southern California, the number of residences on the market was at the lowest level in ten years, but houses remained on the market longer than usual. Deeds recorded in the city of Los Angeles were down 4.3 percent from the previous year. The problem was that it was very hard to get a mortgage, even at interest rates of between 8.5 and 9 percent. Lenders asked for bigger down payments, larger fees to get the loans, and applied more stringent credit standards. "[Borrowers] may have to put 30 percent or more down instead of 10 percent to 20 percent," said John Lawrence, the author of an *LA Times* article.[23] Previously, it was not uncommon to put 10 percent down, get a 10 percent second loan, and get a first trust deed for 80 percent of the price of the house. Appraisals of homes also became more conservative, often coming in below the purchase price, forcing the price down or the down payment up. In some cases, lenders were refusing to give builders any new long-term commitments on financing home sales, and often "we include in the contract that interest rates will be renegotiated every one to three months [as the property was developed]," according to an S&L executive.[24]

New housing starts in 1970 dropped 10 percent from 1969. Twenty-nine percent of respondents to a survey of members of the Home Builders' Economic Council (HBEC) thought construction financing was hard to get. "The S&Ls have been making loans far above their intake of savings, and builders have been living on past financing commitments," said R. Gene Conatser, vice president and senior economist for Bank of America. Money for construction loans and mortgages increased by the end of 1971, however. Only 13 percent of HBEC members thought construction loans were difficult to get in 1971. "Prices were at their highest during the boom years of the early 1960s, then financing deteriorated." But by 1971, "financing is easier to get, interest rates have dipped, and housing is on the upsurge," according to Richard Van Dyke in an *LA Times* article.[25] A survey of HBEC members revealed that the members planned an average 28 percent increase in production in California for 1971, although they did not think it would be as large an increase in the rest of the nation. They anticipated that the biggest increase in production would be in townhouses and multi-family rental units. A government assistance program would help stimulate building, they thought, but this assistance was an incentive to build more low-cost housing, so the average housing price would fall.[26]

Dick Turpin, in an *LA Times* article in 1973, reported a "break in the credit crunch as the rate slipped a notch to 9 percent from 9.25 percent on low-risk loans for the most marketable dwellings."[27] The same article reported the prices of all homes were rising. In Orange County, it was "skyrocketing." This area, one of the nation's "hottest" housing markets, experienced an increase in average sales prices for single-family, three-bedroom, detached dwellings between 1,400 and 1,500 square feet from $28,000 in the first half of 1971 to $35,800 in the first half of 1973. By then it was reported that "soaring home prices are killing the American dream. Most folks no longer can afford to own their own home."[28] Growth continued at a feverish pace through the middle of the decade.

In 1978, while many experts predicted nationwide housing prices were in danger of imminent collapse, the prices in California, particularly Southern California, continued to climb. That year, *LA Times* reporters throughout Southern California interviewed lenders, real estate agents, and recent home-buyers. They reported the strength of real estate prices was based on the ability of families to pay and the lack of sufficient home construction to meet the demand. California was particularly expensive because there were higher incomes and more severe building restrictions than in other parts of the country. In the seven counties of Southern California, prices rose at an annual rate of 23 percent during the six months ending April 1978. The six months before that saw an increase in prices of 30 percent. The average house that sold for $30,000 in 1970 was selling for $83,200 in the spring of 1978.[29] Ken Agid, a housing market researcher, quipped "Houses in Orange County make more money than their occupants."[30]

Supply and demand in the housing market

Higher housing prices were attributed to both supply and demand—that more people wanted houses, while there were fewer units offered for sale. But until mid-1982, inflation and the ease of borrowing on real estate drove demand up, while government energy and other regulations added layer upon layer of cost onto the price of a new home, lowering supply. And, increasingly, what people expected to get with the purchase of a "typical" house expanded. For example, a two-car garage became a standard item, as did central heating and air condition-ing, dishwasher, built-in cooktop and oven and, often, decor options. Builders now automatically designed homes with newer "energy-saving" windows and non-asbestos insulation, which came at a higher price. These factors were becom-ing important to the consumers, newly aware of their rights as purchasers.

Consumerism affects lending

In 1964, activist lawyer Ralph Nader had set off the modern "consumer movement" with his assault on auto giant General Motors. By the 1970s, consumers' rights and concerns about unethical or, at the very least, "un-consumer friendly" busi-ness practices had spread into almost every area of manufacturing and service, including banking. Certainly financial institutions were interested in pleasing their customers, but banking traditions were designed to make it easy for the banker to compete for loans. Interest rates were the first issue to be attacked by consumer groups. As interest rates started to rise with other prices in the late 1960s, people paid more attention to the rates they were paying. The normal practice was to state interest rates in "simple" terms. The simple rate was the dollar interest paid as a percentage of the amount borrowed. On installment loans, this would be inaccu-rate, since after the first payment the borrower did not owe the entire amount. To its credit, Congress mandated a formula, called "APR" (annual percentage rate), similar to the financial calculation of internal rate of return, which is now the standard in the financial world.

The "Fair Credit Reporting Act" became effective on April 25 1971.[31] This APR interest rate required could not be calculated easily when the electronic calculator was a novelty even to bankers. Bankers sought out tables showing the APR for various circumstances, and lessons were given in their use. While few would question the advantage of a law that allowed better comparison of the interest consumers paid, lenders found it difficult to comply, slowing the lending process.

Even in 1976, the California Superintendent of Banks emphasized that "a banker's only product is service" and that "bankers should be fully alert in this age of consumerism and consumer activism to what the consumer thinks." In his view, the past reluctance of bankers to sell their products—such as loans and depository services—on a straightforward basis resulted in confusion and friction on the part of the consumer:

> By clinging to old traditions such as the "360-day year," "add-on interest," "the rule of 78," and no interest on real estate loan impound accounts, the banker is widening the credibility gap and swimming against the rising tide of consumerism. This has resulted in his being enmeshed in a web of new rules and regulations, and he is inviting further regulation if he fails to look at what he is doing from the standpoint of how consumers react.[32]

Banks undertook major advertising campaigns during the year 1975 to improve their image. United California Bank conducted two major campaigns—a series of full-page advertisements in daily and weekly newspapers, and television commercials using the line "we don't give credit to women—we give credit to people," which addressed the then-widespread practice of discounting or disallowing the income of a female spouse when considering capacity to repay a loan, especially on a home. They also started a six-month advertising campaign in about 200 newspapers to give consumer information on banking, including comparisons between commercial banks and S&Ls, the different ways banks can compute interest, the cost of using credit cards, how to shop around for a loan, and what consumers can do when a bank makes a mistake.[33]

Other reactions to the emerging consumerism included Hibernia Bank using radio and newspapers to compare its loan rates, passbook savings rate and checking account fees with other San Francisco area banks. San Fransico's "Consumer Action" (a non-profit consumer group) published "It's in Your Interest: The Consumer Guide to Savings Accounts" after contending that banks were deceptive in their advertising. In response, four consumer-oriented bills were passed by the state legislature in 1975.[34]

Demographics increase demand for housing

Near the end of the decade, the basis for housing affordability was profoundly changed. In a 1978 *LA Times* article, John Lawrence contended that support for the rapidly rising home prices was provided by the "astounding" growth in the number of two-income families. In 1960, 27.6 percent of married women held jobs in households where the husband and children were present. In 1978, the figure was 46.1 percent.[35] The "baby boomers" were maturing and fueling the demand as well. The first of this bulging generation was born in 1946. By the mid-1970s, most of the early boomers were having children and buying homes. Another factor was the impact of federal income tax deductions for mortgage interest, which became increasingly significant in reducing home ownership costs as income rose, pushing marginal income into higher tax brackets, making the tax deduction for interest paid on home loans more valuable.[36]

The rate of inflation was an obvious factor in increasing the desire to own a home. The late-1970s housing boom progressed in the face of mortgage interest rates of 9.75–10 percent. The fear of higher prices in the future was greater than the fear of paying 10 percent interest. Banks and S&Ls became more creative in their financing, contributing to the boom by permitting borrowers to commit a higher percentage of their income to home payments than previously. The "old rule" was that income had to be four times the payment. The new guideline was closer to three times. Bankers abandoned other formulas in lending. "Balloon" mortgages returned. Like typical mortgages of the 1920s, these loans were for short terms of three to five years. The bank and the customer understood that these loans could be renewed, but at the prevailing interest rate at the time of renewal. Bankers also developed new types of mortgages. The *Los Angeles Times* noted that "Some [lenders] are beginning to experiment with new forms of mortgages with reduced payments in the early years, bigger ones later on." The article also noted another trend: "A more important contribution by the lenders is the development in recent years of the so-called secondary market in mortgages, which is keeping huge sums of money flowing into California for use in meeting home buyers' demands."[37]

Speculators were blamed for the price increases, as they are in most booms. They certainly were a factor for a while, particularly buying tract homes not yet built, then later selling them at a profit when the builder finished them. However, this could not have been a strong factor in the boom, as when a tract was finished it often happened that too many of these speculators' homes came on the market at once, dampening the appreciation.[38]

But it was two legal issues that created a little-noticed, but powerful, effect on the demand for residential real estate. The first was the Wellenkamp decision of the California Supreme Court. This decision gave "property rights" to the borrower for a residential mortgage. The second was more recognized; a voter-initiated change in law known as Proposition 13, which limited taxes on owner-occupied housing.

Court decisions and mortgage types increase demand for housing

Wellenkamp decision

In 1974 and 1978, rulings of the California Supreme Court gave additional impetus to residential real estate purchases. The 1974 decision allowed homeowners to sell property "on contract" without giving up low-interest loans secured by the property. The original borrower would still be responsible for payment of the loan, but could give up control of the property that served as collateral for the loan. The 1978 decision strengthened this and gave the homeowner the additional right to sell the loan on the property with the property itself. Thus, the "assumable loan" was born.

The *Wellenkamp vs. Bank of America* decision of the California Supreme Court in the 1970s made unenforceable the "due on sale" clause in most mortgages. As interest rates fluctuated violently in the 1970s, sellers of property often had lower interest rates on their loans than the current prevailing rate. Banks routinely had a clause in the loan contract that specified that the loan be paid in full when the property was sold. These "due on sale" clauses were routine, more for the control the bank would have over the quality of a new borrower's credit scores, than to update the interest rate, but the issue came up when Cynthia Wellenkamp bought property and agreed to assume the previous owners' loan payments to Bank of America. The bank notified Ms. Wellenkamp of its intention to accelerate the debt (i.e., make her pay the full balance due), but offered to let her keep the loan if she agreed to pay the higher interest rate then prevailing on new loans. Wellenkamp argued that this indicated that the concern was not with her ability to repay the loan, but merely an attempt to raise the interest rate. The Supreme Court viewed the due on sale clause as an inhibition on the property owner's right to sell the property and ruled in her favor.[39]

In 1974, in *Tucker vs. Lassen Savings and Loan Association*, the court also held that automatic enforcement of a due on sale clause following transfer via a sales contract, where the owner took cash or a note for his equity, and the buyer assumed the payments, was an "unreasonable" restraint of the property owner's rights.[40] In 1976, the California legislature set limits on prepayment penalties on real estate loans secured by single-family, owner-occupied dwellings. Penalties were limited to six months' interest on that portion of a prepayment during a twelve-month period in excess of 20 percent of the original loan amount, if such prepayment was made within five years of the date of the loan.[41] In *Wellenkamp*, the court ruled that there was no significant difference between the contract sale, and the outright sale of property.[42] This ruling then granted the property rights in a residential loan at below current market interest rates to the borrower, providing additional incentive to purchase and leverage residential property in a time of uncertain (but, at the time, rising) future interest rates. If the interest rates rose, the loan's owner gained value in his or her loan. However, if interest rates dropped, the borrower could usually refinance the property. Occasionally, the lender prevented this refinancing by a "lock-in" provision. An additional incentive to home ownership was provided by the perception that Wellenkamp also made the lock-in provision unenforceable. Therefore, when a person bought a house, they could take over the payment of the old owner, regardless of their own circumstances.

There were some complications and uncertainties left. Federal law specifically allowed due on sale clauses in loan contracts for all federally chartered savings and loan institutions until June 8 1976. Therefore, trust deeds executed before that time were not subject to Wellenkamp, so not all loans could be assumed. Because not all loans could be assumed, some "creative financing" developed. Sales contracts allowed buyers to take over payments in return for a cash deposit, while the original borrower retained title to the property to avoid a required loan pay-off. Variable-rate (adjustable-rate) mortgages became a way for the banks to get back a portion of the gain in loan value when interest rates dropped. The majority of new loans in the late 1970s took this form, soon called "ARMs." The institution then offered lower rates at the beginning of the loan, knowing they could raise the rate when market rates increased. With fixed-rate mortgages the lender had to forecast interest rates for long periods (residential loan life was at the time estimated to be seven to ten years[43]) and charge above the expected average. State usury laws slowed this activity somewhat by putting caps on the total amount of increases, lags on the time between interest increases, and other requirements for these loans.[44]

A wrap-around mortgage was an innovation created by *Wellenkamp*. A home-owner with a house for sale might have an existing mortgage that was well below the price of the property. Under Wellenkamp, this was assumable. To allow a buyer to acquire the existing mortgage, the seller would offer to supplement the assumable trust deed with a second trust deed or with a "wrap-around" loan that included the unpaid balance of the existing first mortgage. Because of the seller's equity in a lower-interest first trust deed, he or she could compete with a financial institution on interest rate and still receive an attractive return. Of course, many people who sold a home needed the cash from the sale to buy another home. A market of private buyers developed for second trust deeds and wrap-around loans. Professional lenders also entered the market. Investment companies that created pools of second trust deeds became popular. These pools started with "pass-through" clumps. "Securitization" of the loans was not a feature of 1970s investing, but the pools did add to the mortgage funds available. Ultimately, the *Wellenkamp vs. Bank of America* decision stimulated innovation in the mortgage market, and created more channels for out-of-state funds to support real estate.

Proposition 13

Proposition 13 was a reaction to rapidly increasing public spending. Through the 1970s, state and local governments increased their spending and employment far faster than the private sector. In California, the higher home values brought higher assessed values on homes and more property taxes to fund this government spending. In California, laws can be passed at the initiative of the voters. In a campaign led by Howard Jarvis, petitions qualified an initiative, Prop 13, on the June 1978 ballot. The law passed. In an analysis of the action, Joan Baratz and Jay Moskowitz attributed this to three factors: 1) property value inflation coupled with high per-capita taxes; 2) a legislature that seemed unresponsive to pleas for tax relief; and 3) a governor with Presidential aspirations who was sitting on a surplus.[45] Under that governor, Jerry Brown, government expenditures were growing at a 17 percent rate and employees were increasing at the rate of 10 percent.

However, Brown, famous for rejecting the governor's Victorian mansion in favor of a snug apartment, felt the surplus was a symbol of his financial success.[46]

Prop 13 set a maximum tax on property of 1 percent of fair market value on 1975 assessment levels. This immediately decreased the taxes by 57 percent. More importantly, it limited growth in the assessed market value to 2 percent per year. It ensured its own longevity by requiring a two-thirds vote of the legislature for any new state tax to substitute for lost local revenues.[47] This last provision, although under constant attack, has kept Prop 13 in place at least until 2016.

Reduced taxes granted increased security to existing homeowners: although when a home was sold it was reassessed at the current market value, the restriction on the increases in the property tax made the cost of owning the home more predictable. The future tax bill was now completely known.[48] This increased the attractiveness of home ownership. While Prop 13 was part of a nation-wide "tax revolt," a study calculated that from 1977 to 1987 the average property tax rate on single-family homes with FHA mortgages fell in California by 75 percent, compared to a decline of 31 percent in the United States overall.[49]

The California Legislature reacted to Prop 13 by a transfer from the state treasury to local governments' coffers that would become permanent. State funding came mostly from sales and income taxes, which eventually rose to offset the loss of local property tax funding. The legislature also sloughed off many of its expenses by authorizing special funding districts to levy assessments for roads, lighting, flood control and other infrastructure costs. In addition, fees were allowed where they were identified with specific properties or were approved by local taxpayers.[50] Communities with homeowners' associations became more common, and permits to build homes in previously undeveloped areas now most often required the builder to assume the cost of constructing roads, sewers, and other public goods previously provided by municipalities. The long-run effect of Prop 13 is uncertain, but it is clear that when it passed it increased the desirability of home ownership, and that this pushed housing prices up. In addition to the pressure from demographics, Wellenkamp, the Coastal Commission, and Prop 13, there were changes that made it impossible for supply to catch the rising demand.

Housing supply limitations

Not only was demand pushing housing prices up, supply was slowing and contributing to higher real estate prices. In 1978, the California Building Industry Association estimated California's need for housing for replacement and population increase to be above the current rate of construction. Security Pacific Bank made a similar forecast of shortages.[51] The building industry blamed shortages and rising prices on regulations. Other factors, including difficulty obtaining financing, increased cost of building materials and a growing trend for municipalities to limit growth, reduced the increase in the number of housing units available to California residents.

Building costs and restrictions

Building material costs started rising at the beginning of the decade.[52] The post-war building boom had finished the sources of "old growth" lumber in the United States. There were few timber companies left relying on forests that were not "managed" (new trees planted) to sustain the timber source. In addition, there was a national shortage of cement caused by restrictions on building new cement plants.[53]

Californians were also seeing their formerly agricultural state becoming increasingly urban and suburban—or developing "urban sprawl." An anti-growth sentiment strengthened. Arnold Sternberg, former director of the State Department of Housing and Community Development, pointed to coastal conservation, prime agricultural land preservation, and open space requirements as causes of rising housing prices.[54] In a 1978 book, Bernard Friedan labels California as the most "mature" in its no-growth policies, estimating that around San Francisco local policy may have blocked the building of a year's-worth of housing between 1970 and 1977.[55] By 1978, builders were claiming they were afraid to buy land for development. They contended that it took three years to develop from bare land to completed houses. One Rancho Bernardo developer estimated the cost of complying with government regulations added $6,000 to $8,000 to the cost of developing the raw land and building an $80,000 to $95,000 house.[56]

A study of the San Francisco Bay area the same year attempted to measure the impact of local building restrictions.[57] Using 1975 data, David Dowall and John Landis found that over 50 percent of the ninety-three cities in the San Francisco bay area were actively limiting population growth.[58] Their methods included:

- establishing urban limit lines to currently developed areas;
- bargaining with builders to reduce densities;
- reducing hillside development by slope requirements;
- establishing twenty-year agricultural preserves;
- increasing development fees, and
- directly limiting developments.[59]

Dowell and Landis found that the average direct fee paid by developers to the cities increased between 1976 and 1979 by 35 percent, after adjusting for inflation. In addition, developers faced longer periods between acquiring land and selling houses. This caused increased interest payments on the funds developers borrowed to acquire the land, increased opportunity costs for the funds invested, and actual protection and maintenance costs for unoccupied land and buildings—all passed along to the home-buyer in the soaring prices.

Environmental protections

The National Environmental Policy Act (NEPA) of 1969 required that any planned, federally funded project have an "Environmental Impact Report" that would detail the impact of the project on the community. The scope of this report increased throughout the 1970s. The new report plus associated public hearings made the land developer's project far more difficult than it had ever been. Various endangered species emerged in the process of these reports and hearings, including a rare type of kangaroo rat that could only be distinguished from its very common relatives by its chromosomes. The state supplemented the national law with the California Environmental Quality Act (CEQA). This required any public work projects to also present an environmental impact report. Delays associated with CEQA compliance were estimated to add between 4 and 7 percent to the selling prices of new housing units in 1974.[60]

The Coastal Commission Act 1976

The state legislature created a requirement to plan and regulate the use of land and water in the coastal zone of the state in the Coastal Commission Act of 1976. Development activities had to be reviewed by the newly formed Coastal Commission to ensure public access to beaches, protect wildlife, and even protect the ocean to three miles from shore. The new rules and process for construction of buildings, divisions of land, and activities that changed the intensity of land use or public access to coastal waters, like building, subdividing, improving or even maintaining property, initially covered an area larger than Rhode Island.[61] It seemed at the time that existing property would become more valuable, as building would be restricted, so purchases and prices rose. Eventually many owners found the regulations onerous, and it may have decreased the value of affected waterfront property from what it would have been.[62]

Low-income housing requirement

With the decade's rapid rise in housing prices, concern developed that California would lose workers who could not afford to live in the state and that this would make it difficult to retain businesses. The California Housing Finance Agency, created in 1975, raised $290 million through tax-exempt revenue bonds for use in providing below-market interest rate loans to developers and homeowners in (presumably deteriorating) urban areas, and for promoting construction of low-income housing.[63] This supplemental financing raised by bond sales was soon changed to requirements that developers provide some low-income housing in each of their developments, an experiment in social engineering that tried to force different income groups to live in the same neighborhoods. A lawsuit against the city of Irvine was settled after the city agreed to provide more low-income units. Requiring developers to respond to forces other than the market put an additional strain on them. Low-income housing requirements would become an even more important factor in the 1980s.

Lender liability

A probably minor, but additional, factor reducing supply was a much-publicized legal case, *Connor vs. Great Western Savings and Loan*, where a lender on a construction project was held liable for the failure of a builder to insure the stability of the structures. While this case involved houses built on clay, insuring stability on California hillsides is a notoriously difficult problem, and many parts of the state had little flat land left to build on near population centers.[64]

Community reinvestment

In 1976, Carl J. Schmitt, then the State Superintendent of Banks, stated that:

> the Superintendent has the responsibility to assure not only that State-chartered banks are operated in a safe and sound manner and in compliance with the law, but also that they are responsive to the needs of the public. Since a bank has, through the chartering process, some exclusivity of market, the banker has, in turn, a responsibility to respond to the needs of the community in which he operates. A banker who is too conservative in his lending policies or *who seeks (to make) loans outside his service area* may not be answering the needs of his community.[65]

Schmitt was expressing a widespread concern about the practice of "redlining." Redlining was defining an area where real estate values were considered endangered, the claim that banks and S&Ls would not lend on real estate in these neighborhoods. The result was a self-fulfilling prophecy. Buyers or existing occupants who wanted to improve a property in the area could not borrow the funds, so the values slid. Residents of Watts, Richmond, and other low-income, and often racially segregated neighborhoods, protested.

The Community Reinvestment Act (CRA) passed Congress in 1977. The Act represented another trend to endow the consumer with new rights which would have unforeseen repercussions. By banning "redlining," borrowers were granted the right to borrow against real estate regardless of whether that real estate was in a geographical area where values were rising or where values were falling. For CRA purposes, the number of loans in each nearby zip code was indicated by pins, representing loans, on a map. It was a safe report if the pins evenly surrounded the bank. Regulators granted "excellent" and "satisfactory" rankings. The penalty for failure to achieve at least a satisfactory rating interfered with plans to merge with, sell or buy another bank.

CRA's effect in the 1970s was to introduce uncertainty, and awareness, but it would become costly for lenders, as they were required to prove that they were serving businesses and consumers in low- and moderate-income geographic areas as well as they served higher-income areas. Later, CRA would have even more significant effects.

A changed world for finance and real estate

The 1970s were a complicated decade for real estate lending in California. Nationwide, homeownership became more attractive because of inflation.

In California, demand for homeownership was additionally increased by two very dramatic changes in 1978: the passing of Prop 13, which limited property taxes on housing, and the California Supreme Court's Wellenkamp decision, which granted residential property owners the right to retain their mortgage even when they had yielded control of the property.

While the demand for housing increased, S&Ls had difficulty providing the funds to loan. The limit on interest paid on deposits, and the changed rights of homeowners to keep old, low-interest loans even after they sold their homes, were particularly damaging to the S&Ls. Their inability to satisfy the demand for home loans led to the commercial banks increasing their real estate lending and also to new structures and products in the financial markets. By the 1980s, the S&L industry was in decline (see Graph 8.2).

In addition to demand factors, the supply of housing was limited by the lack of funds for builders to develop property, and also by high materials costs. In California, supply was also limited by movements in several communities (notably the San Francisco Bay area) which restricted the amounts and types of housing built.

In California, the total assets of financial institutions rose dramatically in the late 1970s. However, the increase was faster in commercial banks, with S&Ls' growth beginning to decline in total assets in 1980 (Graph 8.2). As the S&Ls' assets were nearly all in real estate loans, the commercial banks seemed to take over this activity, and their growth accelerated. The S&Ls began to suffer more from disintermediation, the need to pay high interest on deposits (including raising money from costly NCDs), and falling income from the older, low-interest loans on their books.

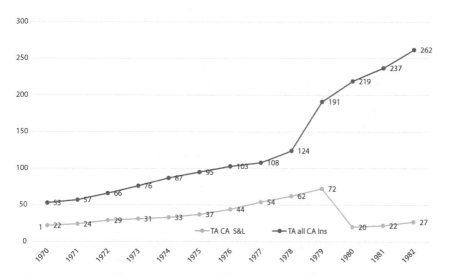

Graph 8.2 Total assets in $ billions of savings and loan associations and financial institutions in California, 1970–1982.

Source: Computed from FDIC and state regulator reports.

The financial institutions found that the decade changed their basic business models permanently. The S&L industry faltered after its rapid growth in the early post-war period, and by the 1980s would be in a serious decline. All real estate lenders found that politics favored the consumer, and emerging consumer movements had to be monitored and accommodated.

Notes

1 Superintendent of Banks of the State of California, *Annual Report* (Sacramento: State Printing Office, 1971), 9–10.
2 Interest on certificates is provided in Superintendent of Banks of the State of California *Annual Report* (Sacramento: State Printing Office, 1966), 9–10.
3 Ibid.
4 Lynne Pierson Doti, "Nationwide Branching: Some Lessons from California," *Essays in Economic and Business History* (May 1991), 141–61.
5 Savings and Loan Commissioner of the State of California, *Annual Report* (Sacramento, California: California Department of Savings and Loan Associations, April 15 1970), 1.
6 Savings and Loan Commissioner of the State of California, *Annual Report* (Sacramento, California: California Department of Savings and Loan Associations, April 1 1972), 3.
7 Savings and Loan Commissioner of the State of California, *Annual Report* (Sacramento, California: California Department of Savings and Loan Associations, April 1 1971), 3.
8 Consumers viewed the tax as temporary, so reduced their savings rather than cut consumption, supporting Milton Friedman's "permanent income hypothesis." Savings and Loan Commissioner of the State of California, *Annual Report* (Sacramento, California: California Department of Savings and Loan Associations, April 1 1971), 3.
9 Savings and Loan Commissioner of the State of California, *Annual Report* (Sacramento, California: California Department of Savings and Loan Associations, April 1 1972), 3.
10 Savings and Loan Commissioner of the State of California, *Annual Report* (Sacramento, California: California Department of Savings and Loan Associations, February 27 1973), 3.
11 Ibid.
12 Savings and Loan Commissioner of the State of California, *Annual Report* (Sacramento, California: California Department of Savings and Loan Associations, March 7 1975).
13 Lynne Pierson Doti and Larry Schweikart, *California Bankers 1848–1993* (Needham Heights, Massachusetts: Ginn Press, 1994), 145–7.
14 Superintendent of Banks of the State of California, *Annual Report* (Sacramento: State Printing Office, 1976), 27.
15 Savings and Loan Commissioner of the State of California, *Annual Report* (Sacramento, California: California Department of Savings and Loan Associations, March 7, 1975). Letter from Commissioner Saul Perlis to the Honorable Edmund Brown, Jr, Governor of California, included in the 1975 Report.
16 Savings and Loan Commissioner of the State of California, *Annual Report* (Sacramento, California: California Department of Savings and Loan Associations, May 1 1977), 19.
17 Savings and Loan Commissioner of the State of California, *Annual Report* (Sacramento, California: California Department of Savings and Loan Associations, May 1 1978), 12.
18 Dennis Dingemans, "Redlining and Mortgage Lending in Sacramento," *Annals of the Association of American Geographers* 69, no. 2 (June 1979), 225–39.
19 Savings and Loan Commissioner of the State of California, *Annual Report* (Sacramento, California: California Department of Savings and Loan Associations, May 1 1978), 12.

20 United States Census Bureau, Housing and Household Economic Statistics Division, "Historical Census of Housing Tables: Home Values" (June 6 2012). Available online at www.census.gov/hhes/www/ housing/census/historic/values.html.

21 United States Department of Commerce, Bureau of Economic Analysis, "National Income and Product Accounts Tables." Available online at www.bea.gov.

22 Richard Forstall, Population Division, United States Bureau of the Census, "Population of Counties by Decennial Census: 1900 to 1990" (March 27 1995). Available online at www.census.gov.

23 John Lawrence, "Homes, Loans Scarce; Worst May Be Ahead," *Los Angeles Times* (1923–current file, July 11 1969). ProQuest Historical Newspapers *Los Angeles Times* (1881–1987), A1.

24 Ibid., A12–13.

25 Richard S. Van Dyke, "Mortgage Bankers Forecast," *Los Angeles Times* (1923–current file, January 22 1971). ProQuest Historical Newspapers *Los Angeles Times* (1881–1987), E14.

26 Ibid.

27 Dick Turpin, "Waiting Costly in Purchasing Home," *Los Angeles Times* (1923–current file, October 21 1973). ProQuest Historical Newspapers *Los Angeles Times* (1881–1987), H2.

28 John Lawrence, "2-Wage family: U.S. Housing Buyers Keep Up With Pace," *Los Angeles Times* (1923–current file, September 3 1978). ProQuest Historical Newspapers *Los Angeles Times* (1881–1987), A1.

29 Turpin, H2.

30 Ibid.

31 Superintendent of Banks of the State of California, *Annual Report* (Sacramento: State Printing Office, 1971), 16.

32 Superintendent of Banks of the State of California, *Annual Report* (Sacramento: State Printing Office, 1976), 20.

33 Ibid.

34 Superintendent of Banks of the State of California, *Annual Report* (Sacramento: State Printing Office, 1976), 20–1.

35 Lawrence, "2-Wage family: U.S. Housing Buyers Keep Up With Pace," A30.

36 Ibid., A30, A-1.

37 Ibid.

38 Ibid., A3.

39 David A. Gauntlett, "Wellenkamp v. Bank of America: Invalidation of Automatically Enforceable Due-on-Sale Clauses," *California Law Review* 67, no. 4 (July 1979), 886–915. Cited information on pages 886–7.

40 *Tucker v. Lassen Savings and Loan Association*, described in Gauntlett, ibid., 890.

41 Superintendent of Banks of the State of California, *Annual Report* (Sacramento: State Printing Office, 1976), 21.

42 Gauntlett, 890.

43 Ibid., 910.

44 Ibid., 904.

45 Joan C. Baratz and Jay H. Moskowitz, "Proposition 13: How and Why It Happened," *The Phi Delta Kappa* 60, no.1 (September 1978), 9–11. Jerry Brown never became president, of course, but he was elected Governor of California again in 2008 and reelected for a third consecutive term in 2014.

46 Ibid., 9.

47 Ibid., 10.
48 An amendment in November 1978 insured that homes were assessed for property taxes at the lower of market or Proposition 13 rate. Other modifications: 1986 Proposition 58 allowed transfer of the assessment base to children upon the death of the parent. Proposition 60, 1986, allowed homeowners fifty-five and older to take their assessments with them if they move to another house within the same county if the new residence is of equal or lower value. This essentially was extended to all counties in 1988. See Nada Wasi, Michelle J. White, Steven M. Sheffrin and Fernando Vendramel, "Property Tax Limitations and Mobility: Lock-In Effect of California's Proposition 13," *Brookings-Wharton Papers on Urban Affairs* (Washington, D.C.: The Brookings Institution, 2005) 59–97. Cited information is on page 61.
49 Arthur O'Sullivan, Terri A. Sexton and Steven M. Sheffrin, "The Future of Proposition 13 in California," *California Policy Seminar* 15, no. 4 (1993).
50 Werner Z. Hirsch, "The Post-Proposition 13 Environment in California and Its Consequences for Education," *Public Choice* 36 no. 3 (1981), 413–23. Cited information is on page 415.
51 Lawrence, "2-Wage family: U.S. Housing Buyers Keep up with Pace," A29.
52 Van Dyke, E14.
53 Lawrence, "2-Wage family: U.S. Housing Buyers Keep up with Pace," A29.
54 Ibid.
55 Bernard J. Friedan, *The Environmental Protection Hustle* (Cambridge, Massachusetts: MIT Press, 1979).
56 Lawrence, "2-Wage family: U.S. Housing Buyers Keep up with Pace," A29.
57 David E. Dowell and John Landis, "Land-Use Controls and Housing Costs: An Examination of San Francisco Bay Area Communities," *Journal of the American Real Estate and Urban Economics Association* 10, no. 1 (1982), 67–93.
58 David E. Dowell and John Landis, *Local Government Planning Summary: 1975* (Sacramento, California: State Office of Planning and Research, 1975), 68.
59 Adapted from Dowell and Landis. Ibid., 69.
60 Environmental Analysis Systems, Inc., "*The California Environmental Quality Act,*" prepared for the State Assembly Committee on Local Government, 1975.
61 "What we do," *California Coastal Commission*. Available online at www.coastal.ca.gov/whoweare.html. The Commission's authority was later extended to all waterways and wetlands in the state.
62 For example, private beaches became public property and adjacent property owners had to make modifications to their property to provide for public access.
63 Lawrence, "2-Wage family: U.S. Housing Buyers Keep up with Pace," A30.
64 Court Decision: *Connor vs. Great Western Savings and Loan Association*, 69 Cal 2d. 850 (12/68). The court held in a four-to-three decision that a construction lender was liable on a negligence theory to the purchasers of a tract home which developed major structural defects from expansive soil conditions when the lender actively participated in the development and failed to exercise due care in supervising an inexperienced builder. See Savings and Loan Commissioner of the State of California, *Annual Report* (Sacramento, California: State of California, April 1 1970), 4.
65 Superintendent of Banks of the State of California, *Annual Report* (Sacramento: State Printing Office, 1979), 24.

9   Crisis, crime, and more mortgages
1980–1992

What started as a dip in the assets of S&Ls in the 1970s became a deep, collapsing trough in the 1980s. S&Ls were failing at an alarming rate. The problem of the older real estate loans that languished on the books paying low interest rates became severe when mortgage interest rates rose to the teens in 1980 and 1981. To help the S&L industry, Congress loosened regulations on them, and California loosened them even more. While S&Ls were allowed into more areas of business, other businesses moved aggressively into their traditional realms. Even more problems resulted for the S&Ls, and they began to fail in large numbers. California had more than a proportionate share of these failing S&Ls, and a few cases where liberalization became an opportunity to stretch the margins of legality.

Savings and loan associations decline and fail

High interest rates, caused by inflation of the 1970s, were peaking in 1981. There was a brief spell in the fall of 1981 that thirty-year fixed loans went for 18 percent![1] Because inflation was slowing, many predicted that the interest rates would fall. The resulting "flipped yield curve" meant that investing for a long period would let you continue to receive the high interest rate. Of course, long-term investment became more desirable than short-term, so ended up with lower interest rates than short-term investments. Since savings deposits were for short periods relative to mortgage loans, the result was deadly for S&Ls who earned long-term interest rates and paid short-term. Whereas normally the difference between the long-term interest they received and the short-term interest on deposits they paid produced income, now it only produced losses.

The S&Ls knew they had another problem that was not entirely visible to the rest of the world. Even though at that time accounting rules allowed institutions to keep loans on the books at "book value" (the amount owed on the loan), the market value on many of these old loans had declined due to the low interest rate they paid.[2] Interest paid on deposits remained low, even as Congress began to phase out the limits, but the S&Ls were often unable to make a profit on their existing loans and could only make it up by issuing new loans at higher interest rates.

Commercial banks made mostly short-term loans and could adjust the rates they earned frequently, but the savings banks made mostly twenty-five- to thirty-year loans on real estate, and had locked themselves into long-term inflexible commitments, with fixed interest rates for the life of the loan. Many of these loans had been granted when interest rates were below 6 percent, and in the 1980s were not earning enough to allow the banks to pay interest that was high enough to attract depositors. Plus, brokerage firms began to offer new financial products that, while not protected by FDIC insurance, nevertheless competed with bank deposits.

The S&Ls were still limited to raising funds mostly through savings accounts, paying interest on them limited by Congress. So Congress and state regulators tried to help the industry by liberalizing the powers of S&Ls, and also commercial banks. They authorized S&Ls to make a variety of other types of loans in addition to mortgages. Despite good intentions, the changes in the laws made survival even more difficult for savings and loan institutions. Through the 1980s, they failed in steeply increasing numbers.[3] California did not present the worst situation for failures; Texas was far worse, but the problem there was oil-related, and the FDIC attributed the causes of failure in California to weak real estate prices.[4]

When interest rates were rising due to inflation, the high rates were not a deterrent to purchases of long-lasting assets such as real estate. When interest rates stayed at high levels from 1980 to 1982, but inflation began to slow, the real estate market changed, adding to the S&Ls' struggles. The high interest rates devastated the construction business. It also nearly halted the sale of existing homes, as few people would pay the high mortgage rates on new loans. As construction dried up, so did the other industries supporting it: lumber, hardware, furniture, and appliances. Inventories fell in every business, and auto dealers and real estate developers disappeared. According to a study by BankAmerica, existing home sales in California plummeted from 1978 to 1982.[5] Lending on real estate declined (see Graph 9.1).

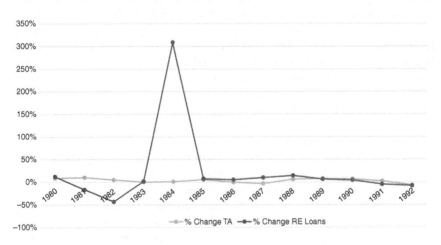

Graph 9.1 Change in total assets and real estate financing of financial institutions in California, 1980–1992.

Source: Computed from FDIC and state regulator reports.

Federal regulatory changes

Congress made most of the major changes in the laws affecting the financial industry in the spirit of the Ronald Reagan presidency. "Deregulation" was the solution to every problem. Already, airlines, telecommunications, trucking, and natural gas had seen deregulation lead to dramatic gains. Unfortunately for the financial industry, the new changes were not deregulation that eliminated restrictions, but re-regulation, which only made disruptive changes in the business of lending. Several changes in federal regulations impacted real estate financing.

The Depository Institution Deregulation and Monetary Control Act (DIDMCA)

In 1980, Congress passed the first of these laws, the Depository Institution Deregulation and Monetary Control Act (DIDMCA). The main feature that affected the real estate market was the plan to gradually phase out interest rate controls on deposits to allow S&Ls and commercial banks to compete with rival sources for funds. DIDMCA was rushed through Congress with a phase-in period eliminating interest rate ceilings.[6] Other provisions of DIDMCA would directly or indirectly affect the ability of financial institutions to provide funds for real estate. DIDMCA:

- pre-empted state usury laws for federally related mortgages secured by first liens;
- granted S&Ls the power to hold trust accounts, interest-bearing checking accounts, consumer loans and unsecured construction loans;[7]
- increased FDIC and FSLIC insurance from $40,000 to $100,000;
- removed dollar limits on some single-family mortgage loans; and
- granted S&Ls access to the Federal Reserve System equal to that of commercial banks' for all services, and allowed them access to the discount window for borrowing.

Federal Home Loan Bank liberalizes product offerings

Having failed to help the industry the first time, Congress quickly passed new, more lenient regulations to allow savings institutions to expand into other sources of funds. In 1981 the FHLB, which regulated nationally chartered S&Ls, removed restrictions that had limited borrowing from the FHLB by member institutions to 50 percent of their assets. These extra funds allowed thrifts to increase their newly allowed product offerings. They introduced new deposit products that would bring them higher income: Money Market Certificates, Eurodollar Certificates, and especially, an important longer-term deposit called a Negotiable Certificate of Deposit (NCD).[8] This was a deposit with a minimum duration of thirty days and minimum amount of $100,000. It could be sold to someone else before the thirty-day maturity, so it offered depositors a very liquid, and insured, deposit that competed with investments in commercial paper. These NCDs became popular offerings for California S&Ls, which employed brokers to market them to financial institutions nationwide.

The Act also allowed them to lend for consumer leasing (mostly for autos) and to offer certain stock brokerage and investment advisory services within their branches. In addition, they could own data-processing companies.

Garn-St Germain: Savings and loan associations moving into more new businesses

In 1982, Congress tried to help the commercial banks and S&Ls by passing another law. The Garn-St Germain Act also reflected Reagan's push for deregulation.[9] The law provided for another liberalization of the types of assets S&Ls could hold. A provision allowed federal associations to make secured or unsecured loans for agricultural, business, corporate or commercial purposes. Lending authority for commercial, rather than residential, real estate increased to 40 percent from 20 percent of total assets. Federal S&Ls were given the ability to offer demand, or checking, accounts to corporate, commercial, business or agricultural concerns. The Garn-St Germain Act reduced the minimum lending on real estate for S&Ls from 75 percent to 50 percent of assets to allow S&Ls to move into other, more profitable lending categories. By the mid-1980s, S&Ls were taking advantage of the new laws and were diversifying into construction lending, consumer lending, commercial lending and real estate direct investment.[10] As interest rate maximums on the largest deposits were phasing out, with large deposits losing the limits first, S&Ls used NCDs to attract funds from around the country and even from foreign sources. New technology and brokers allowed the advertisement of the rate to reach buyers quickly. FDIC insurance covered all the $100,000 deposits, so there was no need for the NCD buyer to know anything about the institution. The money flowed in when the S&L offered the highest going rate, and it flowed away if the institution did not keep up with other institutions on the rate. This made these deposits extremely volatile.

As to the new lending powers, a lack of management talent proved to be a barrier to moving into these new types of loans. To finance auto leasing, make loans to businesses to finance inventory, and to develop raw land into houses or apartments, required different skills than the old business of lending to individual home-buyers. Many lenders thought they knew about land development, since they had made loans to the developers. Most were wrong. They had fewer illusions about business loans. To lure experienced talent for business and consumer lending from the commercial banks, S&Ls had to offer higher pay, or use less experienced talent. Either cost or risk on these loans became higher for S&Ls than it was for the commercial banks.

Financial institution deregulation in California

In the 1980s, California made changes that allowed California state-chartered institutions the same, or more, powers than federally chartered institutions had.

There was a blanket law which made the changes automatic. Any state restriction was cancelled if the federal rival institutions were allowed to engage in the activity. So, for example, California federally chartered institutions had limited ability to make adjustable-rate mortgages in the early 1970s, but when federal regulations changed in 1981, the California Superintendent of Banks made the state regulations more liberal to match the federal changes.[11]

Real estate investment allowed

In 1982 California allowed commercial banks to become a direct partner in real estate development. Plus the legislature amended another law to allow banks and S&Ls to buy capital stock and other securities (bonds) of real estate development companies. Commercial banks could also invest in real property up to the amount of total shareholder equity in the bank.[12] Both commercial banks and S&Ls could, and did, become real estate developers. This had worked in the days of Isaias Hellman, the late 1800s, but 100 years later, real estate development was complicated by environmental, low-income, housing standard, and zoning laws that made it a highly specialized business.

Real estate brokers join California banks

An American Bankers Association study in 1984 concluded that bankers had the skills necessary to move into the consumer real estate brokerage market and that the customer base for both was the same, since most real estate loans that banks and S&Ls made were in the residential category. In most states the savings banks were allowed to hold brokerage companies. The US League of Savings and Loans identified full-service realty brokerage as one of the essential new powers if S&Ls were to compete effectively in a newly deregulated, integrated financial services marketplace. Influenced by this argument, in 1985 the federal regulations allowed federally chartered financial institutions to engage in financial and home-ownership counseling.[13] These powers were interpreted by some S&Ls' attorneys as permitting franchises of real estate brokerage companies to open offices in their branches. In California banks and S&Ls the idea was embraced enthusiastically and the state-chartered institutions also quickly joined realtors in selling houses, then offering financing, all in the branch office.

California was an attractive partner for real estate brokers, as it was one of the more liberal states. State-chartered institutions were allowed to engage in third-party realty brokerage if they were parent institutions, or service corporations, with the permission of the state regulator. Only three other states allowed savings banks to directly own real estate brokerages.[14] Several California banks and savings banks partnered with existing real estate brokerage franchises. Franchising was copied from the fast food industry to gain better corporate image and more efficient office procedures, and was eased by better communications technology.[15] In the long term, however, this affiliation did not appeal to customers.

The Nolan Bill opens new ventures

State law AB3469, introduced by Ross Johnson, was the wedge that brought in the most dramatic change in the state's real estate market in history. Effective in 1982, it relaxed the asset and liability mix available for state-chartered depository institutions. State banks, through a subsidiary corporation, could become real estate developers, as the act let them subdivide, build residential housing or construct commercial improvements. They could use up to 10 percent of the institution's total assets to buy property to own, rent, lease, manage or operate it for income. The law also allowed thrifts to make agricultural, business, corporate and commercial loans as well as personal family and household loans, with the same 10 percent limit.[16] California thrifts gained the power to invest up to 5 percent of their assets in an unrestricted range of equity securities in 1984.[17] Then the legislature allowed state banks, thrifts, credit unions, and industrial loan companies to form and operate investment companies that could underwrite, distribute, or sell any type of security.[18]

But the most far-reaching change in financing real estate came from the 1982 Nolan Bill.[19] Effective January 1 1983, it eliminated the 10 percent restriction on investment in service corporations. This allowed S&Ls to use insured deposits or any other source of funds and put 100 percent of them into a service corporation which could engage exclusively in real estate development, real estate brokerage or any other business activity approved by the state. The bill also allowed the thrifts to directly invest in real estate for residential purposes with *no limit.*[20] This bill came just after Wellenkamp was overturned, an event which re-established the rights of the lenders to force loan pay-off and a new interest rate when property was sold. The existing mortgage no longer "came with" the house when the owner sold it. Now a house sale meant the mortgage had to be paid off, and lenders more quickly reduced their portfolios of older, lower-yielding mortgages.[21] To avoid this trap in the future, most banks and S&Ls had been making adjustable-rate mortgages. For these mortgages, the interest rate would vary along with other interest rates over the life of the loan. ARMs cushioned the bank and the borrower from fluctuations in the economy. To the S&L industry, the future seemed promising.

The last step to complete liberalization of financing real estate came with the Johnson Bill, AB2332. Effective June 1984, it permitted any state bank to directly engage in subdividing, developing, building upon, owning, renting, managing, operating for income or selling real property, up to the limit of the total stockholders' equity. With the Commissioner's permission, this limit could even be exceeded.[22] It is estimated that $5 billion to $6 billion became available for real estate development by the state banks with the passage of these bills. Federally chartered financial institutions still did not have the ability to buy any equity securities, but even national banks could engage in real estate development with these new laws by acquiring a California-chartered bank. In May 1983, Security Pacific Corporation, the holding company for Security Pacific National Bank, which was one of the largest banks in the United States, bought the failed Bank of Irvine, to conduct real estate investments.[23] Many California commercial banks and S&Ls

jumped on the emerging real estate boom by undertaking development projects, either directly or through subsidiaries.

The jump in lending is visible in Graph 9.1. Again, lack of experience in these new activities created a high-risk, expensive environment for banks and savings and loan associations, but few recognized the changes as anything but opportunities.

California savings and loan associations a hot commodity

The series of state deregulatory measures enacted between 1982 and 1984 that reduced restrictions on the investments of California state banks and S&Ls made some Wall Street investors consider these financial institutions as "the most valuable financial franchise in the country."[24] Applications to open state-chartered S&Ls in California skyrocketed, jumping from forty-three in 1982 to over 200 by the start of 1984. The almost total deregulation of asset powers in California had made owning and operating a savings institution a very attractive, albeit, in retrospect, uncertain, proposition.[25]

At the end of 1986, there were 1,336 federally chartered saving banks and S&Ls in the United States, with 66 headquartered in California. By the mid-1980s, federally chartered S&Ls were taking advantage of the new laws and were moving aggressively into construction lending, commercial lending and real estate direct investment.[26] Congress moved to compete with California deregulation. In the mid-80s, Congress increased the limit on federally chartered thrifts' investment in service corporations from 1 percent to 3 percent of the institution's assets. Through a service corporation structure they could indirectly invest in real estate by lending to a wholly owned subsidiary up to 50 percent of their net worth. In 1984, a Garn-St Germain provision allowed up to 10 percent of assets to exist in secured or unsecured commercial, corporate, business or agricultural loans. The limit on loans secured by liens on non-residential real property was lifted, and during 1984 there was a marked increase in real estate development activities of federally insured S&Ls. These activities included loans for acquisition and construction, direct investment and additions to service corporate equity.[27]

One unintended consequence of allowing S&Ls and commercial banks such wide latitude in real estate lending and property holding was that, given the sudden increase in revenue potential from these institutions, it became profitable to start a small bank, hold it for a year or two, and then sell it. Banks were started for the sole purpose of selling them as soon as possible, an institutional version of the television show *Flip this House*. But even smaller established banks became ripe takeover targets.

Increased competition in the mortgage market

Providing financing for real estate was considered to be such a good investment that even retail establishments bought their way into the activity. Companies starting direct lending operations included General Motors, Ford, Sears, Kmart, American Can, Owens Illinois, Household International, Beneficial Finance, Citicorp, Travelers Insurance, John Hancock Insurance, Prudential Insurance, Metropolitan Insurance, Fireman's Fund Insurance and Merrill Lynch.[28] Sears, Roebuck and Co. bought a controlling interest in Coldwell Banker, the largest commercial real estate broker in the country, in 1981. They also bought Dean Witter Reynolds, one of the nation's largest securities brokerage firms. Sears also owned Allstate Insurance Company, which would allow the retailer to offer all these financial services in their network of stores to their 120 million customers. Sears was targeting 28 percent of the nation's mortgage business for itself by 1990.[29] Kmart started in-store banking operations in 1984 through First Nationwide Bank (FNB), a federal savings bank. Ford bought FNB in 1984, and Kmart installed more kiosks inside their stores.[30] Soon, miniature bank branches opened in supermarkets.

Despite their size and potential clout, most of these efforts fizzled, damaging not only the banking arm, but often harming the parent company. Many were sold off almost as fast as they were acquired, leading Chief Executive Officers who made cars to wonder what they had ever thought they knew about banking.

Security firms

The 1981 Economic Recovery and Tax Act of 1981 shortened the depreciation period on real estate investments to fifteen years. Independent investors wanted into the real estate market, too. One way of investing was to buy houses and rent them to others. This made real estate investment syndicates an attractive tax shelter for those who had larger sums to invest and did not want to directly own individual homes. Small-scale real estate syndicates had always existed. Since the Gold Rush, there had always been a few people pooling funds to buy property. In the 1970s, large national syndicates had developed. JMB Realty Trust, McNeil Real Estate Fund, and Fox-Cascarden Financial Corporation started in the 1970s. Multipurpose investment companies like Merrill Lynch, E. F. Hutton, Shearson-Lehman/American Express, Goldman Sachs and Co., and others developed real estate investment pools and raised record amounts of capital in 1983–4. These produced immediate income to the companies through the fees they collected on the capital raised. The Economic Recovery Act also created Individual Retirement Accounts (IRAs), which attracted a new pool of investment funds to real estate-based securities.[31]

Insurance companies

The percentage of mortgages originated or funded by life insurance companies declined in the early 1980s in the United States, but remained an important source of funds, especially for multi-family and commercial projects. Metropolitan Life Insurance Co., for example, purchased Century 21 from Transworld Corp (the owner of TWA airlines, Hilton Hotels, and so-on) in 1985. Century 21 was the world's largest residential brokerage franchise. Metropolitan Life also owned companies that originated and serviced loans for residential mortgages. In 1986, it built an office tower in Irvine, California, to serve as the headquarters and training center for the real estate operations.[32]

Prudential Insurance Company already operated the largest real estate company in the world when it started plans to build a nationwide network of brokers under the Southern California subsidiary, Prudential Real Estate Affiliates.[33] While statistics on real estate lending of insurance companies is not available for California, these activities indicate that they were a major source of funds. They brought funds into the state, as they had since the 1920s, channeling it through loans to mortgage bankers.

Return of mortgage bankers

A 1986 real estate report said that "some of the biggest changes in the provision of real estate-related service are coming in the area of mortgage lending." As S&Ls experienced increasing difficulties, mortgage companies and commercial banks gained market share at the expense of S&Ls, savings banks, and other thrifts. Between 1976 and 1982, the thrift share of US mortgage-lending activity fell from over 60 to 40 percent of mortgage originations on owner-occupied buildings for one to four families. Commercial banks' share rose from 22 percent in 1976 to 26 percent. The biggest change in real estate financing sources came from mortgage companies. Mortgage companies accounted for nearly 29 percent in 1982, more than double their 1976 volume.[34]

Mortgage companies, which are also called mortgage banks, originate mortgage loans by marketing directly to individuals who buy or refinance a home. Then the company sells the mortgage to investors. These companies served as an important conduit for insurance companies, which used them to bring their funds to California. Private investors and investment companies also used mortgage banks rather than directly investing in real estate. Mortgage companies almost always operated under state law, with little regulation. In the 1980s they imported funds to California from distant investors, enabling funds "in capital surplus areas to be transferred to capital-deficient areas, such as California," according to the California Department of Real Estate. In 1986, mortgage companies had doubled their share of originations over the mid-1970s. According to one survey, mortgage bankers originated 44 percent of all new first mortgages that year. While this percentage declined to 33 percent in 1987, it was clear that mortgage banks succeeded as S&Ls failed, partly by buying their fixed-rate mortgages at low prices.[35] Having been burned by the flipped yield curve between 1978 and 1982, few S&Ls or commercial banks wanted fixed-rate mortgages on their books.

The mortgage bank, originally a "mortgage pool," was making a comeback in the 1980s. First started in the 1920s or earlier, the simplest pools bought a collection of mortgages and shared the payments of principal and interest when the borrowers made their payments on the mortgage. By the 1980s, GNMA created most of these pools, called Mortgage-Backed Securities (MBS), or Collateralized

Debt Obligations (CDOs). Since the 1930s, the FHMA had bought mortgages with money they raised selling government-guaranteed bonds. So technically the bonds were (and are) MBS. The difference was that GNMA bought mortgages and organized them into packages. GNMA guaranteed the MBS's payments of interest and principal represented that buyer's share of the interest and principal repayments on all the mortgages in the package, but did not match individual mortgage-holders with individual investors. Because each security represented a diversified collection of mortgages, pension funds, and other institutional investors bought MSBs as low-risk investments.[36] Mortgage bankers, S&Ls, and banks often "swapped" the mortgages they originated for FNMA and Federal Home Loan Mortgage Corporation (FHLMC) government-guaranteed pass-through bonds that represented ownership interests in the same mortgages.[37] During the period from 1977 to 1983, the dollar value of total mortgages outstanding rose 78 percent, but the total mortgages in pools rose 305 percent.[38]

While in 1984 GNMA still held 56 percent of the total pooled mortgages, institutions began to develop new types of secondary market debt instruments and securities.[39] Investment companies offered Real Estate Mortgage Investment Conduits and CMOs. Like GNMA, the advantage of originating and administering these instruments was an immediate and continuing stream of fee income. By the mid-80s, according to the State Real Estate Department.[40]

> Both federally-sponsored and private conduits repackage mortgages into a variety of securitized forms. These securities then are resold to investors not only in the United States, but also in Canada, Europe and Japan .... Today the nation's mortgage and capital markets are clearly integrated .... they are interdependent and global in nature.

The rise of the secondary market and savings and loan association failures

In 1985, real estate expert Anthony Downs accurately predicted the secondary market would be increasingly important. Increased liquidity, he felt, was needed to make the mortgage market competitive with other investments. He said: "The future ability of real estate to extract debt funding from fully integrated capital markets depends heavily on greater use of MBSs of various types."[41] Originators and holders of mortgage debt increasingly were becoming divorced from one another. The world had changed. No longer would a real estate developer partner with a bank to turn raw land into houses, and the homeowner was rarely in personal contact with the provider of the funds for the home mortgage.

In 1980, twenty-two banks and S&Ls failed in the United States, but two years later the number had nearly quadrupled. While the problem of attracting funds at lower cost than the interest that could be charged on loans was a problem common to all the institutions, local problems soon added to the failures.

Nationally, declining oil and agricultural prices meant that many of the banks that failed were focused on a few industries. California's branch system provided important protection, while most states still did not allow depository institutions to branch. The number of failures dropped a bit in 1983 and 1984, but grew at an alarming rate through the rest of the 1980s, reaching 533 failures in 1989. Of the ten largest federal commercial bank failures from 1980 to 1994, all were outside of California. Nor were any of the ten most costly takeovers, or "resolutions," by Federal Home Loan Insurance Company (FHLIC) located in California.[42] It was far behind the biggest problem state, Texas, where 599 insured commercial banks, with assets of almost $93 billion, failed. Most of these failures were tied to the oil or cattle industries. While California institutions had more diverse portfolios, with 87 commercial banks, worth $5.5 billion, failing, the state ranked third by number of failures. In the California S&L industry, 43 federally chartered institutions, with assets of $39 billion, were resolved by FSLIC/RTC (Resolution Trust Corporation). Another 70 state-chartered savings institutions, with total assets of $95 billion, made California the biggest problem the insurance fund had to deal with among the states.[43] For this reason, the RTC established its headquarters in Southern California.

Congress established the RTC to accept ownership of the property held by closed financial institutions when no one else would. When the FHLIC closed an S&L, loans, deposits, and foreclosed properties owned were sold, or given, to other institutions. If the property could not be disposed of in one of these options, RTC took on the task of managing, and trying to dispose of, the property. As the real estate market improved, they did manage to successfully dispose of all the property and, remarkably, RTC dissolved itself in 1995. During its tenure it "resolved" $394 billion in assets from failed S&Ls.[44]

As the number of failures began to rise quickly, FHLIC learned to act quickly as an institution revealed insolvency. When it decided to resolve a bank's problems, it solicited buyers by making quiet, confidential phone calls to stronger institutions in the same geographic market. Accountants from these institutions would unobtrusively review the failing institution's assets. If a "purchase and acquisition" could be arranged, the acquiring institution took over all the deposits, but FHLIC and the potential buyer would negotiate about what assets would be included in the sale. Fearful of withdrawals by depositors, this process was secretive. On a Friday afternoon, just before closing, a number of serious-looking people quietly gathered outside the failed bank or S&L. Together, they marched into the building and announced the purchase. Records had to be produced and, after a weekend of labor, the new owner's sign would rise over the old sign, before the institution opened on Monday. This process was becoming so common in the 1980s that customers began to realize that it only meant they would eventually have to get new checks.

Misconduct and crime

Receiving the most attention, but probably the least frequent cause of the problems of the S&Ls, was the misconduct of some of the officers of the financial institutions. California provided some of the most prominent examples of this. Exploiting the gaps created by all the legal changes became part of a financial officer's job, but some found they could not only work in the gaps, but spread beyond them.

Charles Keating was probably the most famous of those who stretched the advantages of owning an S&L beyond the law. In 1984 he bought Lincoln Savings, a $50 million institution in Irvine, so he could move into the lenient California market.[45] Leisure World retirement community provided the core existing customers of Lincoln. Keating had worked for American Financial Company (AFC) in Ohio, though after 1976, when there were some questions about his actions from the Securities and Exchange Commission (SEC), he directed a spin-off of the company, American Continental Homes (ACH).[46] He left Cincinnati in 1978 and moved to Phoenix to start over. He took the southwest assets of ACH with him, under the name Continental Homes, and then built this organization into a multi-billion dollar operation, mostly with homes built in Phoenix and Denver. Keating financed a lavish lifestyle with loans from the company.[47]

He was active in politics, donating large sums to the campaign funds of everyone from the local council members in cities where he had developments to federal Senate races. When California Savings and Loan Commissioner Larry Taggart ended his term months after Keating bought Lincoln, Keating quickly hired Taggart as a consultant.[48] When he bought Lincoln Savings, the net worth was about $34 million. Keating paid $51 million. The transaction took about a week.[49] The extra value Keating saw was the Nolan Bill. Eventually banks would all be able to do direct investment without restriction.[50] He quickly grew Lincoln Savings' assets to $5 billion by offering high interest on NCDs. The funds were used to purchase land for development, for investment in Michael Milken's "junk bonds," to speculate in foreign currency and to put into investment funds. The home-building division was sold in 1985; however, in 1986 the FDIC claimed that he had exceeded the limits for direct investment in real estate by a considerable amount.[51] Keating started a 22,000-acre planned city of 200,000 near Phoenix.[52] He was even building a 600-room hotel in Phoenix that remained as one of the world's most luxurious for decades.

In 1986, Keating had $3 billion in deposits invested and FHLBB had $2 billion of that classified as risky investments.[53] A plan was approved to sell bonds in the parent company (then American Continental Corporation, "ACC") through the bank's branches. This plan was implemented in December 1986 and the sale of ACC bonds continued in his branches for two years, totaling about $250 million.[54] During that two years, when customers came in to reinvest their insured six-month maturity certificates of deposit, the bank tellers referred them to an "investment desk," where they were offered bonds with higher interest rates than CDs. Of course, unlike deposits, the bonds were not insured by the FDIC. Among the many who took advantage of this offer were large numbers from the retirement community of Leisure World, a mother of a disabled twenty-four-year-old girl who invested all her daughter's settlement funds, and others who later claimed they thought that their investment was as safe as FDIC-insured money in the bank.[55]

In May 1987, the San Francisco office of the FHLBB completed a year-long audit of the Keating Empire and decided to place it in conservatorship. When it looked like the S&L might be seized, Keating enlisted the support of his political friends, including five prominent Senators, Alan Cranston, John McCain, John Glenn, Donald Riegle, and Dennis DeConcini, afterward known as the "Keating Five," who met with Ed Gray, the director of the FSLIC, demanding to know why Keating was being harassed. Keating already had a large dedicated law team that worked to block investigations into all of his businesses. But by April 1988, The FHLBB had evidence that documents at Lincoln have been backdated and even forged.[56] In July, the auditors arrived at Lincoln's headquarters. In September, the "investment desks" were moved out of the branches. Keating decided to sell Lincoln Savings and Loan.[57]

The audit of Lincoln proceeded slowly, impeded by intervention from members of Congress, an arson fire in the Los Angeles office of the California State Banking Department (where only documents related to Lincoln burned), and the distraction of Michael Milken's indictment in January 1989. By March 1989, the FHLBB finished an exam of Lincoln and asked for increased reserves of at least $50 million. On April 10, Keating talked to California Senator Alan Cranston and told him that ACC was in danger of failing, and that there may be as many as 50,000 people in the state who bought the $200 million in bonds sold through the branches of Lincoln. Cranston started calling people who could help the sale of Lincoln go through.[58]

However, on April 14 1989, the federal regulators seized Lincoln Savings and Loan. ACC went into bankruptcy. In September, a Racketeer Influenced and Corrupt Organization (RICO) complaint was filed against Charles Keating and many of his family members and associates.[59] Keating's law team fought the takeover of Lincoln, but, in August 1990, the courts ruled it was justified.[60] In September, Keating went to jail for selling the junk bonds without making it clear that they were not insured deposits. He couldn't make the $5 million bail, and it was thirty-three days before it was reduced to $300,000 and the family raised the money. In 1993, Charles Keating was sentenced to ten years in jail, convicted of seventy-three counts of racketeering, fraud, and conspiracy. There were also civil suits and fines. The public was astonished that such a crime could actually put a person behind bars. Even while Keating was under attack, Lincoln depositors remained strangely calm. Deposits trickled out at a leisurely pace.

The "Keating Five" Senators faced the Senate Ethics Committee. Both John Glenn and John McCain (both of whom had ceased contact with Keating after criminal behavior was mentioned) were exonerated. Don Riegle and Dennis DeConcini were questioned, and Alan Cranston was censored. They all tried to return money Keating gave them.

There were others who exploited the leniency of California's laws restricting S&Ls' activity. Tom Spiegel, head of Columbia Savings and Loan Association, and close associate of Michael Milken, became known as "a leader in the newly deregulated thrift world and a gluttonous consumer of junk bonds."[61] In 1986, his salary was $10 million a year, about the same amount as the bank's total assets.[62]

In Lodi, Ranbir Sahni bought American Diversified Savings Bank in 1983. He quickly shut the doors and moved up to a ninth-floor office, where he accepted brokered NCDs and invested the funds in companies he controlled. He liked federally subsidized energy projects, such as a chicken farm with methane production. Windmill farms were another favorite, and he was instrumental in putting the first giant turbines in the vortex near Palm Springs.[63] But he also invested in condominiums and shopping centers, and put $300 million in junk bonds. The FDIC ended up acquiring $800 million in deposits when it closed Sahni's operation.

In Santa Ana, Duayne Christensen and Janet McKinzie opened North American Savings and Loan in 1983. Christensen loaned freely to real estate projects he and McKinzie owned. They inflated the profits of these companies by selling properties from one company to another. When the regulators took over, the loss was $209 million. Christensen's untimely death in a solo auto accident prevented a full investigation of the pair's activities.[64]

Junk bonds played a role in the failure of many of the S&Ls. They had a high rating for safety, but allowed association with the very exciting world of tech start-ups. Michael Milken, "the junk-bond king" himself, had a close association with California. Milken grew up in Southern California. Marked as a genius at a young age, he started working in the large securities firm Drexel Harriman Ripley (Drexel) while a student at Wharton Business School.[65] During the 1970s, Milken developed junk bonds into a modern financing technique for start-up companies, especially in the tech industries like fiber-optic cable, cellular phones, and computers. Since these companies were start-ups, traditional funding sources would not lend to them, so, at first, they had to grant shares of their company to investors.[66] Product developers always felt they had a revolutionary idea (although most ideas did not pan out), so they did not want to give away shares in their company. Milken offered loans instead, by creating and selling bonds for the start-up companies. To make the high-risk loans attractive to lenders, the bonds offered very high interest. He created these bonds through Drexel Burnham Lambert in New York. Drexel was founded in 1871 and stood for tradition, so many Drexel executives must have found the rapid growth of the junk bond business disconcerting. It was just as well that most of the start-ups and bond sales were on the west coast. Investors visited the start-up companies' booths at Milken's investment fairs ("Predators' Balls") in Los Angeles, to where he relocated in 1978, to try to guess which companies would survive long enough to pay the promised high interest.[67] A diverse collection of different companies' bonds seemed to offer safety for individually risky investments. The fair was popular with S&Ls as soon as they were able to buy corporate bonds.

Milken himself was controversial. Some attributed this to the fact that he was so successful, and that he dominated Drexel. A high-interest, high-risk bond was not a new idea, but Milken improved upon it. To increase the safety of the firm, he sometimes issued more bonds than were strictly necessary. Some of the funds from the extra bonds could buy bonds of other companies issuing junk bonds. Milken helped sell the bonds by forming various investment pools.[68] In 1986, Drexel, driven by Milken's division, became the most profitable investment-banking firm in America.[69] On Friday in November of that year, the announcement came that Ivan Boesky, a major Drexel client who used the junk bonds to acquire entire firms, had pleaded guilty to insider trading, which involved using information not available to the public to determine whether to buy or sell bonds or stock to make a profit. He agreed to pay a fine and help the government investigate what was perceived as widespread illegal activity on Wall Street. The next year, Boesky led the SEC to a deal he had made with Milken to let Milken own stock in Boesky's name. There would be several legal reasons that Milken would want to do this, but the government investigation settled on an illegal one: that Milken "parked" the stock with Boesky because he had bought it using insider trading.[70] The April 1987 investors' conference was the biggest ever.[71] But when the stock market crashed in October 1987, a stream of investors headed for safer invest-ments. Under the cloud of increased SEC scrutiny, the financial firms were pulling out of high-risk areas. Finally, in September 1987, the SEC charged Milken, his brother Lowell, and four others with numerous securities violations. Milken plea-bargained, paid a fine, and spent four years in jail. Drexel agreed to plead guilty to six felony counts of fraud, and later went bankrupt.[72] Needless to say, banks and S&Ls that held large amounts of the junk bonds failed as well.

While the S&L industry suffered a meltdown in the 1980s, commercial banks in California did somewhat better. Since their loans were shorter term, they more easily raised the interest rates they charged to cover the higher interest they had to pay depositors. At the end of 1989 they were doing well. The bank stocks had outperformed Standard & Poor's (S&P) Index over the previous several years. As the larger banks were trying to get bigger to compete internationally, they were leaving a hole in the $1 billion to $10 billion market. Individual smaller banks worked to grow enough to fill that hole, mostly through mergers and acquisitions. The commercial banking world was not without problems, however.

Examiners increase standards on real estate loans

In April 1990, former FDIC chairman William Seidman listed California met-ropolitan areas as sites of potential real estate problems.[73] In May 1990, S&P downgraded $3.7 billion in Wells, Fargo & Co. debt, citing concerns over the high concentration of real estate in their portfolio, among other concerns about their exposure to risk.[74] By summer 1990, bankers reported that the FDIC was perform-ing longer and more detailed audits, particularly on real estate lending. "They looked at every one of our (real estate) loans," one banker reported (anonymously).

The short period of prosperity was ending. Bank examinations were the topic of conversation at "Dialog '90," a conference for California bankers, in November.[75] There wasn't much to celebrate by then. Steve Scholzer of the FDIC addressed the bankers and warned, "bank-bashing is the 'in' thing" and "underwriting stand-ards need to be reevaluated—asset appreciation isn't going to bail you out .... Create adequate reserves to cover risk," and, most ominously, "we want to exam-ine each bank every year."[76] William Stolte of the Office of the Comptroller of the Currency responded to a question: "Have we tightened standards on real estate lending? No. We have been applying the same standard for ten years, but the economic climate has changed. It is the recognition by regulators of the changes in the environment [that you are noticing]."[77] He went on to say California commercial banks were becoming increasingly reliant on real estate lending. In 1985, 31 percent of loans were in real estate, and in 1990, 54 percent of the loans were in real estate. Stolte further warned that the collapse of real estate prices that occurred in Texas and Arizona raised the question as to whether that might not happen here. He warned that "many say that the California economy is too diverse to experience the same problems." Much of what happened in Texas was due to oil prices falling, "but Arizona? They are still experiencing in-migration. What happened there? Just over expansion funded by S&Ls and banks." Then he advised the bankers: "Take a look around at your own portfolios and your own areas and see what you want to do."[78]

Bankers, of course, did not need to look around after this little pep talk. Bankers mostly listened thoughtfully to the message, undoubtedly mulling over some of their previously only mildly troubling real estate loans, but others responded vigorously. Pre-eminent bank consultant Carter Golembe, for example, responded sarcastically, "They never change. Bankers change, the climate changes, but they [the regulators] never change!" And Tom Phelps, who played a large role in founding many of California's independent banks charged: "You [regulators] don't make the rules, Congress does, but they have given you nuclear weapons to solve family quarrels."[79]

The crisis came in August 1989, when Congress was convinced that huge amounts of money would be needed to save the S&L industry. They passed the Financial Institutions Regulation and Reform Act. This eliminated the FHLB, which was in danger of failing, and the FSLIC, putting both under the control of the Federal Reserve banks and the FDIC. The RTC was formed to take over those assets of dissolved banks that couldn't be immediately sold. By the end of 1990, the problem was clear: regulators were scaring the banks into restricting their lending, and this was keeping the nation in a recession. The banks and S&Ls felt real estate values were particularly hard to support, and their lending dropped in 1991.

Notes

1 Freddie Mac Mortgage rates survey archives. Available online at www.freddiemac. com/pmms. html.
2 "Book value" is the amount of money owed on the loan. Starting in the 1990s, financial institutions had to change book value to match the "market value," which is the amount that the loan would bring if sold. See Chapter 10.
3 The term "S&Ls" will be used to also cover the few saving banks and building and loan societies still in the state. Nationally, the common term "thrifts" covered all three of these types of financial institutions.
4 The Federal Deposit Insurance Corporation, *History of the Eighties—Lessons for the Future* (Washington, D.C.: Federal Deposit Insurance Corporation, 1997), 14–15. Available online at www.fdic.gov/bank/historical/history/211_234.pdf. Of US

failures from 1980 to 1994, Texas had 43 percent of the assets and 29 percent of the institutions.

5 California Department of Real Estate, *Deregulation of Financial Institutions: How Has it Affected the Real Estate Industry in California?* (Sacramento, California: California Department of Real Estate, 1988), II-7.

6 Ibid., II-15.

7 Trust accounts held funds that had a contracted pay-out. Negotiable Order of Withdrawal (NOW) accounts allowed limited numbers of checks to be written on interest-paying savings accounts. Checking accounts at the time paid no interest. Auto purchases were the biggest category of consumer loans.

8 Money Market Certificates were also allowed to pay higher interest because they were longer-term accounts with larger balances. On Eurodollar accounts, deposit interest was based on the interest rate banks paid for dollars borrowed from foreign banks. Consumer leasing was mostly for automobiles. Data processing companies that financial institutions owned mostly cleared checks or credit cards. California Department of Real Estate, *Deregulation of Financial Institutions*, II-18.

9 Ibid., II-15.

10 Ibid., III-15–21.

11 Ibid., II-20–1.

12 CA 751.3 Real Estate Development and Investment Act. Investment was limited to 10 percent of the financial institution's assets.

13 Harold B. Olin, *Realty Brokerage Operations by Savings Institutions* (Chicago, Illinois: United States League of Savings Institutions, 1986), Executive Summary.

14 Ibid., 16.

15 Ibid., 33.

16 CA AB3469. California Department of Real Estate, *Deregulation of Financial Institutions*, II-21–2.

17 CA AB1434, effective 1984. Ibid., II-22.

18 CA AB3192. Ibid., II-22.

19 CA AB3469. Ibid., II-21–2.

20 Ibid., II-22.

21 The US Supreme Court ruled in 1982 for *Fidelity Federal Savings vs. De la Cuesta* in appeal against the Wellenkamp decision by upholding the enforcement of "due on sale" clauses originated by Federal thrifts. The Garn-St Germain Law pre-empted state laws prohibiting the enforcement of "due on sale" clauses. California Department of Real Estate, *Deregulation of Financial Institutions* II-23.

22 CA AB2332. Ibid., II-23.

23 Ibid., III-4.

24 California Department of Real Estate, *Deregulation of Financial Institutions*, II-23.

25 Ibid., II-20–3.

26 Ibid., III-21.

27 Ibid., III-6.

28 Ibid., III-20.

29 Ibid., III-13–20.

30 Ibid., III-15.

31 Anthony Downs, *The Revolution in Real Estate Finance* (Washington, D.C.: The Brookings Institute, 1985), 94–5.

32 California Department of Real Estate, *Deregulation of Financial Institutions*, III-23.

33 Ibid., III-17.

34 Ibid., III-18.

35 Ibid., III-19.

36 Downs, 238.

37 California Department of Real Estate, *Deregulation of Financial Institutions*, II-12.

38 Downs, 238.

39 Ibid., 238.

40 California Department of Real Estate, *Deregulation of Financial Institutions*, II-12.

41 Downs, 250.

42 The Federal Deposit Insurance Corporation, *The FDIC and RTC Experience: Managing the Crisis* (Washington, D.C.: August 1998), 860–1.

43 Ibid., 832–6. The Texas financial system virtually collapsed, with 226 failures. Texas banks were all independent, as branching was not allowed. This limited their size. Also, Texas problems were specialized, as they related closely to lower oil prices.

44 Available online at www.investopedia.com/terms/r/resolution-trust-corporation.asp.

45 Later renamed Lincoln Savings and Loan.

46 The company was also known as AFC, ACH and ACC. Michael Binstein and Charles Bowden, *Trust Me: Charles Keating and the Missing Billions* (New York: Random House, 1993), 139.

47 Binstein and Bowden, 148–9.

48 Ibid., 251.

49 Ibid., 166.

50 Ibid., 173.

51 Ibid., 191–9.

52 Ibid., 186–7, 317.

53 Ibid., 252.

54 Ibid., 273.

55 Ibid., 320.

56 Ibid., 225, 285–8.

57 Ibid., 342–3.

58 Ibid, 349–50.

59 The RICO Act allowed the seizure of assets used in a crime. Ibid., 350, 365.

60 Binstein and Bowden, 383.

61 Ibid., 164.

62 Ibid., 268.

63 Kitty Calavita, Henry Pontell and Robert Tillman, *Big Money: Fraud and Politics in the Savings and Loan Crisis* (Berkeley, California: University of California Press, 1997), 52–3.

64 Ibid., 53.

65 Connie Bruck, *Predators' Ball: The Inside Story of Drexel Burnham and the Rise of the Junk Bond Raiders* (New York: Penguin, 1989), 24.

66 Larry Schweikart and Lynne Doti, *American Entrepreneur: The Fascinating Stories of the People Who Defined Business in the United States* (New York: Amacom, 1999), 378, 394, 435.

67 In fact, Milken brought the whole company with him to Los Angeles.

68 Bruck, 68.

69 Ibid., 247.

70 Ibid., 320.

71 Ibid., 331.

72 Ibid., 369.

73 Susan Futterman, "Outlook: Banks and S&Ls," *California Business* XXV, no. 8. (August 1990), 33.

74 Ibid. Wells Fargo recovered from these issues and acquired California's First Interstate Bankcorp in 1996. This merger did not go smoothly. Norwest Bank of Minneapolis purchased Wells Fargo in 1998, but soon adopted the name Wells Fargo.

75 "Dialog '90," a seminar presented by Western Independent Bankers, Southern California Independent Bankers, and the Conference of State Bank Supervisors, Los Angeles, California, November 1990.

76 Gary Findley, "The Findley Reports California Banking Newsletter and Director's Compass," vol. 15, edition 16 (August 30 1991).

77 Ibid.

78 Ibid.

79 Ibid.

10 Derivative chaos
1992–2008

It is now widely accepted that the burst of the bubble in the real estate market contributed to the overall financial crisis of 2008 and the subsequent recession.[1] Very few people anticipated the depth of the connection between the real estate bust and the financial crisis, so the events surprised even a highly respected former chairman of the Federal Reserve Board of Governors, Alan Greenspan.[2] Nationally, the real estate bubble years were 1997 to 2006, then housing values plummeted somewhere between 30 and 40 percent from 2007 to 2011.[3] California, arguably the epicenter of the expansion and collapse, saw its real estate loans rise faster than the total assets of financial institutions in the state until 1999. There were brief dips, but generally the mortgages grew at increasing rates until 2005 (Graph 10.1).

When lending fell, California housing prices began to fall, and fell faster each year. The FHA showed a drop of 30 percent in 2008 alone. The declines decreased

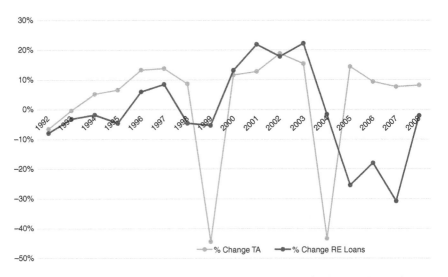

Graph 10.1 Change in total assets and real estate loans of financial institutions in California, 1992–2008.

Source: Compiled from FDIC data at https://www5.fdic.gov/hsob/.

after that, but housing prices in California did not increase again until 2010, and that was only a temporary uptick (Graph 10.2). Housing prices in large parts of the state had not regained their 2008 levels by 2015.[4]

By the 1990s, California lending laws for financial institutions were far more lax than national laws. The variety of assets available to state-chartered financial institutions brought investment funds from domestic and, due to the large trade deficit, international sources. One of the easiest, least-regulated ways to attract funds for mortgages was to find people who wanted to borrow on real estate, originate a new mortgage, and then sell these mortgages to Fannie Mae and Freddie Mac. The newly originated loan could be for new property, change of ownership of existing property, or to refinance an old loan to lower the interest rate or change the amount or payment timing. The state did not regulate these "mortgage originators" as financial institutions. The more sophisticated mortgage originators created derivative securities based on the mortgages they issued. Creating a derivative security was difficult, as it involved combinations of the mortgages, but was a way to attract more funds directly from investors. Three of the largest originators of mortgages opened in Southern California: Countrywide, Ameriquest, and New Century Financial. Their growth was spectacular and their failures preceded the financial crisis by only a short time.

Charles Calomiris and Steve Haber describe the period just prior to the 2008 crash in their book, *Fragile by Design*, as "fraught with regulation; piles and piles of ineffectual regulation."[5] They traced the 2008 financial crisis back to a series of regulatory changes dating to before the S&L crisis of the 1980s. As noted earlier,

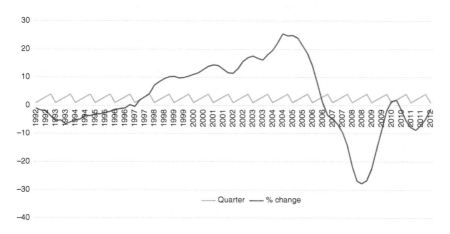

Graph 10.2 Four-quarter percentage change in Federal Housing Finance Agency (FHFA) State-Level House Price Indexes (Seasonally Adjusted, Purchase-Only Index, 2012 Q1).

Source: The HPI is a broad measure of the movement of single-family house prices. The HPI is a weighted, repeat-sales index, meaning that it measures average price changes in repeat sales or refinancings on the same properties. This information is obtained by reviewing repeat mortgage transactions on single-family properties whose mortgages have been purchased or securitized by Fannie Mae or Freddie Mac since January 1975, http://www.fhfa.gov/Default.aspx?Page=215&Type=compare&Area1=CA&Area2=&Area3.

the decline of the S&L industry created a lack of available funding in that market. A virtual flurry of laws attempted to help them survive, but to no avail. And while the industry died, the regulations lived on with unanticipated results.

Federal re-regulation of the financial system

Financial Institutions Recovery and Reform Enforcement Act (FIRREA)

In 1989, Congress mandated the Federal Home Loan Banks to begin a special program of support for low-income housing. The act required S&Ls and savings banks to set aside 10 percent of their net earnings in support of housing for low- and moderate-income individuals and families. When banks made these riskier loans available, they usually required bigger down payments and more mortgage insurance than they would on less risky real estate loans. To support low-income housing, Fannie Mae and Freddie Mac purchased the riskier loans from the banks, providing funds to replace the loans made by the S&Ls, and inducing lenders to make loans on housing for low- and moderate-income families. Both Fannie Mae and Freddie Mac were now private companies, although they still had an implied backing from Congress. Both entities' political as well as their economic power had increased in the 1980s with the S&L industry collapse. In 1990, Fannie Mae and Freddie Mac had one third of all single-family home mortgages; by 2003, their share had risen to half. As these Government-Sponsored Enterprises (GSEs) grew, the public questioned their structure. The bonds issued by the GSEs to fund the purchases of mortgages were treated as if the government still guaranteed them, in effect subsidizing the interest paid by the GSEs with the implication of taxpayer backing. Congress discussed the need to limit their growth. As the GSEs were coming under attack, they moved into buying more real estate loans for low- to moderate-income housing, especially from large banks. Members of Congress continued to grumble, but low-income housing is an attractive cause and no one in Congress seemed to be in favor of any changes limiting it.[6]

Community Reinvestment Act (CRA) developments

The Community Reinvestment Act of 1977 was designed to eliminate "redlining," the supposed practice of financial institutions that excluded lower-income neighborhoods from eligibility for loans. In theory, it was to serve as an incentive for banks to generally support their local neighborhoods. At first, banks satisfied the law by "involvement," supporting local youth programs or not-for-profit organizations. Beginning in 1996, the CRA requirements were applied differently to small banks, judging them only on actual lending: loan-to-deposits ratios, percentage of loans in assessment area (census districts of lower or moderate income), distribution among borrowers of different income levels, and the location and sizes of businesses receiving loans.[7] This change would gradually apply to all banks. But of course, one could only lend to customers who actually came in and sought a loan, and if there were no such customers, meeting federal guidelines was nearly impossible.

With a lot of the merger activity occurring in the 1990s, there was another provision in the law that would create an opportunity. Even if the banks involved in a merger had the required "satisfactory" rating for community lending, CRA required the governing agency to allow testimony of "the community" whenever there was a proposed merger. This gave community activist groups leverage, and gave lawmakers more incentive to encourage lending to lower income groups these activist groups represented.

Community activist groups

Since CRA required that public input be allowed when financial institutions planned to merge, community activist groups were beginning to feel their power. Associations like the Association for Community Reform Now (ACORN) in Chicago organized and coached people in appropriate testimony for prospective financial institution mergers. In 1991, Senator Alan Dixon of Illinois invited ACORN and other activist groups to testify before a Senate subcommittee. In his testimony, the director of ACORN explicitly drew a link between the ability of banks to sell their loans to the GSEs and the willingness of those banks to participate in CRA lending partnerships with ACORN. He also observed that extra security requirements on low-income loans were "at a minimum, income discriminatory and may, by extension, be racially discriminatory."[8] Congress did not argue with this inflammatory rhetoric. Instead, they promptly enacted significant changes in the rules governing Fannie Mae and Freddie Mac, giving them substantial new responsibilities to promote homeownership by low-income and inner-city Americans. The changes came in the Federal Housing Enterprise Safety and Soundness Act (also known as the GSE Act) signed into law by President Bush in 1992. In 1993, empowered by this Act, the Department of Housing and Urban Development (HUD) required the GSEs to devote 30 percent of their loans purchased to those for low- and moderate-income borrowers. HUD also required 1 percent of the loans to be in the "low- and very low-income" category. The mandated GSE purchases of "very low-income" loans were raised to 12 percent in 1996 and about 15 percent in 2001. The overall percentage of the low- to moderate-income loan purchase quota went from 0 to 30 percent in 1992, 40 percent in 1996, and 50 percent in 2001, then rose even more after 2004. It was difficult for GSEs to meet these quotas. Fannie and Freddie had to play games, like buying and selling mortgages to primary lenders, buying them back and counting each repurchase as a new purchase when calculating the quota. Originators didn't mind: they collected fees for collecting payments and sold the eligible loans at high premiums.[9]

Beginning in 1994, Fannie and Freddie started buying loans where down payments of only 3 percent had been made. By 2007, two out of every five mortgages had an equity-to-value ratio of 3 percent or less. Most of the loan purchases were from just a few originators. Ninety-three percent of $4.5 trillion in post-1995 transactions came from Bank of America, Citibank, JPMorgan Chase, and Wells Fargo.[10] Originators linked to Bank of America included Washington Mutual and

Countrywide. In 2004, Fannie and Freddie removed limits on purchases of "no-doc" loans, in which the borrower did not have to provide proof of income, and aggressively moved to buy loans where the monthly payment was interest-only, and didn't reduce the loan amount at all. By 2006, 15.2 percent of the two GSEs' loans were interest-only. Oversight of these two agencies was held at bay by their spending over $200 million on lobbying.[11] The FHA, specifically created by the government to fund low-price housing, also stepped up its lending to lower-income home-buyers.[12] Brent Smith found that the FHA loans served the high-risk housing mortgage market well from 2003 to 2006, but the quality of their loans deteriorated after that in the face of competition from more nimble private lenders.[13]

Glass-Steagall Act revision

The Glass-Steagall Act was passed in 1933 to separate deposit banking from investment banking. Investment banks took the word "bank" out of their names, and deposit banks could not own stock or bonds in companies unrelated to their business. The rationale behind the Act was that banks encouraged their deposit customers to buy the stocks the bank owned. This turned out not to have been a factor in bank failures in the 1920s and '30s, and opposition to the act rose in the 1960s.[14] In 1986, The Glass-Steagall Act was weakened by allowing J. P. Morgan to engage in investment banking. Through the 1990s, debate continued on the repeal of the Glass-Steagall Act.[15] The separation rule kept being stretched: Citicorp bought Travelers Insurance; Morgan Stanley, mostly an investment bank, became the issuer of the "Discover" credit card, and so-on. Finally repealed in 1999 by the Gramm-Leach-Bliley Act, mergers of investment banks and commercial banks were finally allowed. Citigroup put Travelers' red umbrella over the word "Citi." The resulting change was described by Nobel Prize-winning economist Joseph Stiglitz:

> Commercial banks are not supposed to be high-risk ventures; they are supposed to manage other people's money very conservatively ... It is with this understanding that the government agrees to pick up the tab should they fail. Investment banks, on the other hand, have traditionally managed rich people's money—people who can take bigger risks in order to get bigger returns. When repeal of Glass-Steagall brought investment and commercial banks together, the investment-bank culture came out on top. There was a demand for the kind of high returns that could be obtained only through high leverage and big risk-taking.[16]

The instruments of risk: derivative securities

Advances in computers in the 1980s had made a new type of security possible. Derivatives were complex financial instruments developed to provide a way for big companies and financial institutions to protect themselves—hedge—against very specific risks. As with any hedging instrument, investors also bought these securities for speculation. By 1992, outstanding derivative securities amounted to $11 million in value.[17] During the 1990s, they grew to $69 trillion. Many of them were composed of bonds issued by Fannie Mae and Freddie Mac, which the GSEs sold to get the funds to buy mortgages from the original lender (originator). In spite of their rising popularity, derivatives were not well known until the bankruptcy of Orange County, California.

Robert Citron, the treasurer of Orange County, a prosperous Southern Californian suburban community, was facing jail time at the beginning of 1995. The treasurer had invested not only county funds but also the reserve funds of other public entities into sophisticated derivative securities issued by Fannie Mae.[18] His investment strategy depended on falling interest rates to continue his high yield. When interest rates rose in 1994, he reacted by taking on even more risk.

The 1994 election for treasurer was the only one where there had been opposition in Citron's twenty years in office. His opponent, accountant John Moorlach, lost the election, but in the campaign he brought some of the treasurer's high-risk investments under scrutiny. In November 1994, the county's assistant treasurer Matthew Raabe privately went to top county officials to explain the dangerous position the county was in. The market value of the investment portfolio had dropped over a billion dollars. Although, at that time, the value of the securities did not have to be written down unless they were sold, agencies which had loaned the county money to invest on their behalf had begun demanding their funds back. The Orange County Board of Supervisors responded by declaring bankruptcy in December, and defaulted on payments due in the summer of 1995.

The Orange County bankruptcy was one of the largest in municipal bond history. It shook the foundations of the national financial market. Municipal bonds (or "munis"), obligations of local governments, were considered among the safest of investments. Not only were they backed by the taxing power of their issuing agencies, they often funded revenue-generating projects. In this case, Citron had borrowed several cities' and districts' "fund" money, which is essentially savings for replacement of capital stock like water pipes and police cars, and used a lot of it to buy bonds from Fannie Mae. These were "derivatives"—securities backed by other securities. They had a fairly tame market until in 1971, when Fannie Mae was listed on the New York Stock Exchange and began a more aggressive investment policy.[19] Citron didn't invest in ordinary Fannie Mae bonds, either. A victim of his own hubris and a fast-talking broker from Merrill Lynch, he bought large percentages of exotic Fannie Mae issues like "reverse stepped bonds." Unlike most bonds, which offered the same dollar amount of interest each year, these bonds were designed to pay less interest each year than in the year before. If interest rates in the economy fell at the same rate as the interest payments on the bonds, the bonds would retain their initial value. This fit Citron's idea that the interest rate in the United States was falling. When the interest rate actually increased, the bonds' values fell even faster than those bonds with level interest payments.

After the news broke about the debacle in Orange County, risk-averse institutions unloaded anything resembling a derivative product quickly. These exotic securities did not disappear, however. In fact, the Orange County bankruptcy called attention to the customized asset, and derivatives would proliferate and grow more exotic. Securities investment companies hired mathematicians to custom-design derivative securities from existing securities, to protect their clients against very specific risks. Derivatives became the instrument of choice in financing the next cycle in the real estate markets. However, without an increase in mortgages, there would be no raw material to create derivatives. A new, unregulated financial entity, the originator, made sure mortgages would be available.

The players: Non-bank mortgage originators

Commercial banks came under increased scrutiny in the early 1990s as a new FDIC director declared his intention of examining every bank, every year. Scrutiny of bank assets increased even more after the Orange County derivative crisis. Yet Congress and President Bill Clinton continued to pressure the GSEs for more low-income home loans.

Banks, thrifts and investment funds created new mortgage banks. The mortgage banks would find borrowers, originate mortgages and sell them to Fannie Mae and Freddie Mac. Some sold shares of the entire pool of mortgages directly to investors. Some mortgage originators were small, but several of these funds grew at an astonishing rate. Three of the most famous, Ameriquest, Countrywide and New Century Financial, started in Southern California. New Century Financial Corporation, in Orange County, California, was featured on *60 Minutes* in 2004 for its phenomenal growth to become the second-biggest mortgage lender in the country behind British-owned Hongkong and Shanghai Banking Corporation (HSBC). Ameriquest's founder, Roland Arnall, was appointed Ambassador to the Netherlands by George Bush, with the approving remarks of future President Barack Obama. Countrywide's founder, Angelo Mozilo, bragged that his company did more to help American homeowners "achieve and maintain the dream of homeownership" than any other entity in the nation.[20] According to Alan Greenspan, these and other companies were "pressed" to originate mortgages and sell them to securitizers, who "sliced and diced" the mortgages into complicated derivative securities which could be sold to investors who were too risk-adverse to directly loan on real estate.[21]

Subprime loans proliferate

Ironically, with the creation of securities designed to reduce the risk of investing in mortgages, even more risky mortgages could be issued. "Subprime" loans were based primarily on the (rapidly rising) value of the homes rather than the credit-worthiness of the borrower. Purchasers of properties were called "prime" customers when they had a good credit rating, put at least 20 percent of the equity as a down payment and took out a fully amortized loan.[22] For subprime loans, the mortgage applicants may not have had a high credit score (these were called "Alt-A" loans). They may have a sole proprietorship or other reason not to be able to document a steady, adequate income ("no-doc" loans). For people who expected rising incomes, the adjustable-rate mortgage seemed reasonable, especially when the payments could be "interest-only" for the first years, or payments could be "negative amortization" (payments wouldn't even cover the interest on the loan, instead letting the balance owed rise). Since home prices were rising rapidly, it even made sense to make "zero equity" loans for the full value of the property.

To find buyers for these subprime loans, they had to be "securitized." While the risk on each loan was high, if hundreds were bundled into securities and only a little of each bundle was owned, the risk seemed small. In fact, the two largest credit rating agencies, Moody's and Standard and Poor's, gave most mortgage-backed securities their highest ratings. One study showed that, when weighted by value, 80 to 90 percent of securities in a typical non-prime transaction had initially received the highest possible rating from these agencies.[23] These securities were a newly available source of financing which stimulated the real estate market. Especially in the lower end of the housing market, prices rose dramatically.[24] In the United States, home-building increased from 1.6 million new homes in 2000 to 2.1 million in 2005.[25]

Securitization becomes prominent

While the Orange County bankruptcy made investors fearful of the word "derivative," the product itself nevertheless became more common and more elaborate. As practiced by securitizers, the original real estate loans could be packaged into securities of any desired level of risk. The primary principle was that of diversification. Owning a small portion of several loans is less risky than it is to own a single loan. If a company bought a collection of loans, then sold bonds based on these loans, these bonds were safer investments than any of the loans. By putting the mortgage loans into silos, or piles of loans, and then issuing bonds against different mixtures of the silos, securities could literally be tailored to the desired amount of risk. Less than 250,000 subprime loans were securitized in 2000, but the number grew to about 225 million in 2005.[26]

Exotic as this securitization process was, most of the early packages, called mortgage-backed securities or "collateralized mortgage obligations" (CMOs), were, like the ones sold to Robert Citron, made up of bonds issued by Fannie Mae and Freddie Mac. This increased the perceived safety considerably. While their bonds were no longer insured by the government, there were implied guarantees. By the early 2000s, rather than purchasing individual mortgages, Fannie Mae and Freddie Mac were the biggest purchasers of MBO and CMO derivatives. Of course, to create derivative securities, there had to be raw material. Raw material consisted of mortgages.

California subprime originators

As California was one of the four states to experience the most defaults of mortgage loans at the end of the boom, it is not surprising that three of the largest subprime mortgage originators located in the state as the bubble expanded. The stories of these lenders shows how financing was channeled into real estate in the early 2000s.

New Century Financial

New Century Financial Corporation started in Irvine, California, in 1995. By 2001, the founding team of Robert Cole, Brad Morrice, and Edward Gotschall owned 15 percent of the company, worth about $42 million. Fannie Mae and Freddie Mac bought subprime mortgages to increase access of low- and moderate-income families to homeownership; however, New Century's borrowers were not poor. From 2004 to 2006, their borrowers' average income was about $80,000 and the average loan was for 80 percent of the property's value.[27]

In spite of the income of the borrowers, their company made subprime loans almost exclusively. Almost a quarter of their loans were made to borrowers or property located in California. Texas and Florida each got a little less than 10 percent of the loans, and the rest of the funding was distributed all over the country.[28] The company grew at a phenomenal rate. By the end of the first year of business, it had 300 employees and had originated $350 million in mortgages. The company went public in 1997 at $11 a share and hit a high price of $51.97.[29] By 2003, the company had approximately 3,700 employees and originated more than $27 billion in loans. By 2006, it originated $50 billion in loans.[30] From 2001 to 2006, it gathered originations at a stunning rate, analyzing 20,000 loan applications in 2001, 100,000 in 2003 and 160,000 in their last good year, 2004.[31] Its rapid growth also meant that it was always leveraged. The money had to be loaned first, most often to pay off an old loan on the property, then the loan could be sold.

There were several sources of the funds needed to fill the gap in timing. Short-term borrowing and bonds were the main source of working capital. New Century borrowed at least $17.4 billion from investment bankers.[32] While, traditionally, mortgage banks were subsidiaries of savings banks, commercial banks or other financial institutions, for New Century most of the funding came from companies whose main purpose was to enter the mortgage market indirectly. Greenwich Capital Financial Products provided as much as $150 million while New Century was in bankruptcy, apparently backing previous investments. CIT Group/Business Credit Inc. and Carrington Capital bought New Century's mortgages. In the twisted financial environment, New Century had helped finance the creation of Carrington, apparently for the purpose of buying the loans originated by New Century and securitizing them into bonds which Carrington then sold to investors. The New York Teachers' Pension Fund invested funds into New Century, as it later led investors in a lawsuit where a federal court awarded common stock shareholders $125 million.[33]

While the company sold many of its loans to investment banks which "securitized" them, between 2001 and 2003 it started keeping many of its loans on their own balance sheet.[34] This created a mini-whirlwind of risk. The riskier the loans New Century made, the riskier (and more profitable) the loans in the company's assets were. The executives not only worried about the risk that real estate borrowers would not make payments (credit risk), they worried about interest rate risk. Any drop in interest rates would make the loans they held less profitable. When the loans became less profitable, their value dropped. Both earnings and the value of the company would fall.

Even the loans New Century sold had hidden risks. When it sold a loan to another entity, it guaranteed that the payments would be made for the first month or two.[35] New Century knew when payment was not made, as, like most lenders, they "serviced" or collected payments on most of the loans it had sold. If the bank had to buy back a loan, it put it on their books at face value, even though the mortgage was obviously not as valuable as if the borrower were making the payments.[36] In another type of transaction, the company would originate a loan, but then sell it to itself at a discount. The discount was booked as income. This was actually legal, and happened to 10–12 percent of the originations in 2005.[37] It might have been a desperate attempt to maintain income at that point.

When the Federal Reserve System tightened monetary policy in the spring of 2004, New Century's portfolio experienced a severe shock, and it reacted by expanding deferred amortization loan contracts ("zero equity" loans).[38] The customers for these loans tended to be higher-income individuals, and the company increased their focus on California, Texas and Florida.[39] These loans typically had a "reset" date, typically twenty-four months after origination. At that point, the borrower had to get a new loan. During the boom, the home value would rise, providing equity to use for a new loan. If the property value fell below the amount of the loan, the home was referred to as "underwater," and cash might have to be paid to the lender.

The company's demise was as spectacular as its growth. When the Fed allowed interest rates to rise in 2004–5, the margin between the rate the company received on the mortgage loans and the rate it paid to get funds to make loans fell. Since New Century had grown so fast, most of the mortgage loans were still in their first two years, paying a low fixed-rate interest. New Century's income fell. The market value of the portfolio of loans the company owned also fell. Worse, the origination business dropped sharply.[40] The base of the business was weakening. Ed Gotschall resigned in 2006, but Brad Morrice, CEO, reacted by increasing the risk profile of their business even more.[41] After 2004, the company began to specialize in "interest-only ARMS" and balloon loans. The first loan required payment of only the periodically adjusted interest for the first years of the loan. Once, this period lasted two years; now it was five. After that, the loan had to be renewed. The balloon loans amortized the initial loan amount over forty years, to create lower payments. However, the loan was due after thirty years. By the end of 2006, these two types of loans accounted for about 60 percent of all New Century's originations.[42]

When interest rates increased, the appreciation in the housing market slowed. With higher interest rates, the monthly payment on a house rose. To keep the payment down, the value of the house had to fall. Homeowners whose house fell in value, possibly below the amount owed on the mortgage, also became less motivated to keep making payments on the house, and foreclosures rose. Subprime loans, with their variable interest rates, and/or high values relative to the home value, were the first to start failing. The nation's largest subprime lender, HSBC, exited that market in February 2007, taking a huge loss.[43]

Rumors were floating about New Century's stability. Internal reports warned that payments were not being received in a timely manner on loans in the company portfolio. The company was selling more and more "80/20" loans, a type of loan that mortgaged the full market value of the real estate by making the normal loan of 80 percent of the appraised value of the property, then adding another loan for the required 20 percent equity. By the end of 2006, these loans made up more than 30 percent of the outstanding loans.[44]

On February 7 2007, New Century announced that it would be restating its financial reports for the first three quarters of 2006. Its stock price dropped precipitously. On March 8, the company stopped accepting new loan applications. In a few days the company's stock was delisted from the New York Stock Exchange and the US Attorney announced an investigation.[45] On April 2, 3,200 employees streamed out of the sleek headquarters shown on *60 Minutes*, their well-paid jobs gone. Twenty-seven thousand loans in the pipeline were cancelled.[46]

When the company entered bankruptcy, an examiner was appointed by the Department of Justice. The examiner's team found "significant improper and imprudent practices" in virtually everything the company did. Some of the language in the report is startling: [New Century] had a "brazen obsession with increasing loan originations without due regard to the risks associated with that business strategy." New Century had created a "ticking time bomb" by its risky loan products, loans to high-risk borrowers, and by using deficient appraisals. The examiners noted that, instead of reporting a profit of $63.5 million in the third quarter of 2006, it should have reported a loss; and that in the second quarter of 2006, when New Century reported an increase in year-to-year earnings of 8 percent, they should have reported a decline of 40 percent. The examiners opined that incompetent personnel and inadequate technology created these problems. The focus of the company seemed to be on producing more loans, and the company seemed to measure quality of the loans more by saleability than by repayment potential.[47] The board wanted to continue the practice of basing employee pay on getting new business even in bankruptcy, by granting up to a $3.48 million bonus if Morrice or other top level managers could sell the company's assets.[48] The SEC later charged Morrice, along with two other top executives, with securities and accounting fraud, and tried to get back some of the bonuses they had been paid.[49] "The calculations misled investors by implying that virtually all of New Century's borrowers had considerable equity in their homes, whereas, in fact, by 2007, nearly one-third of New Century's borrowers had no equity in their homes whatsoever," the SEC said.[50] "Defendants knew this negative information from numerous internal reports they regularly received, including weekly reports that Morrice [received] ominously entitled 'Storm Watch'," the SEC said in its statement.[51]

But New Century was hardly alone in this quicksand. Other mortgage bankers, including Los Angeles-based Countrywide, hurriedly assured the public that they were not in danger, as their businesses were "different." Whether they understood it or not, California, and the nation's, two other largest mortgage originators were also in trouble.

Ameriquest

Ameriquest was originating about the same amount of mortgages as New Century Financial when they stopped taking loan applications in September of 2007. At that time, they probably were one of the best-known mortgage banks in the country, with their heavy TV advertising, their name on a baseball field, their dark green sign draped lavishly on sidelines of sporting events and on green blimps which hovered over any large gathering. Their story was very much like New Century's, but there were also differences.

On the surface, Ameriquest started from more traditional roots, as a thrift called Long Beach Savings & Loan. Roland Arnall, born in Paris as his parents fled Eastern Europe and the Nazis, started it in 1979. In Long Beach, he began making subprime mortgages as early as the 1980s. In the mid-1990s, his company was charged with requiring higher interest rates for minorities. After settling this charge, he then moved to Orange County and divided the business into Argent Mortgage, to originate wholesale mortgages; AMC Mortgage Services, to service its own and others' mortgages; and Ameriquest Mortgage, to originate mortgages at the retail level. His lending practices were tough. After the state abolished usury laws, Arnell's companies made riskier loans, took home equity as collateral, and charged high interest rates.[52]

In 1996, the Justice department challenged the Ameriquest mortgage lending practices as gouging and predatory. Arnall settled with a $3 million educational fund, and promised employee training. The Federal Trade Commission reacted to complaints by ACORN against the company by requiring Arnall to offer more low-cost mortgage loans. Reporters at the *Los Angeles Times* broke a story in 2005 about Ameriquest's lending that contended that the lender had engaged in various questionable practices, including "deceiving borrowers about the terms of their loans, forging documents, falsifying appraisals, and fabricating borrowers' income to qualify them for loans they couldn't afford."[53] Shortly afterward, Ameriquest announced that it would set aside $325 million to settle investigations in thirty states of allegations that it had preyed on borrowers with hidden fees and balloon payments.[54] Still, they loaned copiously. When Prentiss Cox, a former member of the attorney general's office of Minnesota, looked at the Ameriquest balance sheet in 2004, he recalls thinking to himself, "The scope of their lending is unbelievable."[55] Yet their loans continued to grow.

In 2006, Arnall began to condense his business. In 2007, Ameriquest closed all but four of its retail branches and fired 4,000 employees.[56] The next year, Citigroup bought most of his companies, including Ameriquest Mortgage, which they closed.[57] The records on the companies sank into the large organization. Arnall himself did well. As his wealth had grown, so did his charitable and political donations, including founding the Simon Wiesenthal Center and Museum of

Tolerance in Los Angeles. Arnall served as Ambassador to the Netherlands from 2006 until shortly before his death in 2008. He was not the only mortgage banker to survive the mortgage meltdown.

Countrywide

Angelo Mozilo was movie-star handsome and as focused on appearances. He cultivated his son-of-a-butcher roots-to-super-success-story image right up to his trial date, which he avoided by agreeing to pay $67.5 million to his investors.[58]

Mozilo went to work for David Loeb in 1960 at United Mortgage Servicing Company, and was soon sent to Florida. There was a housing shortage near Cape Canaveral, and Mozilo arranged financing for a development there. When United Mortgage Servicing was purchased in 1968, Mozilo and Loeb co-founded Countrywide as a mortgage bank.[59] The first few years were spent struggling for funding, but when Fannie Mae increased its purchase of mortgages, Countrywide took off. Mozilo practically invented refinancing old home-loans at lower interest rates, after the distinction between loans made to buy a house and loans secured by a residence disappeared in 1980.[60] The new rules allowed making home improvements, or, less logically, buying an auto on a loan backed by the value of a home. Refinancing was also fueled by the fact that as inflation and interest rates fell in the 1980s, many people wanted to share in the benefit of lower interest rates without moving.

Loeb became less involved in the company and Mozilo moved it to Los Angeles, California, following the location of the loans made.[61] By 1992, the $40 billion issued in new mortgages made the company the largest originator of single-family mortgages in the country.

When President Clinton announced his housing initiative in 1994, Mozilo signed a pledge to increase lending to minorities by $1.25 billion, calling his plan "House America."[62] He was enthusiastic and the company aggressively advertised, but the loans applications started dropping. He only needed to look to Long Beach to see why. Countrywide was making traditional thirty-year, fixed interest rate, amortized loans, and Arnall's newly restructured Long Beach Saving & Loan, now called Long Beach Mortgage, offered low-income borrowers more flexibility, with various subprime products. Mozilo started a new division of Countrywide to compete.[63] This division offered subprime loans, then sold them.

In the early 2000s, as the bubble expanded, Countrywide began securitizing its own loans rather than selling them to others. Soon he had a department of "quants" (quantitative analysts) who could combine the loans into structured securities that could be sold to buyers who only wanted low-risk investments. This operation was so successful, Mozilo changed CEOs and reversed his plan to retire. He moved to even more aggressive growth. The company's maximum subprime loan amount was $400,000 in 2001. By 2006, it was $1 million.

Subprime loans were more profitable for the company than conventional loans. Countrywide had a 1 to 2 percent return on conventional loans. The return was up to 15 percent on subprime loans. The practice of pushing subprime loans was often encouraged by Commission structures.[64] In 2001, the minimum homeowner's equity was 10 percent. By 2006, it was zero. Countrywide started making loans on which the borrowers made payments of the interest only (pay-option ARMs). By 2006, this type of loan amounted to 23 percent of their portfolio. Thirty-six percent of the loans were "Alt-A" with no proof of income. Twenty-four percent were 80/20 (zero equity) loans. Two-thirds of the loans actually were refinancing of already owned property. "It was hard to imagine anyone who wouldn't qualify for a Countrywide subprime loan during the final throes of the housing bubble," according to Bethany McLean.[65]

Starting in 2005, like New Century Financial, Countrywide started keeping more of its subprime loans on its own books, rather than securitizing and selling them. For example, between 2004 and the end of 2006 the pay-option ARMs on the balance sheet went from $4.7 billion to $32.7 billion. The market for these types of securities wasn't growing fast enough. The company increased its short-term borrowing to finance more mortgages using overnight "repos" (repurchase agreements), which are one-day loans, with the mortgages as collateral.[66] This is a dangerous strategy, grossly violating a financial tradition of matching the time to maturity (payment) of liabilities and assets. As at New Century, risk levels spiraled up. The very short-term borrowing strategy continued into 2007, when Countrywide began buying loans from failing mortgage banks. The first quarter of the year was profitable, but profits were falling and delinquencies were rising. Countrywide stock prices started dropping and some top executives left. By August, a Merrill Lynch specialist warned that Countrywide might fail.[67] Mozilo fought back with a constant blitz of pronouncements. His theme was persecution against a company founded to help people become homeowners. "If the default rate is ten percent," he said repeatedly, "the other ninety percent are people who wouldn't have their own home." At the same time, he was selling his stock options; for $140 million between November 2006 and August 2007.[68]

On August 23 2007, Bank of America announced it would invest $2 billion in Countrywide.[69] In January 2008, Bank of America acquired Countrywide for $4 billion. In 2009, Mozilo was charged with misleading investors and had a sanction imposed of $67.5 million. Countrywide paid $20 million of the fine for him, but the courts were still after Mozilo in 2015. A widely repeated comment called Bank of America's purchase "the worst acquisition ever."[70] Those who believe this must not have considered the previous involvement of Bank of America, or the fact that the bank continued the business Mozilo had developed, including making subprime loans and securitizing them.

The demise of these three companies in 2007 was the beginning of the end of the economic expansion. The housing boom ended in 2006, and by the end of 2008 the country was deep into the worst financial crisis since 1929. By 2006, areas of the country were experiencing sharp housing declines. California's "Inland Empire," consisting of San Bernardino, Riverside, and their numerous suburbs, was among those areas.[71] The market for all types of mortgage-backed securities crashed in 2008. In one study of 14,000 of these securities, 61 percent were in default in September of that year.[72] In September of 2008, the entire financial market crashed.

Notes

1 Steve Gjerstad and Vernon Smith showed that a housing downturn in 1926 preceded the Depression. "At Home in the Great Recession," *The 4% Solution: Unleashing the Economic Growth America Needs*, edited by Brian Miniter (New York: Crown Publishing Group, 2012), 50–79. Also see Gjerstad and Smith, *Rethinking Housing Bubbles: The Role of Household and Bank Balance Sheets in Modeling Business Cycles* (Cambridge, England: Cambridge University Press, 2014), *passim*. There is also a rising interest in the cause of booms and busts in the housing market itself. See, for example, Craig Burnside, Martin Eichenbaum and Sergio Rebelo, "Understanding booms and busts in housing markets," National Bureau of Economic Research Working Paper no. 16734 (Cambridge, Massachusetts: National Bureau of Economic Research, 2011). Available online at www.nber.org/papers/w16734.
2 Alan Greenspan, *The Map and the Territory: Risk, Human Nature, and the Future of Forecasting* (New York: The Penguin Press, 2013), 64.
3 Peter J. Wallison, "Get Ready for the Next Housing Bubble," *Wall Street Journal*, (Thursday December 5 2013), A19.
4 A. Gary Anderson Center for Economic Research, the George L. Argyros School of Business and Economics, Chapman University, "Shifting Gear: Recovery to Expansion: How Long will the Expansion Last?" *Economic and Business Review* 34, no. 1 (December 2015), 13–17. Information is from page 14. In September 2015, the state as a whole had not reached the peak level of housing price before the recession.
5 Charles Calomiris and Steve Haber, *Fragile by Design: The Political Origins of Banking Crises & Scarce Credit* (Princeton, New Jersey: Princeton University Press, 2014), 265.
6 Calomiris and Haber, 232–3.
7 Gary Findley, "The Findley Reports: Banking Newsletter and Directors Compass," vol. 19, edition 12 (December 1995), 3.
8 Calomiris and Haber, 233–4. From US Senate hearings.
9 Ibid., 234–9. Chart on p. 235 shows lending requirements.
10 Wells Fargo and Bank of America were no longer headquartered in California.
11 Calomiris and Haber, 237–40.
12 Brent Smith, "Lending Through the Cycle: the Federal Housing Administration's Evolving Risk in the Primary Market," *Atlantic Economic Journal* 40, no. 3 (September 2012), 253–71.
13 Ibid., 253.
14 See discussion of this topic in Eugene White, *The Regulation and Reform of the American Banking System, 1920-1929* (Princeton, New Jersey: Princeton University Press, 1983), 164–5.
15 Gary Findley, "The Findley Reports: Banking Newsletter and Directors Compass," vol. 19, edition 4 (April 1995), 1.
16 Roosevelt Institute, "Looking Back at the Repeal of the Glass-Steagall Act," *Report*, May 2011.
17 Alan S. Blinder, *After the Music Stopped: The Financial Crisis, the Response, and the Work Ahead* (New York: The Penguin Press, 2013), 60.
18 One of his investments was in "step-up double inverse floaters." These tongue-twisting securities were tied to interest rates, paying progressively more as interest rates fell. Teri Sforza, "Robert Citron was a hard-to-hate villain in O.C.'s bankruptcy," *The Orange County Register* (January 17 2013, updated August 21 2013). Available online at www.ocregister.com/articles/citron-383795-county-money.html.

19 The government started selling Fannie Mae to private investors in 1968, but its more aggressive investment strategy didn't start until 1974.

20 Bethany McLean and Joe Nocera, *All the Devils are Here: the Hidden History of the Financial Crisis* (London: Portfolio/Penguin, 2011), 305.

21 Greenspan, 64.

22 Each month's payment included a fraction of the original amount borrowed plus the interest on the outstanding loan. At the end of the term of the loan, the balance would be zero.

23 Adam Ashcraft, Paul Goldsmith-Pinkham, Peter Hull and James Vickery, "Credit Ratings and Security Prices in the Subprime MBS Market," *American Economic Review: Papers & Proceedings* 101, no. 3 (May 2011), 115–19.

24 Tim Landvoigt, Monika Piazzesi, and Martin Schneider, "The Housing Market(s) of San Diego," National Bureau of Economic Research Working Paper no. 17723 (Stanford University, Palo Alto, California: September 2013), 1. Available online at http://web.stanford.edu/~piazzesi/segments.pdf.

25 Blinder, 16.

26 Yuliya Demyanyk and Otto Van Hemert, "Understanding the Subprime Mortgage Crisis," Social Science Research Network Working Paper (December 5 2008), Slide 4. Gives data on delinquencies on other slides. Available online at http://ssrn.com/abstract=1020396.

27 Augustin Landier, David Sraer, and David Thesmar, "Going for Broke: New Century Financial Corporation, 2004–2006," Working Paper (Toulouse School of Economics, Toulouse, France: September 2010), 20. Available online at www.tse-fr.eu/sites/default/files/medias/doc/wp/fit/10-199.pdf.

28 Landier, Sraer, and Thesmar, 20.

29 Mary Ann Milbourn, "NYSE to oust New Century," *Orange County Register* (March 13 2007, updated August 21 2013). Available online at www.ocregister.com/articles/new-5772-company-century.html.

30 Michael J. Missal and Lisa M. Richman, "New Century Financial: Lessons Learned," *Mortgage Banking* (October 2008), 1–2.

31 Landier, Sraer, and Thesmar, 20.

32 Julie Creswell and Vikas Bajaj, "Home Lender is Seeking Bankruptcy," *Orange County Register* (April 3 2007), 1.

33 Ibid.

34 Landier, Sraer, and Thesmar, 2. At the end of 2003, they had about 20 percent of the loans they originated still on their own books.

35 "We sell whole loans on a non-recourse basis pursuant to a purchase agreement in which we give customary representations and warranties regarding the loan characteristics and the origination process. Therefore, we may be required to repurchase or substitute loans in the event of a breach of these representations and warranties. In addition, we generally commit to repurchase or substitute a loan if a payment default occurs within the first month or two following the date the loan is funded, unless we make other arrangements with the purchaser." [10k form for fiscal year 2003, p.13] from Landier, Sraer, and Thesmar, 8.

36 Mathew Padilla and John Gittelsohn, "How New Century Sank," *The Orange County Register* (April 13 2007, updated August 21 2013). Available online at www.ocregister.com/articles/company-7261-new-brad.html.

37 Landier, Sraer, and Thesmar, 8.

38 Ibid., 1.

39 Ibid., 45.
40 Ibid., 14.
41 Padilla and Gittelsohn.
42 Landier, Sraer, and Thesmar, 15.
43 Barry Nielsen, "The Rise and Demise of New Century Financial," *Investopedia* (September 4 2007). Available online at www.investopedia.com/articles/07/new-century.asp.
44 Zachery Kouwe, "Civil Suit Says Lender Ignored Own Warnings," *Orange County Register* (December 8 2009).
45 Missal and Richman, 1.
46 Creswell and Bajaj, "Home Lender is Seeking Bankruptcy," 1.
47 Missal and Richman, 2.
48 Padilla and Gittelsohn, "How New Century Sank."
49 Zachary Kouwe, "Civil Suit Says Lender Ignored Own Warnings."
50 Ibid.
51 Dealbook [New York Times], "S.E.C. Accuses 3 New Century Ex-Officers of Fraud," *Orange County Register* (December 7 2009). Available online at http://dealbook.nytimes.com/2009/12/07/sec-accuses-3-new-century-ex-officers-of-fraud/.
52 McLean and Nocera, 29.
53 Mike Hudson and E. Scott Reckard, "Workers Say Lender Ran 'Boiler Rooms'," *Los Angeles Times* (February 4 2005). Available online at www.latimes.com/ameriquest.
54 Jo Becker, Sheryl Gay Stolberg, and Stephen Labaton, "White House Philosophy Stoked Mortgage Bonfire," *New York Times* (December 20 2008).
55 McLean and Nocera, 204.
56 Barry Eichengreen, *Hall of Mirrors: The Great Depression, the Great Recession, and the Uses—and Misuses of History* (Oxford, England: Oxford University Press, 2015), 168.
57 The amount paid was not disclosed.
58 McLean and Nocera, 6.
59 Ibid., 22.
60 This expanded loan use was in the usury section of DIDMC. Loans on home equity became popular because the interest deduction allowed on residences in federal income tax law was becoming more valuable as inflation rose.
61 McLean and Nocera, 26.
62 Eichengreen, 66.
63 McLean and Nocera, 37.
64 Eichengreen, 66.
65 McLean and Nocera, 226.
66 Ibid., 230.
67 Ibid., 300.
68 McLean and Nocera, 12.
69 Ibid.
70 Shira Ovide, "Bank of America—Countrywide: Worst Deal in History?" *The Wall Street Journal* [blog] (June 29 2011). Available online at blogs.wsj.com/deals/2011/06/29/bank-of-america-countrywide-worst-deal-in-history/.
71 Eichengreen, 169.
72 Landvoigt, Piazzesi, and Schneider, "The Housing Market(s) of San Diego."

11 The financial crisis and the future of California real estate financing

2008–2016

While the economy had been experiencing problems since 2005, the signs of trouble were not widely noticed. Unemployment was about 5 percent in 2005, and was still at about that level in 2008.[1] One of the signs of trouble was the over-building of housing. In 2000, US builders started 1.6 million new homes, but in 2005 they started 2.1 million. Yet by 2005, the housing market was slowing. The overall economy was showing signs of strain during the winter of 2007–8. By 2008, housing prices were clearly plummeting.[2] The economy began to fail.

The 2008 crisis

The Great Recession officially started on September 15 2008, with the failure of Lehman Brothers, a huge New York brokerage house. GDP in the quarter ending about then fell 3.7 percent (annualized). The next quarter it would fall 8.9 percent.[3] However, even on September 16 2008, the Federal Open Market Committee (FOMC) decided to keep its target for the federal funds rate (the best rate banks charge on loans to each other) at 2 percent, signaling their uncertainty about the strength of the economy.[4] By October 2008, there was a notable lack of liquidity in the financial markets. The Federal Reserve Board mentioned on October 7 that the short-term market was under "considerable strain."[5] The Fed spent October in a flurry of activity. First, they offered a new tool, the Commercial Paper Funding Facility (CPFF).[6] Remember that mortgage bankers had been borrowing short-term to finance their activities. The Treasury believed this facility was necessary to prevent substantial disruptions to the financial markets, and made a special deposit at the Federal Reserve Bank of New York in support of this facility.[7] They expressed the hope that the plan would not only help the short-term commercial paper market, but, by making lending safer, would encourage longer-term credit. Fed officials stated that "an improved commercial paper market would enhance the ability of financial intermediaries to accommodate the credit needs of businesses and households."[8]

The Federal Reserve Open Market Committee (FOMC) decided to lower its target for the federal funds rate fifty basis points to 1.5 percent by increasing the money supply. Central banks in other countries agreed that credit was literally unavailable. The Bank of Canada, the Bank of England, the European Central

Bank, Sveriges Riksbank, and the Swiss National Bank also announced changes in policy to support reductions in interest rates on October 8. The Bank of Japan expressed its strong support of these policy actions.[9] The same day, the Federal Reserve Board authorized the Fed to take securities from US subsidiaries of the American International Group (AIG) in return for cash. This amounted to, at least, an unprecedented loan to a private company, and in fact was more like a purchase of part of AIG. This was a very unusual transaction, but AIG was the most important source of insurance for bank deposit funds that were not covered by the FDIC.[10] By October 13, a comprehensive plan was being formulated jointly by the Treasury Department, Federal Reserve, and FDIC. One central plank of this effort was a plan for the Treasury to take approximately $250 billion in equity stakes in potentially thousands of banks, using funds approved by Congress through a $700 billion bailout bill. In addition, the FDIC extended its traditional focus from bank deposits to buying new preferred debt issued by banks and thrifts. They hoped that this program would be an aid to companies that needed capital.[11]

Earlier, Treasury Secretary Henry Paulson had summoned the top US banking heads to a meeting in Washington. At the meeting, Paulson discussed details of his new plan to take equity stakes in financial firms. The plan was that the US government would forcibly buy preferred stock in nine large financial institutions. The force was there to remove any stigma the banks might suffer from taking funds from the government. However, one bank, Wells Fargo (no longer a California bank), refused the offer of an "investment." Paulson then, instead of strong-arming the big banks, offered a total of $250 billion to any bank that wanted to sell preferred stock to the federal government and pay a mandatory 5 percent dividend. At first the offer of capital seemed attractive. The interest rate was fair. However, along with the government's involvement came certain restrictions, for example caps on executive pay, bans on new employment contracts containing golden parachutes, and limits on banks' ability to use "excessive" executive salaries as a tax deduction.[12] Paulson gave the banks a one-month deadline to take him up on the offer.[13] While some banks of all sizes took the offer, some refused, and some could not quickly produce preferred stock available to sell.

The FDIC temporarily lifted the insurance limits for non-interest-bearing bank deposit accounts from $100,000 to $250,000, to discourage customers from withdrawing funds from financial institutions.[14] The Fed began to pay interest on depository institutions' required and excess reserve balances on deposit at the Fed. This unprecedented payment of interest on reserve balances unfortunately made it less attractive for banks to make loans.[15] By the end of October, the Fed substantially increased the size of the Term Auction Facility (TAF) auctions, which allowed depository institutions to borrow from the Federal Reserve for a longer, fixed term. These TAF auctions injected $900 billion into the banking system by the end of the year. Also in October, the Fed allowed banks to buy the assets of money market mutual funds if they were previously affiliated with them, then moved to buy up to $600 billion worth of money market mutual funds assets themselves.[16] After this frenzied month, the economy continued its downward path.

Federal Reserve supports the government-sponsored enterprises

As the housing market dropped, The Federal Reserve started purchasing the obligations of all the housing-related government-sponsored enterprises—Fannie Mae, Freddie Mac, and the Federal Home Loan Banks—and mortgage-backed securities backed by Fannie Mae, Freddie Mac, and Ginnie Mae. They stated that this action was being taken to reduce the cost and increase the availability of credit for the purchase of houses, which in turn should support housing markets and foster improved conditions in financial markets more generally.[17] The Fed said it would buy up to $600 billion in mortgage-backed debt issued and backed by Fannie Mae, Freddie Mac, Ginnie Mae, and the Federal Home Loan Banks.

The furious level of federal activity continued. By the end of the year, the Fed had tripled their assets from the September level by lending, and by buying assets of other organizations. The Fed, Treasury, and FDIC made more than $4 trillion of financial commitments through a wide range of rescue programs they launched.

The credit markets responded quickly. Interest rates fell, "spurring a burst of refinancing activity by borrowers eager to lower their mortgage costs," the *Wall Street Journal* reported. "While the initial flurry of calls came from people seeking to refinance, economists predicted lower rates also will spur some home buying among bargain-seekers."[18] While the new programs were supposed to make credit more accessible to nervous consumers, those consumers did not want to spend.[19] The stock market and real estate both suffered continued falling values and it was more and more obvious that the economy was slowing. In December, the FDIC began closing banks. The Fed had already done as much as it could. So much new money was pumped into the economy that the Fed's benchmark short-term interest rate—the federal funds rate—hovered near zero, and policy makers assured the public that the rate would remain low for some time.[20] On February 10 2009, Congress initiated fiscal policy to help the rapidly declining economy by approving an $838 billion economic stimulus plan.[21]

Real estate financing was not a focus of the attempts to stop the financial crisis, as policy makers were more used to thinking about broader aspects of the financial markets. In retrospect, there were plenty of signs that the excessive amount of real estate debt was a problem. In 2003, *Black Swan* author Nassim Nicholas Taleb said that Fannie Mae "seems to be sitting on a barrel of dynamite," with its lending.[22] In 2004, Bush administration regulators investigated Fannie Mae's finances. Fannie was forced to restate $9 billion in earnings and the CEO resigned. Private companies had been cutting out the GSE bonds by securitizing mortgages themselves. Fannie Mae and Freddie Mac had loosened their real estate loan standards to compete.[23]

When the subprime mortgage crisis began in 2007, Wall Street lenders, over-leveraged on extremely risky subprime loans, begin to suffer drastic losses. Fannie Mae and Freddie Mac lost big too, on their substantial holdings of Wall Street mortgage-backed securities. Their losses rose so quickly that the Treasury seized the two GSEs. It was billed as a temporary measure, but they were still government-controlled in 2016, and bigger than ever.

After the crisis

The economy slid until late 2009, and then one of the slowest recoveries in US history began. Growth rates in real (inflation-adjusted) GDP jumped from negative numbers in 2009 to just over 2 percent per year through 2015. In California, GDP estimates dropped from $1,994 billion in 2008 to $1,916 billion in 2009. GDP recovered its 2008 level by 2011, but unemployment growth was slow. In 2007 there were 15.4 million jobs and only 16.2 million in September 2015. Housing in several areas had not recovered to 2005 values by 2015. These areas included the counties of Orange, San Diego, Los Angeles and Sacramento, and the Inland Empire (a combination of Riverside and San Bernardino counties). San Francisco values were higher in 2015, as it was experiencing its own boom fuelled by the growth of the hi-tech industry in the area.[24]

The financial area made a better recovery. Some of the banks which came out of the crisis intact got huge sums from the federal government. Others did not take any of the taxpayer's funds. US Bank grew while other banks failed, because they became cautious about making mortgage loans in 2004, wrote off questionable real estate loans and mortgage securities in early 2009, and then acquired conventional residential mortgages. While the bank is headquartered in Minneapolis, both Chairman Richard Davis and former CEO Jerry Grundhofer started their banking careers in California. "We brought experience and patience from a state with very wild swings," Davis explained. "The best skill we didn't know we had was how to deal with a volatile economy."[25]

What caused the bubble?

Now that time has passed, many studies have indicated that the housing bubble contributed to the deep recession afterward. Attention has also been given to the causes of the housing bubble. There are a few theories. The two most common theories are that the private mortgage banks over-issued mortgages by too generous and/or aggressive lending standards, or that federal pressure on Fannie Mae and Freddie Mac caused them to create a monster which required feeding with more and more subprime loans.

An example of the studies of private mortgage banks as a cause of the housing bubble study is available in one of the early papers for the Social Science Research Network, in which several researchers empirically investigated the validity of this hypothesis versus several other alternative explanations. A model of house price changes over the period 1998 to 2006 was specified and estimated using a cross-sectional time-series data base across twenty metropolitan areas over the period. Results suggested that, prior to early 2004, economic fundamentals provide the primary explanation for house price dynamics. Subprime credit activity did not seem to have had much impact on house price returns at any time during that period, although there was strong evidence of a price-boosting effect by investor loans. However, they did find strong evidence that a credit regime shift took place in late 2003, as the GSEs were displaced in the market by private issuers of new mortgage products. Market fundamentals became insignificant in affecting house price returns, and the price-momentum conditions characteristic of a bubble were created. Thus, rather than causing the run-up in house prices, the subprime market may well have been a joint product, along with house price increases, of the changing institutional, political, and regulatory environment characteristic of the period after late 2003.[26]

An example of research on Fannie Mae and Freddie Mac and federally created demand for subprime loans is available in a study of California and Florida mortgages by researchers at the Federal Reserve Bank of St Louis. This study observes that:

> it is unquestionable that Fannie Mae and Freddie Mac held substantial amounts of subprime mortgages, and that their holdings of these securities played a significant role in their demise, the evidence ... refutes the claim that the affordable housing mandates were responsible for the subprime crisis.[27]

They found no evidence that lenders increased subprime originations to comply with affordable housing goals or the revised Community Reinvestment Act.[28] On the other hand, in 2013 the Consumer Financial Protection Bureau (CFBP) outlined a minimum-quality mortgage that permitted a borrower to get a loan with a 3 percent down payment and a FICO (Fair Isaac Corporation) credit score below 660 (700 is "good"). In opposition to this loosening of standards, six regulatory agencies reviewed the crisis and found that mortgages with these criteria had a 23 percent failure rate between 2005 and 2008.[29]

What is next?

Eight years later, the chaotic resolution of the crisis by the federal government had disrupted the real estate scene dramatically. Eight years ago, treasury secretary Hank Paulson said the bailout of Fannie Mae and Freddie Mac was giving them a "time out." Yet in 2016, more than half of the mortgages in the United States are financed from these two federal agencies.[30] Mortgage bankers are touting zero-equity loans, even loans for 25 percent above the home's value, sanctioned by federal programs. An internet search will reveal the ability to get low-equity loans, zero-equity loans, and even "mirror" home equity loans where you don't have to own a home at all. Housing prices in California are inching upward, even though in some areas they are still below 2005 levels. Future bubbles are still inevitable, but continued research may allow policy that will dampen the force and/or help shield the economy from their effects.

What has California's history taught us about financing real estate cycles?

The previous chapters have covered each of California's real estate cycles. Most have been triggered and halted by the "fundamentals" of housing growth: population growth, jobs or income growth, low interest rates or high inflation. Population growth fed most of California's real estate appreciation. However, California has had some interesting twists. The first known real estate boom was stimulated by the founding of Spanish Missions in 1769. The land of what became California was owned by the King of Spain for centuries, but the grants for the use of the land did not become common until Catholic Missions opened along the coastal regions. Land grants seemed to follow the Missions in geography and time. These land grants became cattle and horse ranches. The Gold Rush turned real estate's advance into a real bubble, as intense as any bubble in history, but also brief. Less gold output caused a collapse. In the next advance, population and trade grew, prompting new, now Mexican, land grants for raising cattle and horses. This appreciation stopped with droughts that decimated the livestock herds. Land values grew next for agriculture, which small-scale irrigation projects extended into Southern California.

The 1920s land boom was part of the larger expansion of the American economy and, like the housing market of the entire country, experienced an unexplained dip later in the decade. Unlike in the rest of the nation, California seemed to experience a recovery before the Depression.[31] Also unlike the rest of the country, there was an inflow of population and demand for additional housing during the Depression. While private financial institutions provided some financing, the bank regulators' scrutiny kept lending to government-issued bonds. All levels of government helped provide housing, as did some creative private individuals. Some of the new housing provided in this period shaped the housing created during World War II and in the post-war land boom.

During World War II, there was a similar influx of population to California and a need for more housing due to the location of manufacturing facilities for military goods. This time, a federal ban on home-building created the barrier to production. Again creative builders and government funding provided partial solutions. One of these solutions was to create a mass production system for residences. As the war ended and pent-up demand brought buyers, financial institutions poured money into residential financing and soon needed out-of-state funding. From 1950 to 1960, real estate rose in value virtually without interruption. For a short time around 1960, military funding shifted to aerospace, causing a pause in the demand for housing, particularly in Southern California. However, after a short pause, the real estate market resumed its upward direction to continue the long boom.

The government influenced the supply and demand for housing in California starting in the 1930s, but regulation of financial institutions and housing would become a major force on the cycles starting in the 1970s. In that decade, two laws, one initiative and a court ruling would create a feeding frenzy in the real estate market. New regulations would also limit the supply as demand rose. Housing prices rose, but so did most prices. Inflation began the erosion of the saving banks, or S&Ls as they were known then, by 1980. The loans they had on their books had twenty- to thirty-year terms, while the money funding them was almost all due in a year or less. This no longer worked when short-term funding interest rates became higher than long-term rates. S&Ls began to fail in the late '80s.

California had more of these institutions than most states due to the fast growth in the housing market of the 1960s. When the federal government changed the financial regulatory structure to try to save the institutions, California added its own helpful laws. The longer-term effect apparently was not foreseeable, as a plethora of changes in the 1980s and 1990s created an unstable and uncertain market for real estate lenders.

This pattern repeated itself in the 1990s: There were changes in regulations with unforeseen reactions from financial institutions and the housing market forces. While research is not yet conclusive, it seems clear that policies favoring real estate loans to low-income families resulted in changes in the method of financing real estate. New derivative securities developed that were complex mix tures of GSE bonds and subprime mortgages. Several large, unregulated mortgage bankers located in California generated raw material for these securities.

When the real estate growth slowed in 2005 and the economy went into the Great Recession in 2008, financial assets in California institutions still grew, but more slowly, experiencing no growth in 2009. Real estate loan growth dropped into negative territory, only resuming growth in 2012 (see Graph 11.1). The housing market dropped accordingly and has not recovered its 2005 levels for the state.

For its entire history, California has been influenced by world events. In each real estate cycle, there has been the feeling that national events and national regulations would eventually overpower anything unique to the state.[32] Yet the most recent events have shown that this is not true. As long as there are variations in regulatory environments among the states, there are opportunities to examine how these varied situations shape results. In spite of the fact that, at this time, Fannie Mae and Freddie Mac dominate real estate financing more than any federal

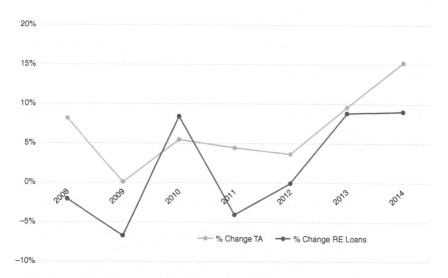

Graph 11.1 Change in total assets and real estate loans of financial institutions in California, 2008–2014.

Source: FDIC, www2.fdic.gov/hsob/hsobRpt.asp.

institution ever has before, California will continue to have a unique real estate situation. In fact, the dominance of the GSEs will make California bankers even more creative than they have been in the past.

Notes

1 Alan S. Blinder, *After the Music Stopped: The Financial Crisis, the Response, and the Work Ahead* (New York: The Penguin Press, 2013), 16.
2 Ibid.
3 Ibid., 19.
4 Federal Reserve Board of Governors, Press Release (September 16 2008).
5 Federal Reserve Board of Governors, Press Release (October 7 2008).
6 Ibid.
7 Ibid.
8 Ibid.
9 Federal Reserve Board of Governors, Press Release (October 8 2008).
10 Banks often bought insurance on account funds in excess of the $100,000 that was the FDIC limit of coverage. In making this loan, the Fed invoked a little-known section (section 13[3]) of the Federal Reserve Act enacted in the 1930s. Normally the Fed loaned only to banks or savings banks. This section allowed companies that were unable to get funds from another source to borrow directly from the Fed. Ibid.
11 Deborah Solomon, Damian Paletta, Aaron Lucchetti, and Jessica Holzer, "Treasury to Roll Out New Approach to Credit Crisis," *Wall Street Journal* (October 13 2008).
12 Federal Reserve Board of Governors, "Press Release" (October 6 2008).
13 Solomon, Paletta, Lucchetti, and Holzer.
14 Ibid.
15 Federal Reserve Board of Governors, "Press Release" (October 6 2008).
16 Federal Reserve Board of Governors, "Press Release" (October 22 2008).
17 Federal Reserve Board of Governors, "Press Release" (November 25 2008).
18 Ibid.
19 "Consumer spending dropped one percent in October, 2008," *Wall Street Journal*, News Alert, *WSJ* online. (November 26 2008). Page no longer accessible online.
20 Jon Hilsenrath and Liz Rappaport, "Fed Weighs Idea of Buying Treasurys as Focus Shifts" *Wall Street Journal*, *WSJ online* (January 29 2009). Retrieved online from http://search.proquest.com/docview/399128831?accountid=10051.
21 Corey Boles and Patrick Yoest, "Senate Passes Stimulus Bill: Lawmakers to Forge Ahead on Details" *Wall St Journal* (February 10 2009).
22 Alyssa Katz, Real Estate Blog. Available online at realestate.aol.com/blog/2010/12/24/the-rise-and-fall-of-fannie-mae-a-timeline/.
23 Ibid.
24 A. Gary Anderson Center for Economic Research, The George L. Argyros School of Business and Economics, "Shifting Gear: Recovery to Expansion," *Economic & Business Review* 34, no. 2 (December 2015), 13.
25 Fran Howard, "How U.S. Bank Saved its own Bacon. The Bottom Line: By Not Making a Pig of Itself," *Twin Cities* (May 2010). Reprint in author's possession.
26 Major D. Coleman, Michael LaCour-Little, and Kerry D. Vandell, "Subprime Lending and the Housing Bubble: Tail Wags Dog?" (Social Science Research Network: September 2 2008). Available online at http://ssrn.com/abstract=1262365.

27 Ruben Hernandez-Murillo, Andra C. Ghent, and Michael T. Owyang. "Did Affordable Housing Legislation Contribute to the Subprime Securities Boom?" Working Paper (St Louis, Missouri: Federal Reserve Bank of St Louis Research Division, August 2012), 36.

28 Ibid. Abstract. The loans studied are all thirty-year, amortized, and originated in 2004–6 in metropolitan areas of California and Florida.

29 Peter J. Wallison, "Get Ready for the Next Housing Bubble," *Wall Street Journal* (Thursday December 5 2013), A19.

30 Bethany McLean, *Shaky Ground: The Strange Saga of the U.S. Mortgage Giants* (New York: Columbia Global Reports, 2015), 22.

31 Lending on real estate recovered.

32 See for example the conclusion of Lynne Pierson Doti and Larry Schweikart, *California Bankers 1848–1993* (Needham Heights, Massachusetts: Ginn Press, 1994), 186.

Index

For Product Safety Concerns and Information please contact our EU
representative GPSR@taylorandfrancis.com Taylor & Francis Verlag GmbH,
Kaufingerstraße 24, 80331 München, Germany

Printed and bound by CPI Group (UK) Ltd, Croydon, CR0 4YY
01/05/2025
01858359-0001